WORDSWORTH CLASSICS
OF WORLD LITERATURE

General Editor: Tom Griffith MA, MPhil

PIERS PLOWMAN

William Langland
Piers Plowman

Translated with notes by Terence Tiller
With an Introduction by Priscilla Martin

WORDSWORTH CLASSICS
OF WORLD LITERATURE

This edition published 1999 by Wordsworth Editions Limited
Cumberland House, Crib Street, Ware, Hertfordshire SG12 9ET

ISBN 1 84022 103 8

By arrangement with BBC Worldwide Ltd.
© Wordsworth Editions Limited 1999.
© Translation and notes copyright Terence Tiller 1981.
The moral right of the author has been asserted.
© Introduction and translation with notes of
the 'Autobiographical Episode'
Priscilla Martin 1999.

Wordsworth® is a registered trade mark of
Wordsworth Editions Ltd

Typeset by Antony Gray
Printed and bound in Great Britain by
Mackays of Chatham, Chatham, Kent

CONTENTS

INTRODUCTION

Piers Plowman is one of the greatest and strangest of English religious poems. Like other theological and mystical literature, it faces the impossibility of describing the nature and expressing the experience of the divine. Like, for example, T. S. Eliot in *Four Quartets*, it treats the difficulty as intrinsic to the subject. Like *Paradise Lost*, it presents a vast panorama of Christian history and debates central doctrinal problems; unlike Milton, the author doubts his own moral and intellectual qualifications to solve them.

We do not know for certain who wrote *Piers Plowman* in the second half of the fourteenth century, during the last years of Edward III and the troubled reign of Richard II. The poem was evidently popular: fifty-two manuscripts survive. In 1550 it was printed, from yet another manuscript, by Robert Crowley, who thought the satirical but orthodox Catholic poem prophetic of the Reformation. Its nineteenth-century editor Skeat (who also edited Chaucer) detected three different stages of the poem which he called the A-, B- and C-texts and thought were composed in that order. On this view, B is a revision and continuation of A and C a revision of B. A dates from about 1367; B, nearly three times as long as A, from about 1378; C, rather longer than B, from about 1385. The major twentieth-century edition, by Kane, Donaldson and Russell, uses the term 'version' rather than 'text', emphasising the lengthy process of composition and revision rather than the scribal complexities and discrepancies. More recently it has been argued that a MS in the Bodleian Library is not an A-text but 'Z', an earlier version still. Fuller than A, more vivid and dramatic than C, B is the version most often studied.

Although there have been theories of multiple authorship, most scholars of the poem believe that the different versions were written by one author, probably called William Langland. A note written early in the fifteenth century in Latin on a C manuscript ascribes 'Perys ploughman' to William 'de Langlond', son of Stacy de Rokayle who was of gentle birth and lived in Shipton-under-Wychwood. This is supported, though not proved, by the internal evidence of the poem. *Piers* opens in Malvern, not far from Shipton. The poem is written in the traditional English alliterative metre, which seems to have enjoyed a revival in the West Midlands in the fourteenth century. Its dialect suggests an author from Worcestershire. The narrator is called Will and the line 'I have lived in this *Land,* and my name is *Long Will*' (15, 148) might be an internal signature by William Langland. Will does present himself as a poet and as the author of the poem in such lines as, 'Thereupon I awoke and wrote down what I had dreamed' (19, 478). Another poet, identifying himself as John But, regarded the A-text as unfinished and wrote a rather lame conclusion in which he reports that 'Wille . . . wrought that here is wryten, and other werkes bothe/Of Peres the plowman' and has died. Presumably the 'other works' Will composed about Piers Ploughman are the B and C versions.

If all the versions of the poem (with the exception of John But's appendix and perhaps some scribal 'improvements') are by one author, he spent most of his adult life writing and rewriting his poem. This suggests an earnest, anxious and obsessive personality, perhaps like that of Will the narrator. If the poet was never satisfied with the poem, Will is chronically dissatisfied with himself and with others. He interrogates almost everyone he meets and usually argues with their answers. He says that he would like to know all the sciences under the sun. He sets biblical and classical authorities and conflicting passages in Scripture against each other. He is questing and questioning, impatient and indignant, critical and self-critical.

A passage in C is known as the 'autobiographical episode'. In it the narrator is questioned by Reason and Conscience, personifications of his own mental faculties, as if he were dramatising his doubts about his life and his work. Will is living with his wife in a cottage in Cornhill, London, an address which may suggest poverty and squalor. He makes himself unpopular by criticising idlers and unworthy hermits in his poetry, yet is attired like them himself and perhaps is as unproductive. It is harvest time, when the able-bodied are obliged to labour, and Reason asks Will what work he contributes. Will claims he is too weak and too tall ('to long', presumably the reason for his nickname Long Will) to do manual work and, being a clerk, need not. The poet certainly has a reasonable knowledge of Latin, the Bible and some of the main theological controversies of the time. In Will's youth his family sent him to school (perhaps implying university) for a clerical education. Since their death, no other way of life has satisfied him. It seems that Will's education may not have been completed and, since he has a wife, that he is in minor orders. He describes his 'tools' as the *paternoster* and other prayers. He ekes out a hand-to-mouth living doing clerical odd-jobs, such as saying prayers for the dead, in and around London. Will defends himself earnestly but his own reason and conscience sound unconvinced.

Another passage in which the narrator is accused by an aspect of his own mind (B, 12) deals more specifically with his role as poet. Imaginatif[1] reminds him that he is middle-aged and must take the opportunity of amending his life before it is too late. He thinks Will's absorption in his poem a waste of time on two grounds: while he composes it, Will is not praying for those who provide for him; and the poem is unnecessary anyway. There are already many devotional and theological works and teachers and preachers to instruct people in virtue. Will has two answers. First, that play is allowed in the intervals of work. Second, that if he could find anyone to tell him what he needs to know about virtue, he would write no more works on the subject. One answer takes poetry more seriously than the other, perhaps implicitly contradicts the other. A silent reconfiguration of terms, characteristic of the poem, has taken place. In the first, poetry is mere recreation, 'play', the opposite of work. In the second, Will's poems are 'works' and perhaps a way of

---

[1] Tiller translates 'Imaginatif' as 'Imagination', the closest modern term. Aristotelians made a distinction between '*imaginatio*' and '*imaginativa*' ('*vis imaginativa*'): the former is passive, the power to receive images; the latter is active, the power to divide and compose images and, aided by Reason, to think through them (see Simpson, 103).

discovering truths he cannot learn by other means. The answer, like many in *Piers Plowman*, seems suggestive, vexing and incomplete. In the history of thought when a vital question is asked for the first time, answers rush to meet it. It seems here as if the question 'What is the function of poetry?' is almost asked and almost answered, as if the self-doubt of the narrator precludes confidence in the poem.

Will, when we first meet him at the beginning of the Prologue, seems, by his own standards, an ambiguous and questionable character. He is dressed as a sheep, suggesting a lost sheep or a pilgrim in sheepskin, or as a shepherd, suggesting the clergy, who will come under heavy criticism in the poem. He is like a hermit unholy of works: is he like a hermit in being unholy or like a hermit except for being unholy? *Piers Plowman* is the account of a spiritual journey, but Will's wandering, wide in the world to hear wonders, may be suspect as mere sightseeing. The poem opens on a sunny morning on Malvern Hills. The narrator falls asleep and has the first of a series of dreams. He finds himself in a 'wilderness' but as he gets his bearings he sees a spiritual topography dominating the landscape. Up on a hill to the East is one castle, down in the valley is another, between them is a 'feeld ful of folk', a plain full of people. The setting is as diagrammatic as that of a morality play: the 'tower' represents Heaven, the 'dungeon' represents Hell and the folk on the field of this life are crucially placed between the two. Unfortunately, most of them seem oblivious of their dangerous position. Some work hard at ploughing but some devote themselves to pride. Some spend their lives in prayer, penance and self-denial, others in greed, fraud, worldliness and self-seeking. The clear visionary light exposes the shortcomings of both laity and clergy: tradesmen, minstrels, beggars, pilgrims, hermits, friars, pardoners, parsons, lawyers. An impressionistic but judgmental parade of all the world's workers and idlers frames (in B and C) a paradigm of government represented by a King and his relationships to the people and a new and topical version of the fable of belling the cat. The King seems to be in the midst of a coronation procession and an ominous gloss is added to the fable: 'when the Cat is a kitten, the Court is wretched'. Richard II was a child when he was crowned in 1377. The scene has changed from the Malvern countryside to the capital and the Prologue ends with the street cries of London. The work of ploughing has diversified into all the occupations of the author's society.

The poem is evidently a dream vision, a genre used for both love poems and religious revelations. The prophetic or apocalyptic dream has a venerable history, Biblical and classical, and Will thinks of the dreams of Daniel and Joseph to give credence to his own. But medieval theory classified dreams into various categories with different causes; Will knows that not all dreams are considered specially meaningful and worries about the nature of his. *Piers Plowman* differs in many ways from other dream poems. Dream visions are not usually as dreamlike as this. Will's experience shares some of the strange but commonplace features of our own dreams: the shifting scenes, the sudden irruption or disappearance of characters, the perplexity about familiar places and people, the unsurprised acceptance of the fantastic and supernatural. Later in the poem characters will sometimes merge, the narrator will be woken by noises within his dream and his mood on waking will be determined by the dream. Unusually, *Piers Plowman* contains a number of dreams, including two dreams within dreams or 'inner dreams', which are of major importance. Between the dreams are waking episodes which often seem rather dreamlike themselves. Both literal and allegorical characters inhabit the poem. One might expect the former in the waking world and the latter in the dreams but very ordinary and lifelike people jostle with personifications in the dreams and allegorical characters can appear between dreams, such as Reason and Conscience in the autobiographical episode and Need in Passus 19. And, as always with this poem, no one description will prove adequate to its scope and complexity. *Piers Plowman* is a dream vision but it also draws upon many other genres, motifs and kinds of discourse: prophecy, sermon, satire, complaint, tableau of sins, confession, pilgrimage, debate.

The first two dreams (usually known as the *Visio*) are particularly concerned with the state of contemporary society. Passus 1, like the Prologue, insists that there are clear moral and spiritual guidelines but shows that people don't recognise or don't understand or prefer to ignore them. A beautiful but intimidating lady comes down from the tower and Will asks her the question that students of the poem have been asking ever since: 'What may this all mean?' She replies that Truth lives in the tower, that he created all people to worship him and told the earth to provide them with the necessities of food, drink and clothing, which they should not abuse. Her teaching sounds authoritative in general terms but it is in its simplicity more suited to an agrarian society (with a paradisal climate) than the more complex and confusing scene with which the Prologue closed. Will promptly asks who owns the world's money, a question which sounds rather childlike but which raises both the issue of 'dominion', a theological topic with immense political implications, and the problem of interpreting traditional Christian teaching in the changing society in which the poet lives. The counsel to render to God and to Caesar what belongs to each suggests that everyone knows what is right and needs only to act on the knowledge. It begs some hotly disputed questions about the temporal powers of Church and monarch, the relationships between the different estates of society, the rights and duties of labourers, the help due to the poor.

Will's conversation with Holy Church takes a form that will be repeated many times in *Piers Plowman*: questions followed by answers followed by further questions; an exasperated instructor and a bemused but insistent enquirer. Will wants to know who lives in the dungeon and who the lady is. When she says that she is the Church and he should recognise her, he falls to his knees and asks, 'How may I save my soul?' Holy Church thinks he ought to have the answers already, either from previous instruction or from the natural knowledge which God has placed in the heart, but she rehearses the standard Christian teaching to him. The poem might have ended here but, as ever, Will wants to know more. He asks about falsehood and is shown Lady Meed and the controversy about her marriage.

This episode dramatises some of the difficulties of defining 'the false' and of promoting a just society. The problems are epitomised in the identity and relationships of Lady Meed. Personification allegory can be tautological and self-evident, merely a way of saying that one is against sin and for virtue, but Langland's use of it is dynamic and analytical. The poem constantly treats linguistic issues as crucial to understanding and action. Meed's name is ambiguous and she exploits the ambiguity. She stands for payment or reward, which might be just or unjust, earthly or heavenly. Various crooks want her to marry Fraud; the King wants her to marry Conscience. This suggests that Meed can be used for good or ill and the King wants to ensure that the economy of his realm will be conducted in accordance with morality. But Conscience refuses this match and in debate and double-dealing Meed exposes her potential for evil. She is implicated in bribery and corruption at Court, in the Church, in local government and in the general venality which the poet perceives as endemic to the growing cash economy.

The second dream begins with the sermon of Reason, the confessions of the seven deadly sins and a wave of mass emotion and penitence in the congregation. Everyone wants to go on pilgrimage to Truth but no one knows the way. God is Truth but they seek a material goal. An inveterate pilgrim, covered, like a medieval youth-hosteller, with souvenirs of his journeys to all the major shrines – Bethlehem, Jerusalem, Sinai, Rome, Compostella – has never heard of St Truth. Langland, like many other educated Christians in the fourteenth century, is suspicious of pilgrimage. The outward physical journey would be merely mechanical without an inner spiritual journey. And perhaps the inner journey makes the outer redundant. The enthusiastic pilgrims who do not know the way to Truth miss the essential. They are at a complete loss until a ploughman appears to tell them.

Piers enters the poem suddenly and with a simple authority. He does know Truth, is indeed employed as ploughman by Truth. He will show the pilgrims the way if they will first help him plough his half-acre. As usual in this poem an apparently straightforward statement, question or command opens out into larger vistas. The ploughing of the half-acre expands into all the work of the world with plans for later hiring and division of labour and defence of the realm. The world's work must be done and takes priority over the pilgrimage. We begin to realise, indeed, when Piers defines his ploughman's garb as that of a pilgrim, that the ploughing is the pilgrimage. The way to Truth is not a geographical route but living and working honestly. Most people, however, do not do this as well as Piers and he soon runs into difficulties with his workforce. Some of the problems are due to the eternal human failings of sloth and selfishness, some to the changing labour relations in the decades after the ravages of the Black Death, which killed at least a third of the population. The reduction in the number of labourers meant that they could seek and command higher wages and there was legislation to control this. Our sympathies are with the labourers but the narrator's position seems conservative, backward-looking to the days of supposed stability in society and loyalty between its members. Piers himself is uncertain. He finds that Hunger will drive idlers back to work but he doubts the virtue of right action based on fear and he feels the Christian obligation of charity. The anxiety, here and elsewhere in the poem, about the duty and the dangers of giving to beggars or supporting the unproductive is an analogue of the great theological paradox of God's justice and mercy. This explodes in the climax of the second dream and the problem of Truth's pardon.

Truth sends a message, confirming that the ploughing has replaced the pilgrimage by telling Piers to stay at home and plough and promising pardon, the reward of pilgrimage, to all who help him. Yet while the paraphrase of the pardon promises mercy, the actual text of it suggests strict justice. The priest finds it 'no pardon', merely, 'Do well, and deserve well ... Do evil, and deserve evil.' Piers' tearing of the pardon is one of the most dramatic and baffling events in the poem. It has been variously interpreted: most often as an outburst of anger against the officious priest, an attack on the system of indulgences, which the pardon misleadingly resembles, or a recognition that nobody can satisfy the claims of justice and a rejection of legalism. Perhaps it marks a transition from the world of the *Visio*, which recognises an Old Testament ethic of good works and law or a basic natural morality common to all societies, to the Christian faith in grace, mercy and redemptive suffering. Piers rejects not only the pardon but also his previous way of life which seemed so virtuous. His plough will now be prayers and penitence and the poem, so concerned in the *Visio* about the problems of society, will journey inward to the problems in the mind and soul of the dreamer.

Will wakes on Malvern Hills thoroughly perplexed about his dream. Piers' startling reaction to the pardon was bold, spontaneous and inspired: the 'ignorant' ploughman tore the document, stood up to the priest and was suddenly able to cite the Bible in Latin. Will's reaction to dream and pardon is timid and anxious: he worries about how much trust to place in either and concludes that it is safest to believe in all the pardons of the Church and to do well. So the first part of the poem has two endings and little sense of closure: Piers' choice, which points forward to another way of life, and Will's nervous inability to choose between apparently conflicting authorities. Neither this poet nor this narrator could leave it there.

During the two dreams of the *Visio*, Will has mainly been an observer. In the rest of the poem, usually known as the *Vita*, he is mainly an active seeker for truth, though often searching in the wrong spirit or the wrong places. He first sets out 'seeking Do-Well', as if the term were a proper noun and a person, rather than a verb and an imperative. Doing well would realise the term in his own experience but Will tries to extract a definition from various sources, first from two friars, then in the next dream from a series of allegorical characters: Thought, Wit, Reason, Study, Clergy[2] and Scripture, aspects of his own mind and personifications of secular and sacred learning, who become increasingly vexed with him while he becomes more confused by them. Will himself could be seen as an aspect of his own psyche, *Voluntas,* the will, fallen and fallible. His problem seems instantly compounded by the first encounter, with Thought, who casually answers his enquiry about Do-Well with definitions of not only 'Do-Well' but the comparative, 'Do-Better', and the superlative, 'Do-Best'. Other speakers add their own definitions of these terms and their own criticisms of Will and his theoretical enquiry. Finally Will loses patience, suggests that salvation and damnation are predestined anyway and God's judgments inscrutable, launches an attack on learning as positively inimical to salvation and declares that illiterate ploughmen and labourers ignorant of everything but the Lord's Prayer will get to heaven sooner than great scholars.

At or near this point the A version ends. After a revised version of A, B continues with the first of the inner dreams, opening with an account of how Will was for many years in thrall to Fortune,

2 Langland's term, Clergy, denotes the clerical estate, those in it and the learning which in his time was mainly confined to them, or the learned in general. In Simpson's view, Langland's 'Clergy, as "cosyn" to Study' represents 'the institution of university theological learning' (Simpson, 106). Tiller translates the name of Clergy the character as 'Clerisy', a term introduced into English by Coleridge to express, as the *Oxford English Dictionary* rather unfortunately puts it, 'a notion no longer associated with the clergy . . . learned men as a body, scholars'.

Lust-of-the-Flesh and Lust-of-the-Eyes until the end of youth and thoughts of death and judgment recalled him to his quest. Assuming A and B are by the same poet, some scholars have read this too as an allegorical autobiographical episode describing a lengthy interval in which the author abandoned his poem and its concerns ('Nor did I find delight in Do-well or Do-better; / I had no wish, believe me, to know anything about them . . . '), perhaps after finding himself at an intellectual impasse. The end of A and the beginning of the continuation in B are the most rewritten part of the poem, suggesting that the poet had most difficulty with, or with expressing, this stage in his argument.

The next part of the inner dream relates Will's emergence from his obsessive introspection and his escapist pursuit of pleasure. Fortune had invited him to look into a mirror called Middle Earth. Now Nature shows him the wonders of the world from a mountain called Middle Earth. It feels like a release from solipsism, as Will is taught through observing all creatures to love their creator. For the first time since the poem opened on Malvern Hills the narrator is moved by the beauty of nature. He is also impressed by its efficiency: animals, in contrast with the disorderly sexuality of humans, observe mating seasons; birds instinctively know how to build nests so intricate that no craftsman could compete. Will, however, moves from feeling reverent awe at the cosmos to criticising the fault in the design. He reproaches Reason, the divine wisdom informing creation, for his inadequacy in directing men and women. Reasoning that Reason is unreasonable is the nadir of irrationality and Reason does not answer Will with reasons. Reason's answer to Will is like a Christian version of God's answer to Job. Job's incomprehension of his sufferings is confronted with the mystery of God's power. Will's presumptuous criticisms of the divine and the human are contrasted with the mystery of God's suffering and patience. Will is overcome by shame and his anger with creator and creatures is punished by his waking from the inner dream.

Will awakes into the outer dream disappointed, frustrated and receptive to Imaginatif's comment that he could have learned much more from Reason if he had not interrupted and criticised. Imaginatif resolves Will's major problems about salvation and the value of learning, though he does not persuade him to abandon the poem. Nor are these anxieties abandoned. Will accepts an invitation from Conscience the more eagerly because Clergy will be there, but he loses his temper at dinner with a learned and gluttonous friar. And, strangely, Conscience leaves his own banquet, choosing to be pilgrim with Patience, despite Clergy's confidence that together they could put right all the ills of the world and prediction that Conscience will return to him. The intellectual talk at table about the 'three lives' and the failure of educated clergy to practise what they preach seem to set learning at odds with virtue, though in an ideal world they would be at one or united could make the world ideal. Next the value placed in the *Visio* on the industrious active life comes under fresh scrutiny: Conscience and Patience meet Haukyn, the active man, who at first seems quite complacent but whose coat proves so spotted with every kind of sin that he collapses in a wild lament that wakes the dreamer.

The next vision takes us into the heart of the poem and Will into the central Christian revelation. Although there will be more and different definitions of the 'three lives', the poem and the dreamer seem to be progressing from the long and exasperating enquiry into 'Do-Well' to a deeper understanding. In some manuscripts Passus 15 is headed with the note *'finit dowel & incipit dobet'* (Do-Well ends and Do-Better begins), which may not be authorial but does mark a transition in the narrative. Will first meets Anima, the soul, who, with his many names, suggests a synthesis of the many aspects of the psyche Will has encountered so far and who instructs him in the virtue of charity. Characteristically, Will is as perplexed after the discussion as before but now charity is revealed as well as explained to him. Charity literally begins at home. It is a tree that grows in the midst of man's body in land leased to Free-Will by Piers Ploughman. Piers has been absent from the poem since the end of the *Visio* while Will has tried to understand its implications with his intellect. At the sound of his name Will faints with joy and awakes in the second of the inner dreams to see Piers Ploughman tending the Tree of Charity. Will echoes the original sin in the first garden. He asks for an apple and sees the devil snatch all the falling fruit. Piers comes to the rescue with a prop called Son and the life of Christ, from Annunciation to Crucifixion, unfolds swiftly before the dreamer until he awakes in tears from the inner vision.

Piers evidently represents more now than the honest ploughman and exemplar of industrious active life that he seemed in the *Visio*. He is closely associated with the power and the life of Christ, perhaps in some sense a figure of Christ, perhaps, as an ideal human being, an image of Christ's humanity. This connection is made more clearly in the rest of the outer dream, where Will meets some richly polysemous characters: Abraham and Moses, who also represent Faith and Hope and the priest and Levite in the story of the Good Samaritan. The poet is making creative use of multi-levelled allegory and of typology, by which events and characters in the Old Testament prefigure those in the New and all times are in equal relationship to the central event in time, the Incarnation. So in Passus 16 and Passus 17 we twentieth-century readers witness the fourteenth-century dreamer talking with the Old Testament Abraham and Moses, who await the coming of Christ, and then watch their failure, as priest and Levite in the New Testament parable, to help the wounded man who can be saved only by the Samaritan/Charity/Christ on his journey to Jerusalem.

Passus 18 presents the next vision and the magnificent climax of the poem. On Palm Sunday, Will dreams of the first Palm Sunday and sees riding into Jerusalem someone who looks like a young knight about to be dubbed, and like the Samaritan, and like Piers Ploughman. Faith explains that Christ is about to joust in Piers' armour, Human Nature, and win back the fruit seized by the devil. The poem presents a simultaneous configuration of the liturgy for Palm Sunday, the entrance into Jerusalem, Old Testament type and prophecy, the parable of the Samaritan, the traditional image of Christ as soldier or as courtly knight come to the rescue of his beloved and the unfolding significance of the figure of Piers Ploughman. At the heart of all the allegories is a literal historical event, the Crucifixion. Will's vision is of the drama of Holy Week and now (like Dante in the *Divine Comedy*) he dreams through Good Friday, Holy Saturday and Easter Sunday. He witnesses Christ's Harrowing of Hell, the release of the souls imprisoned there and the solution of the problem that has troubled the poem for so long: Mercy and Peace are reconciled with Truth and Righteousness. God's mercy and justice are united and for once Will wakes up happy, hearing the bells of Easter and calling his wife and daughter to come to church with him.

It seems as if all pain and problems have been resolved but the rest of the poem is darkly realistic about the subsequent history of humanity and of the Church. The note at the beginning of Passus 19, *'explicit dobet & incipit dobest'* (Do-Better ends and Do-Best begins), describes the structure, not the atmosphere, of the poem. Will goes to Mass (well dressed, for once!) planning to make his communion, falls asleep and has a vision of the bloodstained figure of Piers or Jesus. Conscience interprets their relationship for him and applies the terms Do-Well, Do-Better and Do-Best to the life, death, resurrection and ascension of Christ. After his appearance to Doubting Thomas, Christ 'taught the disciples Do-Best' and gave Piers the power to bind, unbind and grant pardon. Piers now represents St Peter and the Church and Will dreams that Pentecost illuminates Piers and his companions. The last part of the poem seems to be circling back to the world of the *Visio* and remaking it as a Christian society formed and informed by Grace. Grace distributes gifts to its members and, like Piers in the second vision, divides its labour between them. The world is again allegorised as a farm. Piers is to be agent, bailiff, registrar, purveyor and plough-man, with a team of four great oxen called Matthew, Mark, Luke and John to plough and a team of younger oxen called Ambrose, Gregory, Augustine and Jerome to harrow. The land is to be sown with the seeds of the cardinal virtues, Justice, Wisdom, Fortitude and Temperance. At this abstract level all sounds well, until the voices of imperfect literal characters break in with their jarring accounts of how the world actually works and these virtues operate in it: a brewer has no interest in just business practice, cardinals do not exemplify cardinal virtues, a lord's clerks use their wisdom to vet his reeve's accounts and the lord uses his fortitude to rake in all the profit he can. Will wakes up, wretched and destitute again.

In the waking episode before the last vision Will is accosted by the figure of Need, who challenges him with his own interpretation of the cardinal virtue of Temperance. Need's list of the absolute necessities – food, drink and clothing – is the same as Holy Church's in Passus 1, but whereas her emphasis was on God's bounty, his is on human need. Need acknowledges no law and his counsel is questionable. His view that necessity excuses begging or stealing for food and clothing may be theologically correct or an excuse and a perversion of the Spirit of Temperance. His beautiful closing lines on the poverty of Christ sound inspiring but also recall the bitter topical controversy about the theoretical poverty of the friars. Will's own life, his modest livelihood, his immediate problem of where the next meal is to come from raise again the major intellectual issues of interpreting God's law and the moral and economic questions in applying it. He falls asleep again and has the worst dream of all.

In the *Visio*, Piers' work for Truth on the half-acre was impeded by uncooperative humans and the familiar labour problems of Langland's day. Now Antichrist himself attacks Truth's crop and sows falsehood in its place. His coming may presage the end of the world and Conscience seems to be fighting a losing battle against him. In this apocalyptic final passus the forces of evil assault and, more seriously, corrupt the agents of good. Conscience gathers the holy fools who remain loyal into the great barn of Unity, the Church, for protection. At his plea Nature sends admonitory sicknesses and plagues but (like the coercion of Hunger in Passus 6) they have no permanent moral effect. The ravages of Nature do not spare the dreamer: Will loses his hair, his teeth, his mobility, his sexual potency and knows that death is near. But the questions asked all through the poem still haunt him. What craft should he learn? Love, Nature answers, and he will want for nothing, only repeating this counsel when the dreamer asks, 'But how . . . shall I get food and clothing?' Will makes his way through Contrition and Confession to Unity and finds it besieged by the Seven Deadly Sins. But the danger from within the Church is more insidious, as it is infiltrated by Friar Flatterer, a confessor so complaisant that he cheers up and so denatures Contrition himself. 'He's asleep and dreaming,' says Peace, 'and so are many others' (20, 375), as if the visionary enlightenment of the dreamer and the whole form of the poem were being questioned. Conscience calls for Clergy's help, as Clergy predicted at the banquet, but in vain. So, in a leap of faith or despair, Conscience vows himself to another pilgrimage, to seek Piers Ploughman, as if Piers with all he has represented throughout the poem is mysteriously absent from the Church. To the sound of Conscience's cry for grace, the dreamer wakes and the poem ends.

The reader may well feel that *Piers Plowman* breaks off rather than closes, that a D version (or more) was precluded by the poet's death rather than his satisfaction with his work. But such disappointment or dismay have continually been provoked in the course of the poem, by the way that answers are followed by questions and solutions by problems, by the tearing of the pardon, by the departure of Conscience from Clergy, by the absences of Piers, by the sad course of human history after the triumph of the Resurrection. *Piers Plowman* is an overtly deconstructive poem, dismantling its own constructions, abandoning its own narrative structures, finally departing from Unity itself on yet another pilgrimage. It leaves us with its dominant images, the dreamer, the ploughman, the pilgrim and the quest.

PRISCILLA MARTIN
St Edmund Hall, Oxford

FURTHER READING

Editions

George Kane (ed.), *The A-Version. Will's Visions of Piers Plowman and Do-Well*, Athlone Press and University of California Press, 1960.

George Kane and E. Talbot Donaldson (eds), *The B-Version. Will's Visions of Piers Plowman and Do-Well, Do-Better and Do-Best*, Athlone Press, 1975.

George Kane and G. H. Russell (eds), *The C-Version. Will's Visions of Piers Plowman and Do-Well, Do-Better and Do-Best*, Athlone Press, 1997.

Derek Pearsall (ed.), *Piers Plowman by William Langland: An Edition of the C-Text*, York Medieval Texts, Edward Arnold, 1978.

A. G. Rigg and Charlotte Brewer (eds), *Piers Plowman, the Z-Version*, Athlone Press, 1983.

A. V. C. Schmidt (ed.), *The Vision of Piers Plowman. A Complete Edition of the B-Text*, Dent, 1987.

Walter W. Skeat (ed.), *The Vision of William concerning Piers the Plowman*, 4 vols, Early English Text Society, Oxford University Press, 1873.

Selected critical reading

John A. Alford (ed.), *A Companion to Piers Plowman*, University of California Press, Berkeley and Los Angeles 1988.

Robert J. Blanch (ed.), *Style and Symbolism in Piers Plowman*, University of Tennessee Press, Knoxville 1969.

S. S. Hussey (ed.) *Piers Plowman: Critical Approaches*, Methuen, London 1969.

James Simpson, *Piers Plowman: An Introduction to the B-Text*, Longman, London 1990.

Creative works in the Piers Plowman tradition

Piers Plowman was read, copied and imitated in the fourteenth and fifteenth centuries. Its influence is obvious in satirical alliterative poems such as *Richard the Redeless* and possible in the General Prologue to *The Canterbury Tales,* with its panorama of contemporary society and its portrait of an ideal ploughman. It was published by Robert Crowley in 1550 and, on the evidence of his annotations and references to *Piers* in Protestant authors, misunderstood as an attack on Catholic doctrines as well as on corruption in the Church. The poem was then almost unknown until the scholarly editions of the nineteenth century. However, the tradition of the allegorical religious dream vision continued, most notably in Bunyan's *The Pilgrim's Progress*, and has been an inspiration to modern novelists who were also medieval scholars, such as J. R. Tolkien and C. S. Lewis. Interest revived in the accentual metres of Old and Middle English alliterative verse: Gerard Manley Hopkins knew *Piers Plowman* and in the twentieth century the influence of these earlier forms is visible in the free verse and poetic experiment of, for example, W. H. Auden and Derek Walcott.

Helen Barr (ed.), *The Piers Plowman Tradition; A Critical Edition of Pierce the Ploughman's Crede, Richard the Redeless, Mum and the Sothsegger and The Crowned King*, Dent, London, and Charles E. Tuttle Co., Inc., Rutland, Vermont 1993.

P. L. Heyworth (ed.), *Jack Upland, Friar Daw's Reply and Upland's Rejoinder*, Oxford University Press, 1968.

Frances Chesterton (wife of G. K. Chesterton), *Piers Plowman's Pilgrimage: A Morality Play*, Samuel French, London and New York 1925.

Florence Converse, *Long Will: A Romance*, Longmans, Green and Co., London and Bombay 1903; reprinted in Everyman's Library edition, Dent, London 1908, 1910, 1939.

NOTE ON THE TEXT

Terence Tiller's translation of the B-text is based on: W. W. Skeat, *The Vision of William concerning Piers the Plowman: Text-B* (with notes, general preface and indexes), Oxford University Press, 1972; and J. A. W. Bennett, *Piers Plowman: The Prologue and Passus I–VII*, Oxford University Press, 1972. Tiller also refers to the lively and learned prose translation by J. F. Goodridge, Penguin, revised edition 1966.

Priscilla Martin's translation of the 'Autobiographical Episode' (C, 5, 1–104) is based on: Derek Pearsall, *Piers Plowman by William Langland: An Edition of the C-text*, University of California Press, 1979.

TRANSLATOR'S NOTE

This book began as a greatly shortened modern English version of *The Vision of Piers Plowman* arranged serially (and semi-dramatically) for radio. The broadcast version was intended for the general, rather than the specialist, listener; on the whole, therefore, 'difficult' passages were omitted rather than annotated. Even this printed version, which is complete, carries only such apparatus as I believe essential to the reader's understanding and enjoyment. The scholarly reader will detect several occasions on which my translation departs slightly from the literal meaning of the Middle English. This has been done where that meaning was, or would have been, unclear; or sometimes to avoid the need of a footnote. For the most part, however, I have aimed at a literal, as well as an easily readable, translation.

On the whole I have done my best to avoid archaisms, though this avoidance removes (for instance) the valuable distinction between *you* and *thou*. Where archaism cannot be avoided, as in technical terms like 'provisor' or 'limiter', or when the medieval term seemed more vivid than a modern paraphrase or translation, as with 'Meed', I have usually kept the original, with a footnote.

Lines are numbered according to Skeat's edition, though for

several reasons my version does not march quite line by line with the original. For example, I have almost always added an English translation to Langland's longer French and Latin quotations (though sometimes simply omitting the original, when it is short, and giving the English only). When the quotation is from the Vulgate, I have usually given the English of the Authorised Version. Sometimes, however, Langland's memory of the Vulgate has been faulty. On these occasions I have for the most part silently corrected his Latin and, if necessary, adjusted the translation. There are times, of course, when the Authorised Version does not in fact translate what the Vulgate says; if the general intention is clear, I have ignored these discrepancies, rewriting or annotating only when real misunderstanding might result. Sometimes, in the interest of clarity, I have expanded the Latin or the translation, or both.

Langland's use of the English Alliterative Metre is very far from rigid. The rules that he purports to observe are simple enough. The normal line is divided into two parts (the first usually somewhat longer), separated by a caesura or natural break of sense or of emphasis. Each half-line has two − sometimes more − *strongly* accented syllables. Three or more of these alliterate, usually two in the first half-line and one in the second. The alliterating syllable in the second half-line is the *first* strong accent; the letter that begins this alliterating syllable is called the *chief-letter* (and it may be added here that all stressed initial vowels are treated as alliterating).

There is not one of the rules and principles outlined above that Langland does not ignore or distort or break in a variety of ways − including complete inversion of a line. I have not thought it necessary to be more of a precisian than Langland himself; though I have allowed myself no liberties that Langland does not somewhere take. It is true, however, that in two respects I have given myself licence more frequently than Langland has taken it: these are, first, abuse or misuse of the caesura; second, making the chief-letter the latter of the two stresses in the second half-line. Often enough, Langland avoids this only by means of grammatical inversions that are neither necessary to his dialect nor acceptable in modern English. But in any case it feels to me actually more effective, in modern English, to have the alliterating accent as the 'clincher' of the line. And since I had precedent, I indulged myself when it suited me!

PIERS PLOWMAN

Prologue

One summer season, when the sun was soothing,
I shrouded myself in a shaggy sheepskin coat;
Thus habited like a hermit of unholy life,
I walked into the wide world to hear of wonders.
But one May morning in the Malvern Hills,
I met with a marvel that seemed made by magic:
I was weary with wandering, and went to rest
Under a broad bank by the side of a brook;
And as I lay, and leaned to look into the waters,
They sounded so sweetly that I sank into sleep . . .   10
    There I dreamed a dream that was indeed wonderful:
I was in a wilderness, but *where* I knew not.
I set my face eastward, where, high against the sun,
I saw a tower, trim-built on the top of a hill;
And a deep dale beneath it, and a dungeon in it,
With deep dark dykes that were dreadful to see.
A pleasant plain full of people lay between these places,
With every manner of man, poor, middling, and rich,
Toiling or travelling as the world's way took them.
Some spent their lives at the plough, and were seldom idle,   20
Seeding and sowing and strongly labouring
To gather what the gluttony of wastrels would again scatter.
Some spent their lives in pride, and were dressed in apt style,
Coming all tricked-out in conspicuous clothing.
In prayers and in penance many passed their days,
And for love of Our Lord lived rigorous lives
In hope of having happiness in Heaven;
Such are hermits and anchoresses who hold to their cells
And do not care to career about the country
Or flatter their flesh with dainty food and living.   30
    And some were sellers and buyers; they were served better,
For in *our* sight it seems always that such men thrive.

Some came to make men merry, as minstrels know how,
Getting money for glad music – and are guiltless, I think.
But jokesters and jabberers, Judas's children,
With feigning and with fantasy pretend to be fools,
Yet have wits enough to work, at will or at need:
That St Paul[1] has preached of them I shall not prove in full,
Save that 'he who speaks foulness' is in the service of Lucifer.

    Cadgers and beggars were bustling all about,   40
Their bellies and their back-packs crammed with bread;
They were fed by their feigning, and fought over their ale;
And in gluttony, God knows, do they go to bed,
And arise with ribaldry, the robberly rogues:
Sleep and shabby sloth pursue them for ever.

    Pilgrims and palmers were compacting together
To seek Spanish St James's,[2] or saints' relics in Rome.
They went upon their way with much wise talk,
And had licence to lie for the rest of their lives.
I saw some that said they had sought-out saints: 50
Whatever tale they told, their tongues were attuned to lying
More than to speaking the truth, as their style of speech proved.

    Hermits in hordes, with their hooked staves,
Were away to Walsingham[3] – and their wenches followed them.
Great long-bodied lubbers that were loth to work, they were,
And clad themselves as clergy for their kind to be known,
And were habited as hermits to have easy times.

    I found there friars, all the four orders,
Who preached to the people for their own profit,
And glossed the Gospel for the good will of their patrons,   60
Construing it comfortably, they so coveted new cloaks.
Many of these master-friars may dress as they please,
For their merchandise and their money move on hand-in-hand.
For since Charity turned chafferer, and the chief-confessor
                             to nobles,
Many strange things have we seen in the space of few years.
If the friars and Holy Church form no better friendship,
The greatest evil on Earth will come early upon us.

    There was a pardoner[4] preaching as if he were a priest;
He brought forth a pope's Bull, with bishops' seals on it,
And said that he himself could absolve all men   70

From falsehoods, fast-breaking, and forsworn vows.
The unlettered quite believed him, and liked his words;
They came and knelt and kissed his credentials.
He brow-beat them with his brevet, and blinded their eyes,
And raked-in with his great roll their rings and brooches.
Thus people give their gold, to maintain gluttons,
And believe in such wastrels who live in lechery.
Were the bishop truly blessed, and his whole brain working,
His seal would not thus be sent to deceive the people.
But it is not by the bishop's word that this biter preaches,   80
For the parish priest and the pardoner share the plunder –
Which the poor folk of the parish would have, apart from
                                                those two.

    Parsons and parish priests pleaded with the bishop,
Their parishes being poor since the time of the Plague,[5]
To have licence to leave, and live in London,
And sing simoniac Mass there (for silver is sweet).
Brethren and bishops, both masters and doctors,
Curates under Christ, their crown shaven in token
That they should all of them shrive their parishioners,
And preach to them, and pray for them, and feed the poor –   90
There they were, living in London, even during Lent:
Some as the King's servants, counting his silver,
In Chancery or the Exchequer keeping charge of his dues
From wards and wardships and waifs and strays.
And some enlisted as lords' or ladies' servants,
Sitting and making decisions in the office of steward,
Their Masses and their Matins, and most of their set prayers,
Being done undevoutly: and they are in danger
Lest at Christ's final Consistory[6] many are accursed.
I perceived then some of the power in St Peter's charge,   100
'To bind and unbind', as the Bible tells us.[7]
He left that power to Love, as Our Lord commanded –
The greatest Virtue of all, among those four Virtues
Called by men 'Cardinal':[8] hinges that close
The gates of the Kingdom of Christ, or *dis*close to others
All Heaven open, and its happiness at hand.
But the *Cardinals* of Rome's Curia, who claimed that title,
And pre-empted for themselves the power of pope-making,

With all the potency of Peter: impugn then I will not;
For such elections belong to both love and learning;   110
Therefore I may not – though I might – say more of that Court.
    Then there came a King, with a convoy of Knights;[9]
By consent of the common-folk was his kingship gained,
But Mother Wit came amain and found men of learning
To counsel the King and protect the common-weal.
The King and his knightly cohort, and the clergy too,
Planned that the People should provide for all.
With Mother Wit, the commoners contrived crafts for themselves;
And, that all the People might profit, appointed ploughmen
To till the earth, and to toil as trusty men should.   120
Thus the King and the Commons, accompanied by Mother Wit,
Laid down law and fair-dealing, their duties and rights
                                                    known by all.
    Then a lunatic looked in on them – and a long lean
                                        creature he was –
And said, on his knees to the King, in formal style:
'Christ keep you, my lord King, and all your kingdom,
And let you so rule your realm that the loyal shall love you,
And you for your righteous reign be rewarded in Heaven.'
And then, from the air on high, a heavenly angel
Stooped low, and spoke in Latin – for the unlettered had not
The judgment or the jargon for what should gain them justice,   130
But must suffer and serve. Therefore, thus spoke the angel:
        '*Sum rex, sum princeps: neutrum fortasse deinceps;*
        O qui jura regis Christi specialia regis,
        Hoc quod agas melius justus es, esto pius!
        Nudum jus a te vestiri vult pietate;
        Qualia vis metere talia grana sere.
        Si jus nudatur nudo de jure metatur;
        Si seritur pietas de pietate metas!'
    ('I am King, I am Prince, you say: perhaps neither, after today;
        You wield the laws most high of Christ's own Majesty;
        The better so to do, be just and ruthful too!
        Justice in nakedness needs from you Mercy's dress;
        That harvest you would see, such let your sowing be.
        If you strip Justice bare, such too may be your share;
        Mercy by you once sown, *you* shall be mercy shown.')

Then a goliard,[10] a glutton for words, made this a grievance:
And to the angel on high he gave this answer: 140
    'Dum rex a regere dicatur nomen habere,
    Nomen habet sine re nisi studet jura tenere.'
    ('Since by his reign alone the king *as* king is known,
    He holds the name alone if laws be overthrown.')
Then all the Commoners called out a catchword in Latin,
To counsel the King, construe it who wished.
    'Praecepta regis sunt nobis vincula legis!'
    ('All that the King ordains binds us with legal chains.')
    Then all at once there ran out a riot of rats,
And little mice among them, more than a thousand,
Who came to confer for their common profit.
For a Cat from a certain Court came whenever he chose
And lighted on them laughingly, and did what he liked 150
To play with them perilously, and paw them, and toss them about.
'For dangers and dreads of all kinds we dare scarcely stir;
And if we grumble at his games, he will grieve us the more –
Scratch us and scrape us, or seize us in his claws
Till life is not worth living until he leaves us alone.
Were we but wise enough to withstand his will,
We too might be lofty lords and live at our ease.'
    One rat of renown, with a free-running tongue,
Offered an ideal scheme of his own invention.
Said he: 'I have seen certain fellows, in the City of London, 160
Bearing bright golden chains about their necks,
And cleverly fashioned collars; they are unconfined,
They walk in warrens or wastelands wherever they please
(And at other times, I am told, they take themselves elsewhere).
It seems to me, by Jesus, if their bright chains carried a bell,
People would hear where they went, and could run away.
I have reasoned this out,' said the rat, 'and our right course
Is to buy a bell, of brass or of bright silver,
And, for our common cause, to fix it on a collar
And hang it round the Cat's neck. We shall hear him then 170
When he takes the road, or rests, or runs out to play.
If he is disposed for sport, we may spy on him,
Present only in part while his mood is playful;
And should he wax wroth, beware, and avoid his ways.'

All that rout of rats agreed with his reasoning.
But when the bell had been bought, and hung on the chain,
There was never a rat in the rout — not for the realm of France
— That dared to bind the bell about the Cat's neck,
Nor to hang it over his head, for the whole of England.
They confessed themselves fearful, and their plan feeble,   180
And allowed that their labour was lost, and all their long scheming.

    Then a mouse that seemed to me to have much wisdom
Strode forward strongly, and stood before them all,
And, as follows, addressed the assembly of rats.
'Even if we killed the Cat, another would come
To claw us and all our kinsmen, though we crept under benches.
Therefore I counsel the commoners to leave the Cat alone,
And let us never be so bold as even to *show* him the bell.
For I heard my father say, these seven years since,
That when the Cat is a kitten, the Court is wretched.   190
Thus too runs Holy Writ, for anyone to read:
    Vae terrae ubi puer rex est.
    (Woe to thee, O land, when thy King is a child.)[11]
For there no resident can rest, for the rats at night.
More: while the Cat chases conies, he does not covet *our* corpses,
But (not to defame him) feeds on game from the fields.
Better a little loss than a long sorrow,
And the trouble among us today than the *loss* of our troubles.
For then we mice would destroy the malt of many a man,
And all you riot of rats would rend men's clothing,
Could not the Cat in this Court pounce and catch us.
Were you given your own way, you rats could not rule
                         yourselves.   200
For *my* part,' said this mouse, 'I foresee such an aftermath,
My counsel is to vex neither Cat nor Kitten,
Nor collogue about this collar (that cost *me* nothing,
Though even if it *had* cost me cash I should never confess it),
But to let each one of them do as either pleases —
Whether paired or in private — to take what prey he can.
So, a warning to the wise: watch *your own* affairs.'

    Now, the meaning of my dream, you merry men all,
Decide for yourselves, for *I* dare not, by dear God in Heaven!

    Now a hundred men hovered there, in silken headgear,   210

Serjeants-at-Law, it seemed, that served at the Bar
And presented their pleas for pennies or for pounds;
Not for love of Our Lord did their lips ever open;
You might sooner measure the mist on the Malvern Hills
Than get one murmur from their mouths without showing money.

    Barons and burgesses and bondsmen too
I saw in the assembly, as you shall soon hear;
Batches of bakers and brewers and butchers,
Weavers of wool and weavers of linen,
Tailors and tinkers and market-toll-takers,   220
Masons and miners, and many other craftsmen.
No kind of labourer living, but some leapt forward,
Such as ditchers and delvers that do their work badly
And spend the long day singing *Dieu vous sauve, Dame Emme.*[12]
There cooks and their kitchen-boys cried, 'Hot pies! Hot!
Good pigs and geese! Come and get your dinner!'
And taverners told the same tale to the world –
'White wine of Alsace! Red wine of Gascony!
Rhine wine or La Rochelle to digest the roast!'
All this I saw in my dream, and seven times more.   230

Passus 1

Now, what that mountain meant, and that murky valley,
And the plain full of people, I shall presently show you.
A Lady, lovely to look upon, clothed in linen,
Came down from a castle and called to me kindly,
Saying, 'Are you asleep, my son? Do you see these people,
How busily they bustle about their maze?
The greater part of the people that pass through this world,
If honoured upon Earth, ask nothing better;
Of a Heaven, other than here, they have no thought.'

    Her face made me fear her, fair though she was.   10
'Madame,' I said, 'if you please, what may all this mean?'
She said, 'The tower on the hill-top is where Truth dwells,
He who would have your works accord with His word;
For He is Father of Faith, and fashioned you all
With a figure and a face, and gave you five senses
With which to worship Him while you dwell here.
Therefore he ordered the earth to afford all men
Linen enough, and wool, and their livelihood,
That each might in moderate manner be at ease.

    In His kindness He commanded three things common to all;   20
None but these is needful, and I mean to name them,
Reckoning them by reason; and you shall repeat them.
First there is clothing, to keep you from cold;
Then food to furnish your meals, and keep you from discomfort;
And drink for when you are dry: but drink within reason;
Beware of being the worse for it when you should work.
For Lot, when he was alive, from his love of drink
Did things to his daughters that pleased the Devil.
He delighted in drink, as the Devil would have wished,
And lechery laid hold on him, and he lay with them both;   30
And wine it was he must blame for the wicked deeds:

     Inebriamus eum vino, dormiamusque cum eo,
       ut servare possimus ex patre nostro semen.

(The first-born said to the younger, Come, let us make our
    father drink wine, and we will lie with him, that we
    may preserve seed of our father.)[1]
Thus by wine and by women was Lot overwhelmed,
And begat there in gluttony ungracious sons.
Dread, therefore, delectable drink; you will do better to;
Moderation is medicinal, however much you yearn.
Not all that the stomach beseeches is good for the soul,
Nor food for the flesh all that the soul finds pleasing.
Put no faith in your flesh, for a liar instructs it –
Namely, the wicked World, with its wish to betray you;
For the Fiend and the Flesh are fellow-hunters,[2]   40
Each pursuing your soul, speaking sin to your heart.
I tell this by way of warning, so that you shall beware.'
    'My thanks to you, madame,' said I. 'Your words please
                                                    me well.
But the wealth of this world, that men so watchfully cling to:
Tell me to whom, madame, this money belongs?'
    Said she, 'Go to the Gospel, and read God's own word,
At the question put Him with a penny, by people in the temple,
To pay or not to pay to Tiberius Caesar.
And Christ asked whose inscription was upon the coin,
And whose the likeness lying within the lettering.   50
"Caesar's," they said, "as we all plainly see."
"Give unto Caesar," said Christ, "the things that are Caesar's;
And unto God, God's things; you go astray else."[3]
I say, it is Rightful Reason that should rule you all,
With Mother Wit[4] as the warden that holds your wealth,
The guardian of your gold, who gives you it as needed:
Good Management and these two go hand in hand together.'
Then earnestly I asked her, in Our Maker's Name,
'That dungeon in the dale, so dreadful to look at,
What may its meaning be, madame, I beseech you?'   60
    'That is the Castle of Care; and whoever comes there
Indeed may curse the day that his body and soul were conceived.
A creature dwells in the Castle, and is called Wrong.
He first founded the dungeon, and is father of Falsehood.
Adam and Eve he egged on to evil,
He counselled Cain to kill his own brother;

Judas he be-japed with Jewish silver,
And high on an elder-tree he afterwards hanged him.[5]
He sets leashes on love, and he lies to all men;
Those who trust in his treasure, he betrays the soonest.'   70
Then I wondered within me who this woman could be,
Who spoke with such wisdom the words of Holy Scripture.
I asked her, 'In the Name of the Highest, before you go hence,
Who are you, truly, that so tenderly teach me?'

    Said she, 'I am Holy Church. It behoves you to know me;
I first received you, and first taught you the Faith;
You brought me at baptism sureties of obedience,
Loyally to love me while your life should last.'

    On bended knees I begged her then to be merciful,
And in pity to pray for the pardon of my sins;   80
Also to acquaint me clearly with true belief in Christ,
That I might keep the commands of Him Who created me.
'Teach not of earthly treasure,' I cried, 'tell me this only:
How may I save my soul, oh sanctified Lady?'

    Said she, 'When all treasures are tested, Truth is the best;
And the text "God is Love"[6] I take as my attestor.
Truth is a leman as loveable as the dear Lord Himself.

    Whoever is truthful of tongue, and tells no lies,
And is faithful in works as in words, and wishes no man evil,
He is godlike, says the Gospel, both here and on high,   90
And is like Our Lord Himself, as St Luke says.[7]

    Men well taught in this truth should tell it around,
Christians and unChristians too are clamouring for it.
Kings and their cohorts should by rights be its keepers,
Riding forth to repress wrong throughout their realms,
Trapping transgressors and tying them tightly
Until Truth has determined the extent of their trespasses.
That is the profession plainly proper for knights –
Not just to fast on one Friday in five-score winters,
But to stand by him and by her who would uphold Truth,   100
And leave them neither for love nor for latching on to money.

    King David in his day was a dubber of knights,[8]
And made them swear on their swords to serve Truth always;
And apostate from that Order was any who broke that oath.

    But Christ, who is King of Kings, founded *ten* knightly Orders

(Seraphim and Cherubim, seven lower, and last of all, Satan's),[9]
Deputing them power from His might – and the prouder
                                   they were for it –
And over His lesser lieges made them Archangels,
And taught them to know Truth by virtue of the Trinity,
Obedient when He bade them; He asked nothing besides.   110
   Lucifer and his legions also learned this in Heaven,
But for breach of obedience lost Heaven's bliss
And fell from that fellowship in the forms of fiends,
Into deep dark Hell, there to dwell for ever.
Many more thousands than a man could count
Leapt out with Lucifer, in loathsome shapes,
For they believed in him though he lied in these words,
     "Ponam pedem in aquilone, et similis ero altissimo."
    (My foot shall I set upon the North Wind, and be like unto
       the Most High.)[10]
All who hoped it might be so, Heaven could not hold them;
Out they fell, in fiends' forms, for nine whole days.
Till God in His goodness stemmed and staunched that gushing,   120
Fixing the firmament close, to stand fast and quiet.
   When these wicked ones fell, it was in a strange way,
Some into air, some to earth, some deep into Hell.
But Lucifer lies the lowest of them all:
For the pride that he displayed, his pains are endless;
And all evildoers shall go down and dwell,
After the day of their death, with that same devil.
But they who wrought righteousness, as Holy Writ shows,
And whose end is in that Truth I have said is best,
Certain are they that their souls shall ascend to Heaven: 130
The threefold God's is their truth, and He shall enthrone them.
   Therefore I tell you again, and have proved by my texts,
When all treasures are tested, the best is Truth.
Let unlearned men hear this, for the lettered know it:
The treasure of treasures upon Earth, is Truth.'
   'I do not know Truth by nature; you must teach me better
By what faculty it enters my flesh, and where it is found.'
   Said the Lady, 'You doltish dullard, dim are your wits!
Too little Latin, my friend, you learned in your youth!'

Heu mihi, quod sterilem duxi vitam juvenilem!
  (Woe's me! How barren, in truth, was the life I led in my
      youth!)
'In your heart you know by nature the need you have   140 .
To love your Lord better than your own life,
And commit no mortal sin though death might befall you.
Trust me, that is truth; if any can teach you better,
Be sure to listen, and let him speak, and so learn from him.
  Thus witnesses God's word – let your works conform:
Truth will tell you that Love is the tried elixir of Heaven;
They suffer from no sin, who use *that* sovereign balm;
God worked, as He willed, by Love, when framing the world,
And Moses learned from Him that Love is likest to Heaven.[11]
It is the Plant of Peace,[12] and most precious of virtues.   150
  For Heaven could not hold it, it was so heavy in itself,
Till it had eaten all it could of the Earth;
And when it had upon Earth assumed flesh and blood,[13]
Thereafter it was lighter than a leaf on a linden-tree,
And nimble and keen as the point of a needle;
No armour could resist it, nor high ramparts bar it.
  Therefore Love is leader of Our Lord's folk in Heaven,
Our mediator, as mayors are between king and people.
Just so is Love a leader, and a framer of laws;
Its amercement on man for misdeeds is mercy.   160
To know it by nature needs the power of God
At work in the heart, where its fount and high well-spring lie.
For natural knowledge in the heart, a power is needed,
That comes forth and from the Father Who formed us all,
And Who looked on us with love, and let His Son die
Meekly for our misdeeds, to amend us all.
And He called down no curse upon his crucifiers:
Mildly did His mouth beseech God's mercy
And pity on those people, in His pain and death.
  You have an example here, in His own self: 170
He was mighty but meek, and He granted mercy
To them that hung Him high, and pierced His heart.
  Rich people, have pity, I counsel you, for the poor;
Though mighty to command them, let your acts be mild.
For "with what measure ye mete",[14] amiss or truly,

You shall be weighed therewith when you leave this world.
Eadem mensura qua mensi fueritis, remetietur vobis.
For though your tongue be truthful, and you trade honestly,
Though you be chaste as a child that weeps at its churching,
Unless you love Man loyally, and relieve the poor,
Sharing the gifts God sent you, in goodly bounty,   180
You will get no more merit from your Masses and your prayers
Than Molly the Slut from her maidenhead – which no
                              man has tried for.

As noble St James says in his Epistle,
     Fides sine operibus mortua est:
Faith without Works has no worth at all,[15]
As dead as a door-post unless deeds confirm it.
So, chastity without charity shall be chained in Hell;
It has less value than an unlit lamp.
     Many chaplains are chaste, but lacking in charity:
Are any men more greedy than these, once promoted?
Unkind to their kin and to all fellow-Christians?   190
They gulp down all gifts, and grumble for more:
Such chastity lacking charity shall be chained in Hell.
     Parish priests in plenty are bodily pure,
Yet encumbered by covetousness – and cannot get rid of it,
It is hammered hard into them, like a hinge to a door.
This is not the Truth of the Trinity, but the treachery of Hell;
And laymen learn from it to give less readily.
Wisely, then – by Our Lord – were these words said:
"Give and it shall be given unto you; for *I* gave you my all.
This is the latch of love, that releases my grace   200
To comfort the comfortless encumbered with sin."
Love is the healer of life, that stands next to Our Lord,
And the road that leads directly to the realm of Heaven.
     I tell you again what I took from those texts:
When all treasures are tested, Truth is the best.
     Now I have told you what Truth is – that no treasure is better:
I may linger with you no longer. May Our Lord preserve you!'

Again I besought a boon, on my bended knees,
And said, 'Your mercy, madame, for the love of Mary in Heaven
That bore the blessed child who brought our salvation,
Let me now learn some way to distinguish lying.'
   'Look to your left side: lo! there they stand –
Falsehood and Fauvel[1] together, and their many friends!'
   I looked to my left, as the Lady had bidden me,
And grew aware of a woman with splendid clothing
Fringed with rich fur, the finest in the world.
She was crowned with a coronet as good as the king's.   10
Daintily were her fingers adorned with spun gold
In rings, with rubies on them like red-hot embers,
And diamonds of the dearest, and sapphires both deep blue
                                  and light,
And orient pearls, and iolites as antidotes to poison.
Her robe was very rich, a fast-dyed red scarlet,
With rows of red gold and of radiant jewels.
I was ravished by her array; such riches were new to me;
I wondered who she was, and whose wife she might be.
   'Who is this woman,' I asked, 'so wonderfully dressed?'
'That is Meed[2] the Maiden,' said she, 'who has many
                                  times harmed me,   20
And slandered my sweet friend who is called Straight-Dealing,
And lied about her to the lords in the law-courts.
In the palace of the Pope she is as privileged as I –
Though Truth is bemocked by it, for Meed is a by-blow.
Her father was Fraud, of the faithless tongue,
Who never spoke sincerely since he came to Earth;
And Meed is modelled upon him, as is Nature's manner:
    Qualis pater, talis filius; bona arbor bonum fructum facit.
    (Like father, like son; a good tree bears good fruit.)[3]
I ought to be honoured above her; my lineage is higher:
My Father is great God, the ground of all graces,

One God, Who had no beginning; and I am His good daughter,   30
And He gave Mercy to me, to be my marriage-portion.
Whatever man shews Mercy, and loves me loyally,
Shall be my lord, and I his beloved, in Heaven above.
But whatever man takes Meed — I wager my head —
He will lose for love of her his heirloom of Charity.

   What King David conveys, about men who take Meed,
And of others who go among us maintaining Truth,
And how one may save oneself, the Psalter bears witness:

     Domine, quis habitabit in tabernaculo tuo?

    (Lord, who shall abide in thy tabernacle? or who shall dwell
     in thy holy hill?

    He that taketh not reward against the innocent.)[4]

  And now Meed the Maid is to marry an excommunicate villain,
Fraud Faithless-Tongue,[5] offspring of the Fiend;   40
Fauvel first, with fair speech, enchanted these folk;
But Liar was chief match-maker for the wedding of Meed.

   Tomorrow, then, shall this maiden's marriage feast be held;
And there you might learn, if you wished, who the others are,
Both little and great, who belong in their lordships' train.
Contrive, if you can, to know them; but keep your
                        tongue quiet;
Do not abuse them, let them be, till Straight-Dealing becomes
A Justice with power to punish them: put your case *then*.

   Now I commend you to Christ and His immaculate Mother.
Never encumber your conscience by coveting Meed.'   50

   Thus the Lady left me lying asleep;
And how Meed was married, I imagined in my dream.
All the rich retinue that were retainers of Fraud
Were bidden to the bridal by the kin of both sides:
All manner of men, the humble and the mighty,
To see this maiden's marriage, were assembled in multitudes.
Clergy and knights had come; and, of the common people,
Assize-jurors, summoners, and sheriffs and their clerks,
Beadles and bailiffs and bargainers and brokers,
Pre-emptors and provisioners, and advocates of the
                          Arches Court[6] —   60
I cannot recall or count all who came to see Meed.
But Simony and Civil Law and the Assize-Court jurymen

Were of all men, I thought, the most familiar with Meed.
Fauvel went first to fetch her from her boudoir,
And as marriage-broker brought her to be joined with Fraud.
When Simony and Civil Law understood what was wanted,
They assented, for a small fee, to say whatever they were asked.
Then Liar lunged forward, saying, 'Look! A deed of conveyance
That Guile, with his great oaths, has given to the couple!'
And he begged Civil Law to scan it, and Simony to read it.   70
Then Simony and Civil Law both stood up,
And unfolded the feoffment drawn-up by Fraud.[7]
Then Simony started singing-out at the top of his voice,
    'Sciant praesentes et futuri' . . .
     (Be it known to all present and to come . . .)
  'Be it witnessed and warranted by all the world
That Meed has been married more for her money
Than for any quality or comeliness or native kindness.
Fraud is fond of her, for he knows her wealth;
And Fauvel with his faithless tongue empowers them
                              by this feoffment
To live proudly as princes, and despise the poor;
To backbite and to boast and to bear false witness;   80
To be scornful and scurrilous, and to spread scandal;
To be bold and disobedient in breaking the Ten Commandments.
  And the Earldoms of Envy and of Ire, conjoined,
And the Castles of Contention and of Chattering Claptrap,
The County of Covetousness, and the communes adjoining,
To wit, Usury and Avarice: I grant all these,
With their backdoor deals and brokery, plus the Borough of Theft,
And the Lordship of Lechery in all its length and breadth,
As well in words and in deeds as in wanton ogling,
As well in clothes and concupiscence as in fond conceits   90
That endure in the desire though the doing fails.'
  He gave them Gluttony too, and Great Oaths, its twin,
And the right to drink all day at a dozen taverns,
To jabber there, and joke, and judge their fellow-Christians,
And on fast-days to feast themselves before noon
– And then to sit and surfeit until sleep assailed them;
To breed like boars in town-gutters, and bed in luxury
Till Sloth and sleep had sleekened their sides.

In despair they should wake then, but without repentance,
And in their last agonies believe themselves lost.   100
   'To have and to hold, I give them and their inheritors
A dwelling with the Devil, and eternal damnation,
With the purlieus of Purgatory and the pains of Hell:
They in return to yield, at one year's end,
Their souls to Satan, with him to suffer torment
And with him to dwell in woe so long as God is in Heaven.'
   Of the witnesses of which deed, the first was Wrong himself,
Then Pete the Pardoner with his Pauline doctrine;[8]
Bartie the beadle of Buckinghamshire;
Reynold the reeve of the Soke of Rutland;   110
Munday the Miller, and many more such others.
'On Devilsday do I set my hand to this Deed,
With Sir Simony as witness, by right of Civil Law.'
   Now Theology lost his temper at that loud proclamation,
And said to Civil Law, 'Now, sorrow be upon you,
To manoeuvre such marriages in mockery of Truth![9]
You'll be sorry before you see the end of the ceremony!
   For Meed was of honest birth, engendered upon Amends,
And God has already given Good Work His promise of her.
You have given her to a guileful rogue, God damn you!   120
Is *this* how you interpret the text, that is Truth's own words?
     Dignus est enim operarius mercede sua.
    (For the labourer is worthy of his hire.)[10]
And you have handfast Meed to Fraud! A fig for your law!
For you live by lying and by lecherous business.
Simony and yourself are spoilers of Holy Church;
You and your notaries are a nuisance to the nation.
By the God who made me, you shall both buy this dearly!
Well do you know, double-faced ones, unless you are doited,
That Fraud is faithless and treacherous in all his affairs,
And was born in bastardy, Beelzebub's kinsman.   130
But Meed is a maiden well-born of Amends,
Who might kiss the king as her cousin if the fancy took her.
   Then use what wits you have; and if you are wise
You will lead her up to London, where the Laws are declared,
And find if any law will let these two lie together.
Even should the Justices judge her joinable with Fraud,

Still beware of that wedding; for Truth has His wits about him,
And Conscience is His counsellor, who knows you both
                                        quite well:
Should he find you at fault, and siding with Fraud,
Your souls shall both rue it bitterly, at the Bar of Heaven!'   140
Civil Law assented to this; but Simony refused
Until he had silver for his services, and so did the notaries.
    Then Fauvel fetched out a quantity of florins,
And told Guile to give the gold out all round –
To the notaries in particular, so that none should fail them at need.
He gave many florins to False-Witness, as a retaining fee,
For he could well manage Meed, and make her obedient.
With all this gold gathered in, there was great thanksgiving
To Fraud and Fauvel for their fine gifts,
And many came to comfort Fraud in his quandary,   150
Saying, 'Be sure, sir, we shall never slacken
Till Meed is your wedded wife by the work of our wits.
We have overmastered Meed with mild persuasion;
And she has agreed, good-humouredly, to go with us
To London, and look into whether the Law
Will judge you both rightly to be joined in lasting joy.'
    Fraud, at this, felt much happier, and so did Fauvel;
They summoned all and sundry from the surrounding shires,
And bade them, beggars included, be ready
To go with them to Westminster Court as witnesses.   160
    They must cast-about, now, for caples to carry them there,
So Fauvel's men led forth mounts enough for them all.
Meed the Maiden they shoved upon a Sheriff newly-shod;
Fraud sat on an Assize-juror, who trotted softly;
Fauvel's own mount was a flatterer, finely harnessed.
    But the notaries had no horses, and were annoyed
That Simony and Civil Law must slog-it on foot.
Civil Law and Simony both swore
That the summoners should be saddled and serve to bear them.
'And let Pope's-priests[11] be apparelled as if they were palfreys;   170
Sir Simony himself shall sit on their backs.
You deans and sub-deans, let all draw together,
Bishops' officers and archdeacons, and all your registrars:
Have them saddled with silver to excuse our sins –

Our divorces and adulteries and undiscovered usuries.
And let them bear bishops about, on visitations.

Paulines, as privies to the action, shall plead in the Consistory,
Serving myself, who am named Civil Law.
Cart-saddle the Commissary:[12] he shall draw our carriage,
And with fines from fornicators shall feed us all.   180
Tie Liar to a long cart, and let him lug all the remainder,
Such as friars and fakers, who are still on foot.'

Thus Fraud and Fauvel set forth together,
With Meed in the middle, and all those men following.
I have no time to tell you all who trailed behind,
Of so many kinds of men who live in Middle Earth;
But going ahead of them was Guile, who guided them all.

Straight-Dealing, though, understood him and, although
                                                    saying little,
Spurred-up her palfrey and passed the whole troop,
And came to the King's Court, and told the news to Conscience; 190
And Conscience carried the story to the King.

The King said, 'Now, by Christ, could I only catch
Fraud or Fauvel, or any of their followers,
I would have my revenge on those wretches who
                                          rouse-up trouble!
I would have them hanged by the neck, and their whole
                                          horde with them!
Not even the least shall go loose, on bail or licence:
Let the full force of the Law fall on them all.'
And he called for a Constable, who came forthwith,
And ordered them arrested: 'At all costs, I say!
And put that felon Fraud in fetters, refusing all bribes;   200
And get the head off Guile, before he goes further;
And if you lay hands on Liar, do not let him escape,
But put him in the pillory, however hard he pleads.
And bring Meed the Maid before me, no matter what!'

Sir Dread was standing by the door, and heard these decrees;
How the King was commanding Constables and Sergeants
To bind and fetter Fraud and all his fellowship.
So he went away quickly, and gave warning to Fraud,
Bidding him flee for fear, and his followers with him.
And Fraud, being truly afraid, took refuge with the friars;   210

And Guile, aghast at his danger, did not know where to go,
Till certain merchants met him, and made him go with them
To be shut-up in their shop, and show their goods to buyers,
And wear an apprentice's apparel, and serve the public.
   As for Liar, he leapt lithely away
To lurk in the city lanes, and be lugged-about by everyone,
Nowhere welcome, despite his wealth of stories.
Everywhere hooted at and told to 'sling his hook';
Till the pardoners at last had pity, and pulled him indoors.
They washed him and wiped him, and wound him about
                                          with napkins,   220
And sent him on Sundays to the Church, with seals,
Giving pennyworths of pardons for a pound here and there.
The physicians began to frown, and sent off a letter
Inviting him to join them and inspect people's urine.
Spicemongers bespoke him to inspect their goods
(For he knew the tricks of their trade, and their merchandise too).
Then some minstrels and messengers happened to meet him,
And held on to him half a year and eleven days more.
Fair-spoken friars fetched him away,
And clad him in their clothes to conceal him from visitors;   230
But they let him leave and return whenever he likes,
And he is always welcome among them, and stays with
                                          them often.
   Thus all Fraud's rout fled in fear, and took refuge in corners;
Only Meed the Maiden dared to remain.
Even so, to tell the truth, she trembled with terror,
And sorrowed, and wrung her hands when they came to arrest her.

Passus 3

So, then, Meed the Maiden, and no more of the band,
Was brought before the King by beadles and bailiffs.
The King called for a clerk (I cannot tell you his name)
To take charge of Meed the Maiden and make her comfortable:
'I shall examine her in person, and ask her directly
Which man in all the world she would rather wed.
If she conforms to my counsel, and obeys my commands,
I will forgive all her guilt, God helping me.'
   Courteously, then, this clerk (as the King commanded),
With his arm round her waist, took Meed away to her room,   10
Where musicians and minstrels were ready to amuse her.
   All who dwelt in Westminster were respectful to her.
Some law-lords got themselves up with gallantry and
                           good humour,
And bustled along to her boudoir to befriend her
And comfort her kindly. And thus they commenced:
'Do not mourn, Meed, nor make yourself afraid;
Soon we shall speak to the king, and smooth your path for you
To be wedded to whom you wish, and where you please,
Despite the cunning of Conscience, forsooth, and his crafty tricks.'
   Graciously Meed the Maiden spoke of her gratitude   20
For their great goodness; and to each one she gave
Goblets of pure gold, and great silver cups,
And ruby rings, and many other riches;
And even for the lowest of the lackeys, a large coin.
Then lightly did these lords take leave of Meed,
And up came the clergy, to comfort her likewise.
   They told her, 'Take heart! We will serve you truly;
As long as you last, you shall live as you please.'
Courteously, to the clergy, Meed returned the compliment.
'Loyally shall I love you, and make each of you Lord Bishop,   30
Or at least have your names called to Consistory Courts.
Lack of learning shall not hold back the man that I love

From early advancement: I am very well known
Where clever clergy must crawl in the back ranks.'
    Then there came a Confessor in a friar's cope.
To Meed the Maiden he murmured this speech
Mellowly and mildly, as to one making a confession.
'Though men both lay and learned might have lain with you,
And Falsehood have been your familiar these last fifty winters,
For a horse-load of wheat you should have absolution;   40
I will be your beadsman, and spread abroad your gospel
Among cavaliers and clergy, to the ruin of Conscience.'
    Then for all her misdeeds, Meed knelt, and by that man
Had her sins shriven in short order – and without shame,
                                                    believe me:
She told him the tale, and then tipped him a gold noble
To be her beadsman and her go-between.
    He gave her swift absolution; and then he said,
'We are having a stained-glass window made for us,
                                        that's working-out dear.
Were you to give us the glass, and have your name engraved there,
You could safely count on your soul's sitting in Heaven.'   50
Said the woman, 'Were I sure of that, I would spend freely
To be your friend, my dear friar, and never fail you
While you gave licence to lords who follow lechery,
And did not lash those ladies who love it as well.
It's a frailty of the flesh, as one finds in all the books,
An inborn attraction – from which we all originate.
If one escapes a scandal, there's scarcely any harm in it;
Of all the seven great sins, it's the soonest absolved.
If you're friendly, therefore, to folk who enjoy it,
I'll buy coping for your kirk, I'll build you a cloister,   60
Whitewash your walls, and glaze your windows
With pictures, and with portraits of *me*, and pay for the lot,
So that everyone will say I'm one of your Lay Sisters.'[1]
    God forbids all such emblazoning by good people;
Such advertised virtuous deeds may peradventure
Be the paintings of Pride and of worldly pomp.
Christ knows our consciences and our native corruption,
All our costs and covetousness, and to whom the cash belongs.
Therefore my lesson is, all you lords, leave off such boasts

As engraving on window glass all your good deeds,   70
Asking the clergy's attention when you give alms,[2]
Lest you have your reward here on Earth, but not in Heaven:
    Nesciat sinistra tua quid faciat dextera tua:
Let not thy left hand either early or late
Have reason to know what is wrought by thy right.
That is God's command in the Gospel for them who give alms.
All you mayors and magistrates, that are mediators
Between the King and the commoners, in the keeping of laws,
To punish folk on pillories or on penal stools:[3]
Look to brewing-wives and bakeresses and cooks and butchers.
Of all men and women in the world, they work most harm   80
Upon poor people who must buy small portions.
For they poison these people, often but unpublished:
Dishonest retailers grow rich, and become great rentiers
From food that poor people should be putting in their bellies.
Were they truthful traders, they could not build such tall houses,
Nor batten on tenements, be sure of that.
    But Meed the Maiden has begged all mayors
To accept from such sellers whatever silver they offer –
Or presents other than specie, such as plate silver,
Rings, or other rich gifts – to ignore retailers.   90
Said the maiden: 'If you love me, then love all of *them*:
Let them profit just a penny or two more than is proper.'
    Solomon the great Sage wrote a sermon
For the amendment of all mayors and law-keeping men,
And took as his text this that I shall tell you:
    Ignis devorabit tabernacula eorum, qui munera libenter accipiunt.[4]
For lettered and learned people, this Latin means
That fire shall come from Heaven and burn to fine blue ashes
The houses or homes of all those that are hungry
For the annual gift or the odd gift, on account of their offices.
    Well, the King came from his Council, and called for Meed,   100
Sending many servants to escort her forthwith
To his private apartments, in the pleasantest of spirits.
    The King then courteously began the conference,
And explained to Meed the Maiden his full meaning.
'Often enough, my lady, have you acted unwisely;

But never, forsooth, with more folly than when you
                                        accepted Fraud.
That guilt, though, I forgive, and grant you my mercy.
But from now till your dying day, never do so again!
    A knight of mine, called Conscience, lately came from abroad:
If *he* wants you for his wife, are you willing to take him?'   110
'Indeed yes, my liege; Lord forbid but that I allowed it;
Hang me at once unless I heed your slightest behest!'
    So they called Sir Conscience to come and present himself
Before the King in Council, both clergy and laymen.
He bowed low in obeisance, then on bended knee
Waited to hear the King's will, and what he should do.
    'Would you wed this woman,' said the King, 'were
                                        I to consent?
She is eager for the alliance, and to be your spouse.'
    Said Conscience to the King, 'Now, Christ forbid!
To wed such a wife? I would sooner be damned!   120
Her faithfulness is frail, and her speech fallacious;
She has made men scores of times commit misdeeds;
To wives and widows she teaches wantonness,
They are lured to lechery by love of her gifts;
But trust in her treasures has betrayed countless people:
She felled your own father with false promises.[5]
She has poisoned popes, and impaired Holy Church.[6]
There is no bawdier bitch, by God Who made me,
Between Heaven and Hell, though one searched the whole Earth.
She has a teetotum twat and a tale-bearing tongue;   130
She's as common as a cart-track to every crook on two feet –
To monks, to minstrels, to mumping lepers under hedges.
Summoners and assize-jurors – such men prize her;
Sheriffs could shut up shop but for her,
For she makes men lose their land and their lives alike;
She pays to let prisoners loose, to parade at large,
Giving their jailers groats or gold all round
To unfetter felons who are then free of the country;
But the innocent she arrests and securely imprisons,
And hangs for pure hatred those who have done no harm.   140
    To be cursed in the Consistory she considers no risk,
For she keeps the Commissary in copes, and clerks in coats;

She gets absolution as soon as she herself likes,
And with her money does almost as much in a month
As your Privy Seal[7] in six score days.
She has the Pope's private ear — provisors know that —
For she and Sir Simony seal their certificates.

    She bestows on men bishoprics, though they be unlettered,
Gives prebends to parsons, and enables priests
To use courtesans and concubines all their lives long   150
Who bear the priests' babies though God's law forbids it.
Woe to that kingdom where the king thinks well of her,
For she favours falsehood and befouls the truth.

    By Jesus, her jewels corrupt even your Justices
To lie against the Law, and delay its course;
Her florins fly so thickly, the truth is forestalled.
The law is dragged on her leash, and she picks her own love-days;[8]
For love of her, men lose what good law might have won them.
The poor might plead here for ever, and gain only perplexity;
So lofty is the law, and so loth to end a case,   160
Without presents or pence, it will please very few.

    Barons and burgesses Meed brings to grief,
And calamity to common folk who care about honesty;
For clerkship and covetousness she couples together.
Such is the life of this "lady" — may Our Lord bring her low!
And all who maintain her men, may misfortune undo them!
Poor men, because of her, have no power to complain of
                                          their wrongs,
Such mastery has Meed over men of property.'

    Then Meed looked mournful, and asked the king meekly
For permission to put in her defence and plea;   170
And her wish was granted by him very willingly:

    'Excuse yourself if you can; I keep myself neutral;
For Conscience's case, if just, condemns you to exile.'
'No, lord,' said that Lady, 'no longer will you believe him
When you know the facts fully, and where the fault lies.
In moments of misfortune, Meed may help most.
You know quite well, Conscience, I am not here to quarrel,
Nor to disparage your person with a proud heart.
You are well aware, you weasel — unless willing to lie —
That you have hung about my neck half-a-million times,   180

And grabbed at my gold, and given it where you pleased;
So why you wax wroth just *now*, is a wonder to me!
I could honour you now, as always, with awards,
And do more for your dignity than you deem fit to think.
  But you have defamed me foully before the king:
I never killed a king, nor ever conspired to,
Nor anything that you think I did, by the throne I swear it!
  In Normandy⁹ I was in no way a nuisance to the king;
But you, Conscience, a dozen times did him dishonour,
Huddling in hovels to heat your finger-nails,   190
Wondering if that winter would last for ever,
And dreading that a storm-cloud meant your death
And then hastening home because your belly was hungry!
  You pillager! Without pity you have robbed poor men,
And carried off their copper-work on your back, to sell in Calais.
But *I* lingered with my lord, to preserve his life,
And make his men merry, and relieve their misery.
I clapped them on the back, and kept up their courage,
Till they jigged for the joy of judging me their own.
Had I been Marshal of the King's Men, then by Holy Mary   200
I would have laid my life (no less a wager)
He'd have been lord of the length and breadth of that land –
And King, too, of that country, to promote his own kinsmen,
The lowest brat of his blood a baron's equal!
But you, Conscience, you coward, counselled withdrawal!
For a little silver, to let go of that lordship,
The richest realm that ever lay beneath rain-clouds!
  It is becoming in a king, the guardian of his country,
To give *meed* to those men that meekly serve him –
As to aliens, and to all men, and honour them with presents!   210
Meed makes men love him, and respect his manhood.
Emperors and earls and every kind of noble,
By *meed* retain young men to ride and run for them;
The Pope and all his prelates to not scorn presents,
And themselves give *meed* to the men who maintain their laws.
Servants are paid for their service, as is plain to see:
They take such *meed* from their masters as may be agreed
                                        between them.
Paupers promise their prayers in return for *meed*;

Minstrels demand *meed* for the music they make;
The king takes *meed* from his men, for maintaining the peace;   220
Teachers of children all ask *meed* from their charges;
Priests who preach virtue to the people, ask for *meed*
In the form of Mass-fees or their food at mealtimes.
Masters of all kinds of crafts call for *meed* from their 'prentices;
Merchants and *meed* needs must go together:
I am sure no man under the moon can live without *meed!*'

   Said the King to Conscience, 'By Christ, I believe
That Meed has most soundly overmastered your speech!'

   But Conscience cried out, as he knelt to the King:
'By your leave, my lord, there are two kinds of "meed".   230
The one is granted, of His grace, by God in Heaven,
To those who do their duty well, down here on Earth.
The Prophet preached of this, and it has its place in the Psalms:
   Domine, quis habitabit in tabernaculo tuo?[10]
Who shall abide in Thy abode, beside Thy holy saints,
Or rest on Thy Holy Hills?, is how David assesses it;
And David himself gives the answer, as we see in the Psalter:
   Qui ingreditur sine macula, et operatur justitiam.
   (He that walketh uprightly, and worketh righteousness.)
He, that is to say, who is spotless and of steady mind,
Who has ruled his deeds by reason and by rightful dealing;
Who has never lived usuriously, but has ever
Improved the minds of the poor, and pursued the truth: 240
   *Qui pecuniam suam non dedit ad usuram, et munera super
     innocentem.*
   (Who putteth not out his money to usury, nor taketh
     reward against the innocent.)
All who help the innocent and hold by the righteous,
Maintaining truth *without* meed, but for mercy only:
Such are the men, my lord, who receive that meed
From God, in the great need of their going hence.

   But there is another *measureless* meed that the
                       master-classes covet:[11]
The meed that they take for the maintenance of misdoers.
And the Psalter speaks of that, too, at the end of a Psalm:
   *In quorum manibus iniquitates sunt, dextera eorum repleta est
     muneribus.*

(In whose hands is mischief, and their right hand is full of
    bribes.)[12]
He who grabs at their gold, so help me God,
Shall make a bitter bargain, unless the Bible lies.

    The priests and parsons who seek their own pleasure,   250
Taking meed of money for the Masses they sing,
Have *human* meed only, as Matthew teaches:
    Amen, amen, receperunt mercedem suam.[13]
    (Verily I say unto you, they have their reward.)
What labourers and lowly folk are allotted by their masters
Is by no means *meed*, but a *measured* reward;
Nor is there any meed, I may say, in the deals of merchants:
Obviously, that is only exchange – one penny's worth for another.

    Have you never read the record, you recreant madam,
Of why vengeance was sent down upon Saul and his children?
God sent to Saul, by the mouth of His prophet Samuel,
Word that Agag of the Amalekites, and all his people after him,   260
Must die for a deed that their ancestors had done.

    "Therefore," said Samuel to Saul, "God Himself orders
That you be obedient, and act as He bids you.
Go to Amalek with your army; and all that you find there, slay:
Be they men or beasts, burn them to death;
Widows or wives, the women and their children;
Their possessions and plantations, all the property you may find,
Burn it, bearing nothing away with you, be it never so costly,
Neither for meed nor for money: make no exception.
Ruthlessly wreck it – or you shall rue the day."[14]   270

    But because he coveted the booty, King Saul forbore;
He spared both him and his herds, as we hear in the Bible,
Quite otherwise than he was warned by the prophet.
And God said to Samuel that Saul should die;
And for that sin, all the seed of Saul end shamefully.
These were the mischiefs you, Meed, made for Saul,
So that God hated him for ever, and his heirs after him.
My conclusions from that case, I will keep to myself,
And for fear of offending royalty, will find no moral:
For such is the way of this world, with those who have power,   280
That whoever tells them the truth, is the first to find trouble.

    Mother Wit was my teacher, so that *one* thing I know:

That one day Reason shall reign over all Earth's realms,
And we shall find the fate of Agag befalling others:[15]
Again shall Samuel slay him, Saul be accursed,
David assume his diadem and subdue all nations;
And one Christian King shall have care of them all.
   Meed shall no more have mastery, as now;
But love, and lowliness of heart, and loyalty,
Together shall take mastery of the world, and be saviours of truth. 290
Whoever shall trespass against Truth, or take bribes to subvert it,
Loyalty shall bring him to law, and no-one else living.
No Serjeant-at-Law, for his services, shall wear a silken coif,
No fur to fringe his gown, bought with fees for pleading in Court.
Meed makes law-lords of many malefactors,
Then over-rules those lords' laws, herself to reign in the realm;
But Natural Love shall come, as my – Conscience's – companion,
And make Law an honest labourer; and such love shall arise,
Such peace among the people, and such perfect honesty,
That the Jews shall rejoice because in their judgment   300
Moses has returned, or the Messiah come among men;
And wonder shall hold their hearts, at the truthfulness of humanity.
   Whoever bears a bayonet, a broadsword, a lance,
A hatchet or axe or any other weapon,
Shall be doomed to die, unless the smith do it over
Into a sickle or scythe, a ploughshare, or its coulter:
    Conflabunt gladios suos in vomeres.
   (They shall beat their swords into ploughshares, and their
       spears into pruning hooks.)[16]
Every man shall ply a plough or a spade or a pick-axe,
Or spin, or spread dung – or else be ruined by Sloth.
   Fox-hunting priests and parsons will then pursue God's pleasure,
And study away at the Psalms from dawn till sunset.   310
If hunting or hawking is a habit with such men,
Their boasted benefice shall belong to them no more.
Neither king nor cavalier, neither mayor nor constable,
Shall put-upon the people, or drag them into courts,
Nor jury-empanel them, nor press them to swear upon oath;
The criminal once convicted, one decree shall suffice:
A mild sentence or a severe one, as Truth shall decide.

King's Bench and Common Pleas, Church Court and Chapter,
Shall all be but *one* Court, with one Law-Baron as Judge:
And he shall be True-Tongue, an exact man who has
                                    never troubled me.   320
There shall be no more battles or bearers of weapons,
And the smith who smithies a weapon shall be smitten
                                    to death with it:
    Non levabit gens contra gentem gladium.
   (Nation shall not lift up sword against nation, neither shall
     they learn war any more.)[17]
But before this good fortune befalls us, men shall find
                                    foul omens,[18]
Such as six suns in the sky, with a ship and half a sheaf of arrows;
At a Paschal plenilune shall the Jews repent;
And Saracens, at such visions, shall sing *Gloria in Excelsis*:
For both Meed and Mohammed shall fare amiss in those days.
    Melius est nomen bonum quam divitiae multae.'
   (A good name is rather to be chosen than great riches.)[19]
   And now Meed grew gustier than a March gale.
   'I am not learned in Latin,' she said, 'I leave that to
                                book worms.
But see what Solomon, in his Book of Wisdom, says: 330
    Honorem acquiret qui dat munera:[20]
He that giveth gifts shall gain the victory,
And have high honour as well – that is Holy Writ.'
'I well believe, lady,' said Conscience, 'that your Latin is correct.
But you are like that lady who, reading *Thessalonians,*[21]
Found the phrase "prove all things", and was well satisfied.
But those were the last words of a line at the bottom of the leaf:
If she had turned the page, to see the rest of the text,
She would have found not a few words following after –
"Hold fast that which is good"; and the *whole* text is *God's.*
   You have made the same error, madame; you could
                                find no more   340
Even were you to sweat from your study of Solomon.
The text that you have told us would tickle potentates,
But you lacked someone learned to turn the leaf for you.
Study your Solomon again, and see what comes after –
A very troublesome text for those who love Meed:

Animam autem aufert accipientium.
  (But he beareth away the soul of the taker.)[22]
That is the true end of the text you trotted out:
Although we win honour and victory through you, Meed,
The soul of the receiver is ensnared by what he accepts!'

Said the King then, 'Cease! I will sanction no more.
You shall be reconciled, I swear it, and both shall serve me.
Kiss her, Conscience, for I command it.'
  'By Christ I will not,' said Conscience, 'though my
                              banishment be for ever!
Unless Reason says it is right, I would rather die!'
So the King said to Conscience: 'Then I command you
To be ready at once to ride, and bring Reason back.
Command him to come here to my Council;
For he shall rule my realm with correct advice,
And discuss with you, Conscience, as Christ is my witness,   10
How you instruct my people, either clergy or laymen.'
  'I gladly agree,' said the good man.
He rode off directly, to whisper in Reason's ear,
And told him the King's tidings, and began to take his leave.
But Reason said, 'I shall make ready to ride, so rest a while.'
Then Reason called Cato,[1] his servant (so courteous of speech),
And also Tom True-tongue-tell-me-no-tattle-
Nor-lying-tales-to-laugh-at-for-I-never-liked-them.
'Saddle my steed called Stay-till-I-see-my-Chance,
And gird him well with the girths of Witty-Words,   20
And harness him with a heavy bridle, to keep his head low,
For he will whinny twice at least on the way.'
  Then Conscience mounted his courser, and quickly made off,
Reason riding along with him, secretly conferring
About Meed the Maiden and her doings among men.
  A certain Warren Wisdom, and Witty his friend,[2]
Followed them fast, for they had certain affairs
To clear-up in the Court of the Exchequer, and in Chancery.
They rode hard in hope of having Reason's advice
To save them, for a consideration, from serious trouble.   30
Conscience knew this couple well, and their covetousness;
He told Reason to ride faster, recking nothing of either.

'For their words are wily, and they dwell with Meed,
Where rage and wrangling are – their sources of silver.
For where there is love and loyalty, they leave.
>   *Contritio et infelicitas in viis eorum.*
>   (Destruction and misery are in their ways, and the
>   way of peace they have not known.)[3]
For God, they would not give a goose's wing:
>   *Non est timor Dei ante oculos eorum.*
>   (There is no fear of God before their eyes.)[4]
For, God is my witness, they would do more for a dozen hens,
Or an even number of capons, or a horse-load of oats,
Than for love of Our Lord, or all his blessed saints.
So, Reason, let them ride by themselves, rich as they are.   40
Conscience accounts them worthless and so does Christ, I think.'
Then Reason rode faster along the straight high-road,
With Conscience his convoy to the King's presence.
The King came himself to receive Reason courteously,
    And gave him a seat on the King's bench, between himself
                                                      and his son;
And they exchanged words together for a long time.
    Now Peace came to Parliament, and presented a petition:
How against all righteousness, Wrong[5] had run off with his wife;
And ravished Rose, the sweetheart of Reginald;
And had taken Margaret's maidenhead, maulgre her struggles.   50
'My geese, and my grunters too, were grabbed by his blackguards,
But for fear of him I dare not fight or complain.
He borrowed my horse Bayard, and never brought him back,
And Wrong paid not a farthing for it, though I followed him,
                                                      begging.
He permits his men to murder my servants,
Forestalls my goods from fairs, and fights for them at market;
He breaks down my barn doors, and bags all my wheat,
And all I get is a token[6] for ten quarters of oats.
In addition to all this, he drubs me – and beds with my daughter.
But I have hardly the courage to look him in the eye.'   60
    The King could well believe all this; Conscience had told him
That Wrong was a wicked wretch, wreaking widespread sorrow.
    Wrong now grew worried, and asked Warren Wisdom
To buy-off Peace with pence – and he proffered many,

And said, 'If my lord the King only liked me, little I'd care
Though Peace and his party should complain for ever.'
Then Wisdom and his friend Witty were of opinion
That since Wrong had wrought so many kinds of ruin
They should warn him, before they worked, with some
                                        wise words.
'If men do as they please, upon impulse, they will make
                                        people angry;   70
And soon you shall see that this applies to yourself –
Unless Meed makes things easier, your undoing is imminent,
For both your life and your land lie at the King's mercy.'[7]
    Wrong wooed Wisdom with all his might,
And played handy-dandy with his pence for procuring acquittal.
So Wisdom and Witty went off together,
Taking Meed the Maiden with them, to buy mercy for him.
    Peace poked forward his head, with its bloodstained pate:
'For no guilt at all, God knows, I got this wound,
As Conscience will confirm, and all my community.'   80
    But Wisdom and Witty went quickly to work
On the King, to convince him by the power of cash.
    Still the King swore, by Christ and by his crown,
That the crimes committed by Wrong deserved condign
                                        punishment.
He commanded a constable to cast the fellow into irons –
'So heavy, he shall not see his feet for seven years!'
    But Wisdom said, 'By God, that is not the best course.
Were he to make amends, might not Mainprise release him,
And be bailsman for him, so buying him freedom,
Restoring all that Wrong ravaged, and setting all right?'   90
    Witty was well in agreement, and said the same.
    'It was better that bail should bring benefit with it,
Than that bail be denied and there be no benefit.'
    Then Meed had to meddle, and also asked for mercy,
And offered Peace a present of purest gold:
'Have this from me, my good man, to mend your wound;
Never again, I guarantee, shall Wrong be so guilty.'
    Then Peace himself took pity, and prayed the King
To have mercy on the man who had misused him so often:
'He has given me guarantees, as Sir Wisdom engaged,   100

And I forgive him his guilt, with a good will —
So long as the King assents. I can see nothing better:
Meed has made me amends; I have no more to ask.'

   Said the King, 'No! Not so, as Christ is my Saviour!
Wrong shall not wriggle away until I learn more.
If he escaped so easily, he would only laugh,
And be all the more bold to abuse my servants.
Unless Reason reprieves him, he shall rot in the stocks
As long as he lives, or till his true repentance.'

   Some reckoned that Reason should have pardoned the wretch, 110
And have counselled the King, and Conscience as well,
That Meed by rights must be his mainpernor.

   But Reason said: 'No more advice to *me* about having mercy,
Till every lord and lady learns to love Truth
And hate all harlotry, whether of speech or of hearing;
Till Petronella Peacock[8] puts her furs back in the press;
Till parents cherish children with chastisement;
Till harlots' false holiness be held a shame;
Till the covetousness of the clergy be to feed and clothe the poor,
And religious ramblers[9] sing remembrance Masses in cloisters — 120
As St Benedict bade them, and St Bernard and St Francis;
Till prelates practise in their own lives what they preach;
Till the King's Council be for common good;
Till bishops sell their stables to give poor folk asylum,
And their hawks and their hounds for the help of poor clergy;
Till St James be sought where *I* shall assign,
And no man go on pilgrimage to Galicia, unless for good;
Till all who run off to Rome and the robbers of Europe[10]
Take overseas no silver of the King's sterling,
Nor gold neither, engraved or not engraved,   130
On pain of forfeiting the same to any who find it at Dover,
Unless carried by a merchant or his men, or messengers
                                 with letters,
Or a priest or provisour,[11] or a penitent pilgrim.

   Yet still I shall harden my heart, by the Holy Cross,
While Meed has any mastery in this Moot-Hall.
I could cite you examples that I have seen many times.
I say for myself, that if it so were
That I were crowned king and keeper of this realm,

There should be no crime in this kingdom (that came to
                                        my notice)
But within my powers I should punish it, on peril of my soul!   140
Nor should gifts win my good will, God bless us all!
Nor should Meed buy my mercy, but Meekness only.
    For a man named *Nullum Malum* met with one *Impunitum*,
And he bade *Nullum Bonum* be *Irremuneratum*.[12]
Let your confessor, Lord King, construe this riddle plainly;
And if you act accordingly, I will bet my ears
That lawyers become labourers laying dung on the fields.
And love shall rule the land as you, lord, would wish.'
    Then the Court confessors went into conclave,
To construe that couplet for the King's profit —   150
Not for the King's soul, nor the comfort of the common weal.
    I saw Meed in that Moot-Hall wink at the law-men,
And many joined her joyfully, rejecting Reason.
Warren Wisdom winked back at Meed,
And said, 'Madam, I am your man, never mind how I sound:
Fed with florins, I fall about, and my mouth fails me!'
    All upright men agreed that Reason was right;
Even Witty was in accord, and commended his judgment;
And most of the men in that hall, with many of the law-lords,
Thought Meekness a master, Meed a curst vixen.   160
    Love thought little of her, and Honesty still less —
Who said, speaking high so that the whole Court heard:
'Whoever wants her as wife because of her goods and wealth
Will of course be cuckolded, cut off my nose else!'
    Meed now grew melancholy, and her face mournful,
Three quarters of that Court having called her a whore.
But an assize-juror and a summoner still paid suit to her,
And a sheriff's clerk beshrewed the whole company:
'Have I not often helped you at the Bar?
And when have I had from *you* so much as a halfpenny?'   170
    The King called Reason and Conscience to his side,
And ratified that Reason had argued rightly;
He looked with menace at Meed, and with more at Law
That man whom Meed had almost undone.
'It is your fault, Law, I believe, that I lose so many escheats;
Meed overmasters you, Law, and so makes justice slow.

But you shall have Reason to reckon with, if I rule a while more;
And, for your deeds today, you'll get what you deserve.
Meed shall not mainprise *you*, by St Mary in Heaven!
I will have my lawyers loyal, so leave off your jabbering.   180
And since most have said he is guilty, Wrong shall be sentenced.'

   Said Conscience to the King, 'Without consent of the
                                common folk,
You will find it hard, by my head, to uphold all that,
And so righteously rule your whole realm.'
Said Reason to the King, 'By Christ who lay on the Cross,
If I otherwise ruled this realm, wrench out my ribs!
But always bid Obedience be by my side.'

   Said the King, 'I shall assent, by Our Lady St Mary,
When my Council of Clergy and Lords comes together.
And not readily, Reason, shall I let you ride from me;   190
For as long as I live, I shall not let you go.'

   Said Reason, 'I am ready to remain with you always,
If Conscience will be our counsellor – I can think of none better.'
Said the King, 'I agree; God grant that we succeed!
As long as our lives last, let us live together!'

The King, and the knights of his household, now hied
                                              them to church,
Every man to hear the day's Matins, and then the Mass.
Now I woke from my forty winks, and was very grieved
That I had not slept more soundly, and seen more.
But before I had walked a furlong, I was seized by faintness;
My feet would carry me no farther, I felt so sleepy;
So I simply sat down and said my Creed.
While I mumbled over my Rosary, I once more fell asleep.
     Then I saw much more than had met my eyes before.
Now I saw that pleasant plain full of people, that I spoke
                                              of earlier,   10
And Reason preparing to preach to the whole realm,
Carrying a cross in his hand, in front of the king.
     He preached that their pestilences were punishments for sin,
And that South-West wind on a Saturday evening
Was plainly a punishment for Pride, and nothing else.[1]
Their pear-trees and plum-trees were blown prostrate
As a warning, he went on, to amend their ways.
The beeches and burly oaks were blown to the ground,
And turned topsy-turvy, to put them in terror
That Deadly Sins would on Doomsday undo them all.   20
     (On this matter, I myself could muse at length,
But shall say only what I saw, so help me God,
And how plainly Reason preached before the people.)
     He told Waster to go work at whatever he knew best,
And so recover what he had squandered, by some kind of trade.
     He implored Petronella to put away her fur-pieces,
And keep them in her coffer in case of hard times.[2]
Tom Stowe he told to take a couple of sticks
And fetch Felicity home from the fate of the scold.[3]
He warned Walter that his wife was at fault,   30

With a half-mark head-dress,[4] and his own hood not
                                    worth fourpence.
He bade Betts to cut himself a few swishy branches,
And beat his Betty with them if she stayed bone-idle.
He charged all merchants to chastise their children:
'However much money you make, do not molly-coddle
                                    your young,
Nor over-pamper them, though the Plague were at its peak.
  My father used to say this, and so did my mother:
"The dearer you hold son or daughter, the harder your discipline."
And Solomon said the same, in his Book of Proverbs:
     Qui parcit virgae, odit filium suum.
     (He that spareth his rod hateth his son.)[5]
That is the English of the Latin, if you care to know;   40
Or, "He that stints the switch spoils his children." '
  Then he begged the beneficed clergy and bishops:
'That which you preach to the people, practise yourselves –
It will bring blessing to you, if you do as you bid;
And if you live as you lecture, we shall believe you better.'
  Then he told the Regular clergy to respect their Rule:
'Lest the King and his Council cut down your endowments,
And are stewards of your estates till you keep your own statutes.'
  Then he counselled the King to love his common people:
'They are your true treasure in peacetime, and your balm
                                    in times of trouble.'   50
Then he prayed the pope to have pity on Holy Church,
And before granting others forgiveness, first govern himself.
'And all you who look to the laws, covet only the truth,
Not gold or gifts, if you wish to please God:
For they that turn against Truth, as the Gospel tells,
Are no longer known to God, nor to any saint in Heaven:
     Amen dico vobis, nescio vos.
     (Verily I say unto you, I know you not.)[6]
  And you who seek St James, and the saints in Rome,
Seek rather, St Truth[7] – for He can save you all,
     Qui cum Patre et cum Filio . . .
Who dwells with the Father and the Son, and whose
                                    blessing be on those
Who respond to my sermon.' So Reason fell silent.   60

Then Repentance ran in, and recited his text
Till I, William, wept my eyes full of water.

Petronella Proud-heart[8] threw herself prostrate,
And lay long on the ground ere she looked up and cried:
'Lord have mercy!'
She made a vow to the Maker of all mankind
That she would unsew her shift and wear a hair-shirt inside,
To mortify her flesh and its fierceness of sin:
'Never more shall a high heart hold me, but humility;
Yes, even to endure insults – as I never used to.
I will make myself meek, now, and pray for mercy,   70
Since beforehand I hated such things with all my heart.'

Then Lechery cried 'Alas!', and called upon Our Lady
To pray mercy for his misdeeds, as his soul's intermediary with God.
And he swore that every Saturday for seven years thence
He would drink only what ducks drink, and dine only once.

Envy with heavy heart asked for *his* shriving.
In sorrow he began to say his *I have sinned*.
He was pale as a sheep's pelt, and shook as if with palsy;
And was clothed in such coarse stuff that I cannot describe it –
In a kirtle and a cutty coat, a knife by his side.   80
He had cut his foresleeves from a friar's habit;[9]
And like a leek that has lain too long in the sun,
So did *he* look, with his lean cheeks and ugly louring.
  His body was bursting with rage, he bit his lips for it,
Writhing his fingers around while he waited to wreak vengeance
In word or in deed whenever he might see his chance.
He uttered never a word but with an adder's tongue;
Quarrels and complaints were his usual conduct,
And backbiting and besmirching and bearing false witness:
These were all his courtesy in whatever company.   90
  This shit said, 'I *would* be shriven but for shame I dare not.
I would be gladder, by God, to see old Gilbert ruined,
Than to win this very week a waggon-full of Essex cheese.
  I've a near-by neighbour to whom I'm a constant nuisance.
I've lied about him to the law-lords, and so lost him money,

And turned his friends into foes with all my falsehoods;
Any good luck or grant he may get, grieves me horribly.
Between this man and his minions I make such quarrels
That lives and limbs are lost because of me.
Yet when I meet him in the market-place, this man I hate most,   100
I give him a hearty hullo, as if I were his friend –
For he's beefier and braver than I am; I dare not beard him.
But oh, if I had him at my mercy, God knows what I mightn't do!
   When I arrive in church, and should with reverence
                         kneel to the reredos,
And pray for such people as the priest directs –
Pilgrims and palmers, and people who've paid for Masses –
I crouch on my knees and I call on Christ to curse those
Who buggered off with my shaving-bowl and my torn bed-sheet.
   I turn my eyes away from the altar
To see how Helen has got a new coat;   110
And I wish it were mine, and the whole web it came from.
I love other men's losses – they delight my heart –
But weep and wail if I see them faring well;
   And my own "fair dealing" is "dirty work" if they do it.
Take me to task for this, and I'll hate you eternally.
I wish all men and women I meet were my serfs,
For it angers me if anyone has more than I have.
And so I live unloved, like a surly dog,
My body swollen and bubbling with my bitterness.
   It's years since I was able to eat like anyone else: 120
Envy and ill will are not easy to digest.
Have you no sugar or sweet syrup to assuage my swelling,
No twisted canes of candy to clear my heart,[10]
No shame or shriving, but only to shred-out my belly?'
   'Readily!' said Repentance, giving first-rate advice.
'Sorrow for sins is the salvation of souls.'
   '*Sorry?*' said Envy, 'I am seldom anything else!
What else do you think makes me thin, but thoughts of
                     missed vengeance?
But when I was in business among the burghers of London,
I paid Slander as my secret agent to slate their goods.   130
When my neighbour's sold well, and mine did not, I
                made myself ready

To sniff and sneer at their stock, and spoil their trade.
Still, if I may, I will make amends through Almighty God.'

Wrath roused himself now, eyes rolling to show their whites;
He breathed noisily through his nose, and his neck hung awry.
   First, 'I am Wrath!'[11] said he. 'I'm a former friar.
I began as the Friary gardener, grafting shoots.
What I grafted on the Limiters and Lectors[12] were lies,
Till they burst into foliage of flattery for the pleasure of lords,
And blossomed abroad with mild shrifts in ladies' boudoirs.   140
Now the fruit has come to full ripeness, and folk would
                              much rather
Confess to a friar than to a parish priest.
   And now that parsons perceive they must share their profits,
These possessors of preferments preach against friars;
And the friars pick faults in *them*; and everyone finds,
When friars go preaching in public from place to place,
That I, Wrath, go the rounds with them, teaching *my* Holy Writ.
Both sorts speak of their "spiritualty", each despises the other,
Till both are beggars with nothing to live by but me
(Unless both become rich, and career around upon horseback).   150
So I, Wrath, never rest, but must run after
These wicked folk – for such are my fate and my "grace".
   I have an aunt who's a nun – in fact an Abbess –
Who would sooner swoon, or succumb, than suffer pain.
I was once a cook in her kitchen,[13] and served the convent
For many months, as well as the monastery.
I was pottinger to the Prioress and the other "poor ladies",
So I served them up stews of slanders: Sister Joan was a bastard;
Clarice indeed a cavalier's daughter, but her father a cuckold;
Sister Parnel, a priest's whore – "*She'll* never be Prioress;   160
She bore a child in cherry-time, as the whole Chapter knows."
   I, Wrath, seasoned their soup with such wicked words
That "You liar!" and "You liar!" two nuns would squeal
                            out together,
And each of them slap the other across the chops:
Had they had knives, by Christ they'd have slain each other!
St Gregory[14] was a good pope, and had great foresight:
For this cause he ordained that no abbess should ever play priest;

Women cannot keep secrets – in one day the whole
                              convent would be defamed.
   I *might* be found among monks, but I mostly avoid them:
There are too many tough men spying for my type –   170
Priors and sub-priors, and the Father Abbot in person;
And if I tell any of my tales, they hold council together,
And make me fast every Friday on bread and water;
Or I am chidden in the Chapter-house as if I were a child,
And beaten with my breeches down, on my bare arse.
So I do not like living among such lads!
Their food is third-rate fish and feeble ale;
But at times when there *is* wine, and when I have some at night,
I talk a flood of filth for five days afterwards.
All the evil that I know of any of our brethen,   180
I recount in the cloisters till the whole convent knows it.'
   Said Repentance, 'Repent, then, and never again repeat
Any confidences you collect either casually or by right.
Do not drink too daintily, nor too deeply either,
For fear your intentions may turn once more towards malice.
Be sober![15] he said, and then gave absolution,
And told Wrath to weep for his wickedness, and amend his ways.

   Then Covetousness came; and him I cannot describe,
So hungry and so hollow the old hunks looked.
He was beetle-browed, and blubber-lipped as well,   190
Both eyes as bleary as a blind hag's;
Like a leather purse his cheeks lapped down,
And far below his chin they shivered in senility.
His beard was beslobbered like a bondsman's with bacon-fat.
A hood was on his head, and a lousy hat on top of it;
And his turd-brown surtout had seen twelve winters,
All tattered and filthy, and alive with lice.
(Though if only the lice could have found a better lodging
They would not have walked that Welsh flannel, it was
                                        so threadbare.)
'I have been avaricious,'[16] said that wretch, 'and I admit it here.   200
For some time I served under Simon Stiles,
As his apprentice, pledged to take care of his profit.
First I learned to lie by the thickness of a leaf or so,

And the first wickedness I knew was using false weights.
To Weyhill and Winchester I went, on fair-days,
With all kinds of commodities, as commanded by my master;
And but for the grace that Guile gave, in amongst them,
They would not have sold in seven years, so help me God!
   Then I was drawn among drapers, to drink in the rudiments,
And so learned how to stretch the selvedge, making cloth
                                 look longer.   210
I memorised how, handling heavy striped scarlet,
To sew strips with strong needles, seaming them together,
And putting them into a press, pinned closely,
Till ten or twelve yards stretched out to thirteen.
   My wife was a weaver of woollen cloth;
She spoke to the spinsters, and they spun the yarn loosely;[17]
She paid them by the pound, but employed a
                              twenty-ounce weight,
As I tested by my own steelyard, which *did* weigh true.
   I bought her some barley-malt, and she took to brewing;
But penny-ale and pudding-ale[18] she poured together,   220
And laid it aside for labourers and the lower classes.
The best ale was kept in the back room, or my bed-chamber;
And anyone having a nip of *that*, paid through the nose –
No less than a groat a gallon, as God's my witness;[19]
And it came by the cupful, she was so crafty!
She was known as Rose the Retailer[20] – and rightly,
For she'd been at her spivvery ever since she could speak.
   But I swear now, so I do, I will stop sinning,
And never short-weight anyone, or wangle bargains,
But make my way to Walsingham, and my wife with me,   230
And pray to the Relic at Bromholm[21] to remit my penance.'
   'Did you never repent?' asked Repentance, 'or make restitution?'
   'Yes, once,' said he, 'I lodged at a pub with a party of pedlars,
And I rose when they were at rest, and rifled their baggage.'
   'That was no restitution, but rank robbery!
You more deserve hanging for having done that
Than for all the rest that you have told me yet.'
'I thought "restitution" *meant* robbery; I never learned to read;
And, faith, I know no French but that of the far side of Norfolk.'[22]
   'Were you ever in your life guilty of usury?'   240

'Certainly not, except perhaps in my youth.
I learned from Lombards and Jews[23] a lesson or two,
Such as clipping coins I had discovered were heaviest,
Then lending them, for love of the cross,[24] on pledges
                                        I knew were lost.
Such documents did I draw-up, in case the debt fell in arrears.
That more manors became mine that way than by merciful dealing.
    To lords and ladies I have lent goods in place of money,
And redeemed the goods afterwards for almost nothing;
My commerce is chiefly in such contracts and exchanges,
And the people I lend to lose a lot on every deal.   250
By carrying Lombards' letters, I've leaked gold to Rome,
Giving less gold there than I gave tokens for, here.'
'Have you lent money to lords to protect you from the law?'
'Indeed I have lent to lords, but they liked me none the better!
I have made many a knight my mercer or draper,
Who paid for his apprenticeship not so much as a pair of gloves.'
'Have you pity upon poor men who borrow under pressure?'
'I pity poor men as much as a pedlar pities cats –
He'd kill them, if he could catch them, for the sake of their skins!'
'Do you make free among your neighbours with your
                                        meat and drink?'   260
'They think of me as kindly as of a cur in their kitchen;
And the nearer my neighbours, the worse my name is.'
    'Now God forbid but you repent before long!
Else, may you never on this earth use your wealth well,
Nor your issue after you enjoy your earnings,
Nor your executors invest your money advisedly;
And wicked men waste all that you won by wickedness!
If I were a friar, in a House full of good faith and charity,
I could not spend *your* cash on our clothes and repairs,
Nor accept a penny from *you*, by my soul, as part of
                                        my pittance –   270
Not for the best book on our shelves, with burnished-gold
                                        leaves;
Not if I were certain you were such as you say,
Or if I could come by proof of any kind.
    Servus es alterius cum fercula pinguia queris;
    Pane tuo potius vescere, liber eris.[25]

    (Another man's slave must you be,
     If juicy dishes entice you;
     Would you rather call yourself free,
     Let your own plain bread suffice you.)
You are not a natural creature; I can never absolve you
Till you reckon-up all your robberies, and make restitution;
Until Reason has enrolled it upon the register of Heaven
That you have made full amends, I *must* not absolve you:

    Non dimittitur peccatum, donec restituatur ablatum.
    (The sin is not remitted until that which was taken be
      restored.)[26]

And all who have had any part of your wealth, I have God
                        as my witness,   280
Are required by the High Court of Heaven to help you restore it.
If you think this is not so, see the gloss on Psalm Fifty-one,
Have mercy on me, O God – I mean the verse about Truth:

    Ecce enim veritatem dilexisti.
    (Behold, thou desirest truth in the inward parts.)[27]

No man or woman in the world can thrive on what you acquire:
Cum sancto sanctus eris – or, construing that into English,
With the merciful thou wilt show thyself merciful;
With an upright man thou wilt show thyself upright;
With the froward thou wilt show thyself froward.'[28]

    Then the old hunks lost all hope, and would have hanged
                        himself,
Had not Repentance recalled him rather to comfort.
'Turn your mind towards mercy, and your mouth to
                        praying for it;

    Miserationes ejus super omnia opera.
    (The Lord's tender mercies are over all his works.)[29]

All the wickedness that might be thought or worked
                       in this world,   290
Is no more to God's mercy than a little flame in the sea:

    Omnis iniquitas quantum ad misericordiam Dei, est quasi
    scintilla in medio maris.[30]

    Turn your mind, then, to mercy; and give up your merchantry:
It gives you no grounds to buy yourself good bread –
Only if you earn with your own hands, or will beg.
For all the goods you have gained began in falsehood,

And to live by them is not to buy, but to borrow.
  If you have no means to restore the money to the right man,
Carry it to the Bishop and ask him, of his kindness,
To dispose of it himself as will do your soul most good.
Then he shall answer for it at Heaven's High Court –   300
Both for you and for many more, shall that man make account;
What you learned from him in Lent, do not cease to believe,
Nor what he lent you from Our Lord's wealth, to lead
                                          you from sin.'

  Now Gluttony at least *began* to go to his shriving,
And went casually kirkwards to confess his sins.
  But Betty the Brewster bade him good morning,
And with that asked him whither he was going.
  'To Holy Church,' said he, 'to hear Mass,
And so to get my shrift, and sin no more.
  'I have good ale here, gossip. Won't you try some, Gluttony?'   310
'Have you anything in your handbag – any hot spices?'
  'I have pepper and peony-seeds and a pound of garlic;
Or a farthing's-worth of fennel, since it's a fast-day.'³¹
  So in goes Gluttony, and Great Oaths follows him.
There Cicely the shoemaker sat on the bench,
With Walt the Warrener, and also his wife,
Timmy the Tinker, and two of his 'prentices,
Hicks who hired-out horses, and Hugh the needlemaker,
Clarice the Cock Lane Whore, and the clerk of the parish,
David the Ditcher, and a dozen others –   320
A fiddler, a rat-finder, and a Cheapside filth-raker,
Piers the Prelate and his Flemish popsy Parnel,
A rope-maker, a rider, and Rose the dish-seller,
Godfrey of Garlickhithe, and Griffith the Welshman,
And a rabble of rag-sellers. Early in the morning
All welcomed Gluttony gladly, with a gift of good ale.
  Clement the Cobbler threw off his cloak,
And offered it as his forfeit in a game of New Fair;³²
Hicks the Hackneyman hurled his hood after it,
And asked Betts the Butcher to be his agent.   330
Then they chose chapmen to value the exchange,
How much extra should be had by him who owned the cloak.

The two hawkers hurried to have the game over
And, whispering in private, they priced the poor pennorths,
But declared that they could not, on their consciences, agree . . .
So they asked Robin the Ropemaker into the ring,
Enlisting him as their umpire, to avoid strife;
And between the three of them the business was by-and-by settled.

  Hicks the Hostler was to have the cloak
On condition that Clement should stand him a cupful;   340
And have Hick's hood, and shake hands on the deal;
And the first who renegued on the arrangement was required
To give old Gluttony a gallon of ale.

  So they laughed and they lowered and yelled, 'Let's
                        have a drink,'
And sat there till Evensong, singing now and then,
Till Gluttony had golloped a gallon or more
And his guts began grumbling like two greedy sows.
He pissed four pints in the space of a Pater-noster,
And blew the round bugle at his backbone's end
So that all who heard that horn held their noses,   350
And wished he had bunged it with a bunch of whins.
He could neither stir nor stand without his stick,
And then walked no better than a bar-fiddler's bitch,
Sometimes sideways and sometimes backwards,
His course criss-crossing like a man laying bird-nets.

  And when he drew near the door, his eyes grew dim;
He thrumbled on the threshold, and was thrown to earth.
Clement the Cobbler caught him round the waist
To lift him a little, at least to his knees;
But Gluttony was a burly brute, and a bastard to lift;   360
And he coughed-up such a caudle into Clement's lap
There is no hound so hungry in the whole of Hertfordshire
He'd have lapped-up those leavings, so unlovely they smelt.

  At last, with a world of trouble, his wife and his wench
Brought him back home and put him to bed.
There, after all his excesses, he became unconscious,
And slept all Saturday, and all Sunday till sunset.
Then he came out of his coma, and wiped his eyes clean;
And the first words from his tongue were, 'Who's taken my tankard?'
His wife began to upbraid him for his beastly ways,   370

And Repentance was there also to rebuke him.

   'Evil in word and deed alike has your life been;
Be ashamed of yourself, show it in your speech, and be shriven.'

   'Guilty I am,' said Gluttony, 'I grant it freely.
I've transgressed with my tongue I cannot tell how often,
Swearing "by God's soul" and "So help me God and the saints",
Nine hundred times, when there wasn't any need for it.
I've stuffed myself so at supper, and sometimes at noonday,
That I've spewed it all up along the space of a mile,
Wasting what might have been saved for those in want.   380
On fast-days I've both drunk and eaten delicacies,
And sometimes been so long at the table that I slept while I ate,
Or have taken my meals in taverns, to continue talking
                                 and tippling;
And even on fast-days have been off to my food before noon.'

   'So full a confession cannot fail to win you merit.'

   Then Gluttony began to weep and be in great grief
For the loose life that he had been living;
And he made a vow: 'Every Friday henceforward for ever,
Whatever hunger and thirst I may have,
Not even of fish shall my bowels have knowledge
Till my Auntie Abstinence gives her authority –   390
She whom till now I've hated all my life!'

Then came Sloth, all slobbery, with slimy eyes.
'I must sit down,' said the sluggard, 'or I'll fall asleep;
I cannot stand, nor stoop, nor kneel without a stool.
Were I back in bed, you might ring all your bells,
And I'd not rise till ready for dinner, unless my rear made me.'
He began his 'Bless me, father', then belched, then beat
                                 his breast,
Then stretched himself with a groan, and finally snored.
'How's this? Wake up, wretch!' cried Repentance. 'Make
                              haste with your shrift!'

   'Were I to die today, I'm too weary to wake   400
Nor am I perfect in my Pater-noster – not as a priest should
                               sing it –
Though I do know rhymes of Robin Hood, and
                      Randolph Earl of Chester;[33]

But not the least that was ever made of Our Lord or Our Lady.
  Many a time I've made vows, and forgotten them in
                                        the morning;
I have never performed the penances that the priest laid on me,
Nor been seriously sorry for my sins.
If I ever utter a prayer, unless in a temper,
My tongue is two miles from what my heart intends.
Every day, whether holy or not, I employ
In idle chat over ale (or even in church).   410
The Passion of Christ, though – I seldom think of *that*.
  I have never been a visitor of sickbeds, or of folk chained
                                        in bridewells;
I would rather listen to lewdness, or a cobblers' holiday-play,
Or some dirty jokes, or detraction of my neighbour,
Than everything Mark or Luke wrote, or Matthew – not
                                        to mention John.
As for vigils or fast-days, I've bidden them farewell;
I lie in bed all through Lent with my lady-love in my arms,
Till Matins and Mass are ended, then make do at the Friary.
If I'm in time for the *Ite, missa est*, it's enough for me.[34]
I've kept away from confession, unless being ill scared me;   420
Not twice in two years do I tell my sins – and then by guesswork.
  I have been priest and parson these thirty years past,
Yet cannot sol-fa, say Mass, or read the Lives of the Saints;
But I can find a hare in a furrowed field
Better than construe for my congregation a catchphrase of Latin
Such as *Blessed is the Man*, maybe, or *Blessed is everyone*. [35]
I can hold love-days, and hear a reeve's reckoning,
But of Canon Law or the Decretals I cannot read a line.
  If I borrow, or buy on credit, unless a book is kept
I forget it forthwith; and if I am asked for it,   430
Six or seven times I swear it is not so;
And thus I have troubled honest men ten thousand times.
Sometimes my servants' salaries are in arrears,
And a rueful reckoning I find it, when the accounts are read out;
It's only with ill-will and anger that I pay my workers.
  If anyone does me a good deed, or lends me a hand
                                        when I'm down,
I requite him unkindly: I cannot understand courtesy;

For I have, and always had, something like a hawk's manners:
I am not to be lured with love, but with what lies under
                                                    the thumb.
   The kindness my fellow-Christians formerly conferred   440
Scores of times, on myself, I have slothfully forgotten,
Or by silence or by sour speech have spoiled many gifts
Of fish or flesh or other sorts of foodstuff;
But bread and ale alike, and milk and cheese and butter,
I have left lying about until they were useless.
   I ran around in my youth, and neglected my reading,
And ever since have been beggarly, because of my filthy sloth:
    Heu mihi, quod sterilem vitam duxi juvenilem!
    (Woe's me! How barren, in truth,
     Was the life I led in my youth!)'
  'Do you not repent?' asked Repentance. But that
                                        wretch was asleep again,
Till Vigilant Leveilleur[36] threw water over his face,   450
Splashing it into his eyes, and shouting to shift him:
'You're in danger of despair, and that would be your undoing!
Say to yourself, "I am sorry for my sins";
Beat yourself on the breast, and beseech God for grace;
No earthly guilt is so great but His goodness is greater.'
   Then Sloth sat up and crossed himself speedily,
And made oath before God to overcome his acedia:
'Every Sunday for seven years (unless sickness prevents me)
I shall hie to Holy Church before the sun has risen,
And hear Matins and Mass as if I were a monk;   460
Nor shall after-dinner ale keep me out of it,
Till I have heard Evensong: by the Holy Rood I swear this!
I promise to repay – if I have pounds enough –
All the wealth I have wickedly gained since I first walked,
   Even though this may leave me too little to live on.
Each must have his own, ere I join the hereafter;
And if any remains, with the rest, by the Rood of Chester,
I shall turn pilgrim towards Truth, rather than seek Rome.'
   Robert the Robber remembered the text in *Romans*:
    Reddite ergo omnibus debita.
    (Render therefore to all their dues.)[37]
He began weeping bitterly, because he had nothing.   470

But the sinful wretch was saying to himself:
'Oh Christ who died on the Cross at Calvary,
Beside Dysmas[38] my brother, who besought you for grace,
And you had mercy on that man because he said,

"Remember me, Lord":

Reprieve now *this* robber, who *cannot* repay,
Nor has any art by which to earn what he owes.
By your great mercy, mitigate my punishment,
Let me not be damned on Doomsday for doing such evil.'
    What became of this criminal I cannot rightly say;
But I well know that water went streaming from his eyes,   480
And to Christ again and again he acknowledged his guilt,
And swore to polish anew his pikestaff of penitence,
And walk the world with it while his life should last:
For he had lain with Latro,[39] Lucifer's aunt.

Then Repentance took pity on the penitents, and bade them kneel:
'For I shall seek from Our Saviour His grace to all sinners,
That he amend our misdoing and have mercy upon us all.
    Oh God, who of Your goodness began this world,
Making all out of nothing, and Man most like Yourself:
Yet allowed Adam to sin, and bring sickness upon us all –   490
Which was all for the best, I believe, whatever the Bible says:

> *O felix culpa! O necessarium peccatum Adae!*
> (O happy fault! O necessary sin of Adam, that merited such
>   a Redeemer!)

For through that sin, Thy Son was sent to this earth,
And became a man, born of a maiden, to save Mankind,
And make Yourself and Your Son like us sinful men:

> *Faciamus hominem ad imaginem et similitudinem nostram.*
> (Let us make man in our image, after our likeness.)[40]

And elsewhere it is written:

> *Qui manet in caritate, in Deo manet.*
> (He that dwelleth in love dwelleth in God.)[41]

    Since You Yourself appeared in our fleshly suit, and died
For Man's sake on Good Friday, at full noonday,
Though neither Father nor Son felt sorrow in the fact of death,
Except only in the suit of Man's flesh, and Your Son

overcame that:

Captivam duxit captivitutem.

(He led captivity captive.)

Still, in the sorrow of that, Your Son lost the light for a space,
At the middle of the day, then most bright, and the

mealtime of the saints,   500

For then with Your fresh blood You fed our forefathers

in their darkness:

Populus, qui ambulabat in tenebris, vidit lucem magnam.

(The people that walked in darkness have seen a great light.)[42]

By the light that then leapt from You, was Lucifer blinded,
And Your last breath blew the blessed into Heaven's bliss.

And three days after, again You were clad in our flesh,
And a sinful Mary saw You before St Mary Our Lady;[43]
And for the solace of sinners You let this be so —

Non enim veni vocare justos, sed peccatores.

(For I am not come to call the righteous, but sinners to
repentance.)[44]

And your mightiest deeds, told by Mark, or John or

Luke or Matthew,

Were done in the armour of our human flesh:

Verbum caro factum est, et habitavit in nobis.

(The word was made flesh, and dwelt among us.)[45]

And by so much the more, I believe, may we be sure
In begging and beseeching You (if it be Your will,   510
Who are our brother and our father) to have mercy here
On this rabble of wretches who so sorely repent
That they ever in this world offended you by thought,

word, or deed.'

Then Hope set his hands upon the horn of

Deus, tu conversus vivificasti me

(Yet didst thou turn and refresh me),[46]

And he blew it with '*Beati quorum remissae sunt iniquitates*'
(Blessed is he whose transgression is forgiven).[47]

And all the saints in Heaven sang with one voice:

'*Homines et jumenta salvabis, Domine; quemadmodum
multiplicasti misericordiam tuam, Deus.*'

(O Lord, thou preservest man and beast. How excellent is
thy loving-kindness, O God! Therefore the children of
men put their trust under the shadow of thy wings.)[48]

Then a thousand men thronged together,
Crying up to Christ and His immaculate Mother
That grace might go with them in their pilgrimage to Truth.

But no one there was wise enough to know the way. 520
They blundered out like beasts over the banks and hills.
They had wandered long, and it was late, before finding a leader,
A man in pagan apparel, as pilgrims may be.
He bore double staves, and a broad strip to bind them
Wound spirally all the way round, like a withy.
By his side he had a bag and a begging-bowl,
And on his hat he had a hundred little bottles,
And souvenirs of Sinai, and Galician scallop-shells,
And many a cross on his cloak, and the Roman cross-keys,
And a vernicle-badge[49] worn before them: all to bear witness 530
And be signs to let men know what shrines he had sought.

And all the folk asked him first where he had come from.
He said, 'From Sinai, and from Our Lord's sepulchre;
I have been both in Bethlehem and in Babylon;
In Armenia, Alexandria, and other such places.
You may see by the signs that are set on my hat
That I have walked far and wide, in wet and in dry,
Seeking the saints of God for the good of my soul.'
'Can you tell us at all about a saint called Truth?
Can you tell us where he dwells, and the best way there?' 540
Said the stranger, 'So God help me, no.
I never saw a palmer, with staff and scrip,
Who asked after Truth, until here and now.'
'By St Peter!' said a Ploughman, as he pushed through a hedge,
'I'm as close-acquainted with Truth as a clerk with his books;
Conscience and Mother Wit made me come to his country,
And made me swear solemnly to serve him for ever,
To sow and plant his seed so long as I had strength.
I have been his follower for forty winters,
And have sown his seed and seen to his beasts, 550
And indoors and out have had an eye to his profit.
I dig and I ditch, and do all that Truth commands;
Sometimes I sow, and sometimes I thresh;
I work as a tailor or a tinker, as Truth may require,
I weave, I wind yarn – whatever Truth commands.

And though I say it myself, he is pleased with my service:
He gives me good wages, and a gratuity sometimes,
And is the promptest payer a poor man could find:
He never withholds from a henchman his full hire at day's-end;
He is lowly as a lamb, and of loving speech.   560
And if you would like to learn where Truth lives,
I will tell you truly the way to his dwelling.'
'If you please, good Piers,' said the pilgrims, and offered to pay him
If he would go with them and show them Truth's dwelling.
'Not so, by my soul's health,' swore Piers,
'I wouldn't finger a farthing, not for St Thomas's shrine![50]
Truth would love me the less for it, a long time after!
But if what you want is the right way to go,
Then certainly I will describe it, and set you on your path.

   You must start by way of Meekness, men and women alike,   570
Till you come to Conscience – and by then Christ will know
That you love Our Lord God above all else;
And next to Him, your neighbour, whom you will never use
Otherwise than you would wish that he used you.
Turn beside a brook called Be-gentle-of-speech,
Till you find the ford called Honour-your-father-and-your-mother.
   Honora Patrem et matrem . . . [51]
Wade into that water, and wash yourselves well,
And you will leap the lightlier for it all your lives.
   Then you will see a place called Swear-not-needlessly-and-
especially-take-not-in-vain-the-name-of-Almighty-God.   580
Next you will come to a croft: keep away from it,
For the name of that croft is Covet-not-thy-neighbour's-
      cattle-nor-his-wife-nor-his-servants-lest-you-do-him-an-injury.
See that you break no branches there, unless they belong to you.
Two tree-stumps stand near-by; but do not stop there,
For they are called Steal-not and Slay-not: go straight past them,
Leaving them on your left hand, and do not look back.
Hold well to the high-road of observing Holy Days.
Carry on till you come to a hill called Bear-no-false-witness;
It is forested with florins and fenced with fees: 590
See that you pluck no plant there, on peril of your souls.
   Next you will see Speak-truth-and-act-as-you-say-
and-abide-by-it-always-no-matter-who-bids-you-otherwise.

Then soon you will see a Castle[52] as bright as the sun.
The moat around this manor is called Mercy,
And its walls are of wisdom, to keep out self-will,
Crenellated with Christendom, to preserve Mankind,
And buttressed with Believe-or-you-cannot-be-saved.

All the out-houses, halls, and chambers, have been roofed
Not with lead but with love and with Lowly-speech-of-brethren.   600
The drawbridge is Beseech-well-and-it-shall-be-given-you;
Each pillar is made of penance, and of prayers to saints;
And the gates are hung on hinges of gifts of alms.

The gatekeeper is Grace, a good person;
And his man is called Amend-your-life, well known to many.
That Truth may know he can trust you, tell the porter
                                              this password:

I performed the penance that the priest laid on me;
I am indeed sorry for my sins, and shall always be so
Whenever I think of them, even though I were to be Pope!

Ask Amend-your-life to approach his master humbly   610
For leave to throw wide the Wicket-gate that the woman closed
When Adam and Eve ate unroasted apples:

> *Per Evam cunctis clausa est, et per Mariam virginem iterum*
> *patefacta est.*
> (Through Eve it was closed to all men; through the Virgin
> Mary it was once more thrown open.)[53]

For she has the key and the door-catch, even though
                                              the King sleep.

If Grace gives you leave to go in by that gate,
Then you shall see Truth enthroned in your hearts,
Wearing the chain of charity. As if you were children,
Submit yourselves to him; say nothing against your sire's will.

But beware then of Wroth-waxing, who is a wicked wretch,
And envious of him who is enthroned in your hearts.
He will push Pride into your path, and Self-praise;   620
And the brightness of your benevolences will make you blind:
You will be as the early dew[54] – driven out, and the door closed
And latched and locked behind you; and you may linger
Outside perhaps for a century,[55] before your second chance.
Thus you may lose his love by loving yourself too well,
And perhaps have *no* second chance, unless helped by his grace.

Even so, there are seven sisters that serve Truth forever;
They are protectresses of the postern-gate of that palace.[56]
And one is called Abstinence, and Humility another;
Chastity and Charity are his chief maidens,   630
With Patience and Peace, who help many people,
And the Lady Largesse, who has let many enter:
She has plucked many thousands from Apollyon's pinfold.

    Any kinsman of this company, so help me Christ,
Is wonderfully welcomed by them, and warmly received;
But someone who is no kin to any of the seven
Will find it hard, by my head, to have hope
Of getting in at any gate, unless by God's grace.

    'Oh Christ!' said a cutpurse, 'I've no kinsfolk there!'
'Nor I,' said an ape-leader, 'for all I know.'   640
'I call God to witness,' a confectioner said. 'Could I be
                                     sure of all this,
I'd not put one foot in front of the other, for any friar-talk.'

    But Piers said, 'Please listen!' And he prodded them onwards.
'Mercy herself is a maid there, and commands the others:
She and her son are akin to all sinners.
Through the help of these two – do not hope there are others –
You may be given grace there. Only – go quickly!'

    Said a pardoner, 'By St Paul, perhaps I'm unknown there!
I must get my box of briefs and of bishops' bulls!'[57]
And his concubine cried, 'By Christ, and I'll come with you!
You can say I'm your sister.'

    So I saw no more of them.   651

Passus 6

'The way you describe would be hard, without a guide
For every foot of the way.' So said the folk.
But Piers the Ploughman said: 'By St Peter of Rome,
I have half an acre to plough, beside the highway;
Had I ploughed this half-acre, and had I sown it,
I would willingly come with you and show you the way.'
    'That would be a long while to wait,' said a lady in a veil.
'What would we women be doing meanwhile?'
    'Some could sew-up sacks to keep the wheat from spilling;
And all you lovely ladies with your long fingers,   10
Take silks and satins to sew at your leisure
Into chasubles for chaplains, and the Church's honour.
Wives and widows may spin wool and flax.
And turn them into cloth, and teach their daughters how to;
Note then how the needy and the naked fare,
And carry clothes to them, as Truth commands.
I shall furnish their food, unless my field runs barren;
And so long as I live, for love of Our Lord in Heaven,
Both to rich and poor I shall bring meat and bread.
    Come, now, all manner of men who live by meat and drink,   20
Help speed the labours of him who provides your food!'
Said a cavalier then, 'By Christ, he counsels well!
But, truly, I was never taught how to manage a plough-team.
Still – teach me how to, and by Christ I will try!'
    'By St Paul!' said Piers, 'That's so generous a proposal,
That I myself will sweat and toil and sow for us both,
And will gladly do all such work, life-long, as you may want.
You must promise, for your part, to protect Holy Church and me
From the wasters and the wicked who despoil the world;
And be hot in your hunting of hares and foxes,   30
Of boars and badgers that break down my hedges;
And train falcons for yourself, to kill the wild-fowl
That come to my croft and crop my wheat.'

The cavalier's comment was truly courteous.
'By my purview, Piers, I give you my promise
To abide by this bargain to the point of battle;
So long as I live, look to me for protection.
  Said Piers, 'Well, but one more point I must put to you:
Never ill-treat your tenants, unless Truth gives warrant;
And if you must amerce them, let Mercy be your assessor,   40
And Mildness your master, for all Meed's allurements.
And if poor men approach you with presents or offerings,
Accept nothing, ever, in case it exceeds your deserts,
And at one year's end or another you must yield it back
In a truly perilous place – called Purgatory!
  Do not misuse your serfs – you will profit, so:
Though *here* they are your underlings, it may well
                                          happen in Heaven
That the serf sits higher than you, and receives more bliss,
Unless yours was the worthier life; for Our Lord said,
       Amice, ascende superius.
    (When thou art bidden, go and sit down in the lowest
        room; that when he that bade thee cometh, he may say
        unto thee, Friend, go up higher.)[1]
In the church charnel-house, it is hard to tell churls   50
Or serfs from their seigneur; so have that at heart.
Let your tongue be truthful, and hate all tales
But those that are wise and worthy, for correcting your workers.
Licence no jesters, nor listen to their lewdnesses,
And avoid such men above all when you sit at meals:
They are the Devil's discoursers, I do assure you.'
  'I swear by St James,' said the knight in reply,
'To act on your advice as long as I live.'
  Said Piers, 'I shall put on, then, a pilgrim's dress,
And take you all with me until we find Truth.   60
I shall put on my poor clothes, all ragged and patched,
My gaiters, and my gloves to get warmth in my fingers,
Sling my seed-bag round my neck instead of a scrip,
And bring along in it a bushel of bread-corn.
This I myself will sow, and then soon after
Will pilgrim-it like a palmer, in search of pardon.
  And whosoever will help me beforehand to plough or sow,

Shall have leave, by Our Lord, to glean here at harvest,
And make merry with their takings, no matter who grumbles.
And for all kinds of craftsmen, of Christian life,[2]   70
I shall find food if they are faithful and honest.
But Jack the Jester and Jenny from the whorehouse,
Dan the Dicer and Denise the Bawd,
And Friar Faker and his fellow brothers,
And Robin the Ribald with his ruttish jokes:
Truth once told me, and bade me tell it to others,
Have no dealings with them: *deleantur de libro viventium.*
    (Let them be blotted out of the book of the living.)[3]
For Holy Church has been told not even to take tithes from them,
    Quia cum justis non scribantur.
    (For let them not be written with the righteous.)[4]
They have had good luck to get away with it, may God
                         make them better.'
   Now, the wife of Piers was called Dame Work-when-you-can;   80
His daughter was called Do-your-duty-or-get-a-beating;
His son was Be-sure-your-betters-are-obeyed-
and-do-not-dispute-with-them-or-you'll-pay dearly-for-it.
'May God be with you all, as His word teaches;
For now that I am old and grey, and own a little property,
I propose as a penance to be a pilgrim with these people.
And I wish, before I go, to have my will drawn up well.
In the name of God, Amen. I myself make this Will.
He shall have my soul who has best deserved it,
And shall defend it from the Fiend (for so I believe)   90
Till I come to Accounts-Day, as my Creed tells me,
Then to have release and remission from all my back rent.
   The Kirk shall have my carcass and the keeping of my bones:
From my harvest and my havings it would have its tithes,
Which I paid promptly, to save my soul from peril;
It must therefore, I hope, remember me in Masses,
And have me in mind among all other Christians.
   What I honestly earned, and no more, I leave to my wife,
To distribute among herself and my dear children;
For though I should die today, my debts are all paid.   100
Because I always gave back before bedtime whatever I borrowed.[5]
   And any residue or remnant, by the Rood of Lucca,[6]

I will worship Truth with, all my life,
And behind the plough be his pilgrim, for the sake of poor men:
My pilgrim-staff my plough-staff, to cut roots apart,
And help my coulter to carve and cleanse the furrows.'

Now Piers and the pilgrims have gone to plough,
And many are helping him to ear his half-acre.
Ditchers and delvers dug up the ridges
(Which pleased Piers greatly, and he praised them well).   110
But others also were working eagerly,
Every man in some manner making himself useful –
Such as hoeing out weeds, perhaps, which also pleased Piers.

But promptly at nine o'clock Piers stopped his plough,
To oversee his helpers; for those who worked best
He would hire at highest wages when harvest-time came.
And some were sitting and singing over their ale –
Helping him 'plough his half-acre', forsooth, with *Hey,*
nonny nonny!

'Now, by my soul's peril,' cried Piers, in pure rage,
'Unless you're on your feet fast, and flying to work,   120
Not one grain that I grow shall you get when you need it;
And though you die of dearth, devil take me if I care!'
Then the slackers grew scared. Some claimed to be blind,
Or flexed their legs all awry, as such losels know how.
And plaintively whined at Piers, and begged him to pity them.
'We have no limbs to labour with, Lord save you, master!
But we pray for you, Piers, and for your plough as well,
And that by God's grace your grain shall multiply
And yield you a return for the alms you give us here:
For so grave are our afflictions, we are utterly useless.'   130

Said Piers: 'If that were so, I should soon perceive it.
Well I know you are wasters, and so is Truth aware of it;
I am his oldest hired-man, and promised to warn him
Who they were in this world that injured his workers.
You waste what other men earn with toil and worry:
But Truth shall teach you in time how to drive his ox-team,
Or your food shall be barley-bread and the brooks your drink!
The truly blind or disabled, or with legs braced in irons,
He shall eat wheaten bread, and he shall drink at my table
Till God in His goodness gives him a remedy.   140

But you *could* work as Truth wishes, for food and wages,
By keeping the beasts from the corn, or by herding cattle,
Or ditching or digging, or drubbing away at sheaves,
Or helping mix mortar, or carrying muck afield.
    But you live in lechery, and in slander and sloth;
And by God's long-suffering alone are you saved from His
                                                    vengeance.
    Anchorites and hermits who eat only at noon,
And no more till the morrow – they shall have my alms
To clothe them; and so shall the keepers of cloisters and churches;
But Robin Runaround[7] shall receive nothing of mine,   150
Nor any scripture-expounders but preachers with episcopal licence:
I'll give *them* their bread and soup, and seat them in comfort,
For even the religious must by reason be sure of their keep.'
    One waster grew angry, and wanted to fight;
He challenged Piers Ploughman by proffering his glove.
And a braggartly Breton[8] also blustered at Piers:
'Go and piss on your plough, you pitiful bastard!
We'll do what we want, whether *you* like it or not,
And we'll fetch away your flour and your food when we please,
And make good and merry with them, for all your maundering!' 160
    Then Piers the Ploughman appealed to the knight
To preserve him, as he promised, from these curséd reprobates,
Those wolvish wasters who make the world dangerous.
'They use up all, earn nothing; and, in the meanwhile,
The people will never have plenty if my plough stands idle.'
The knight, with urbanity that was his by nature.
Then warned the wasters against evil ways –
'Or you shall be brought to justice, by my Order of Knighthood!'
    'I was never used to work, and I won't begin now!'
Said the waster, and scoffed at the law and scorned the knight, 170
And said Piers and his plough were neither worth a pea-pod,
And menaced Piers and his men should they soon meet again.
    'By the peril of my soul!' cried Piers, 'You shall pay for this!'
And he cried 'come hither' to Hunger, who heard him at once.
'Work vengeance on these wasters who ruin the world!'
    And Hunger took hold of the waster by his belly,
And wrung him so by his innards that his eyes ran water;
And he so buffeted the Breton about his cheeks

That he looked like a lantern all the rest of his life.
He so battered them both, he nearly burst their guts.   180
Had not Piers with a pease-loaf persuaded Hunger to stop,
They would both have needed burying, don't believe otherwise.
'Allow them to live, but let them eat with the pigs,
On bean-and-bran mash; or else be reduced
To skimmed milk and small ale.' Thus Piers prayed for these men.
    In utter fear, these fakers fled off to the barns
And flogged away with their flails from morn till eve,
So that Hunger had not the courage to harm them,
Because Piers had prepared them a potful of peas.
A horde of hermits got hold of spades,   190
And cut up their copes to make short coats,
And went out as workmen with spades and shovels,
And ditched and delved to drive away Hunger.
    Thousands of the 'blind' and 'bedridden' grew suddenly better;
Those who had sat and begged for silver were swiftly healed.
Food baked for Bayard[9] was brought many starving,
And many a beggar, for a few beans, turned biddable workman;
And many a poor man was pleased to have peas for his wages.
They pounced on the work Piers gave them, as promptly
                                        as sparrow-hawks.
Piers was proud of all this, and put them to work,   200
And gave them what food he could afford, and fair wages.
    Then Piers had pity, and pressed Hunger to go
Back to his homeland, and keep himself there:
'I am well avenged now on those vagabonds, thanks to
                                        your vigour;
But I pray you, before you depart,' said Piers to Hunger,
'What is best to be done with beggars and cadgers?
For I know well, once you're gone they'll again work badly.
It is only their misery that makes them so meek now,
Only for want of food do these folk obey me;
Yet they are my blood-brothers, for God bought us all,   210
And Truth taught me once to love every one of them,
And assist them in all things, as their need might be.
So now I would learn from you what the best way is
To make myself their master, and them to work.'
    Said Hunger, 'Hear me, now, and hold on to my words.

The big burly beggars who could labour for their bread,
Give them horse-feed or hounds'-food to keep their hearts high;
Or abase their bodies with a diet of beans.
If they begin to grumble, just say "Go and work":
Their suppers will be more savoury if earned with sweat.   220
    But if you find a fellow truly ill-used by Fortune,
Or by vile men's villainy, learn to know such victims,
And comfort them as you can, for the love of Christ in Heaven;
Love and relieve them, as God's law teaches:
    Alter alterius onera portate.
    (Bear ye one another's burdens.)[10]
And all manner of men whom you may come across,
Who have nothing, or are needy – let your own goods help them.
Give them charity without chiding – leave their
                                        chastisement to God;
If they have done evil, vengeance is His.
    Mihi vindicta, et ego retribuam.
    (Vengeance belongeth to me; I will recompense, saith the
        Lord.)[11]
If you wish for God's grace, obey the Gospel,
And make yourself loved by the lowly; thus you lay hands
                                        on grace: 230
    Facite vobis amicos de Mammona iniquitatibus.'
    (Make to yourselves friends of the mammon of
        unrighteousness.)[12]
    'I would not grieve God for all the wealth in the world;
Is it possible to do as you say, and commit no sin?'
'It is, I assure you, or else the Bible is lying.
Look at the giant *Genesis*, that engendered us all:
"In the sweat of thy face shalt thou eat bread."[13]
"Thou shalt labour for thy living" – so our Lord said.
And Solomon says the same – I saw it in the Bible:
    "The sluggard will not plough, by reason of the cold."[14]
Hence, he shall beg at harvest-time, and have nothing.
    Matthew of the Man's Face mouthed these words:[15]   240
The worthless servant would not set his one talent to work,
And lost the esteem of his master for evermore;
And his master took that one talent away from him,
And gave it to the servant who had gained ten talents;[16]

And let Holy Church hear what he said at that time:
"He that hath shall have, and help at need;
He that hath not shall have nothing, and no man shall help him;
And from him who thinks he has something, I shall
                                        withhold even that."[17]
   Mother Wit would teach us that all men should work
In ditching or delving, or in drudging at prayers –   250
The contemplative life or the active – as Christ commands.
And the Psalter says, in the Psalm *Blessed is every one*,
That the fellow who feeds himself by straightforward labour
Is blessèd (so says the Book) in body and soul:
    Labores manuum tuarum.'
  (Thou shalt eat the labour of thine hands: happy shalt thou
    be, and it shall be well with thee.)[18]
 'If you please, there is one more point,' said Piers. 'If
                                        perhaps you have
Any morsel of medical knowledge, teach it *me*, dear friend:
For some of my servants – and myself too –
Have not worked for a week, we have such belly-aches.'
 'I know all too well,' said Hunger, 'what your sickness is.
You have all been guzzling too much – that's what gives
                                        you such gripes.   260
Here is my advice: if you hope to stay healthy,
Drink nothing, any day, until you have dined a little;
Have nothing to eat until true hunger
Has sent the savour of its sauce to your lips;
Save some of that sauce for supper, and don't sit there too long –
Be up and away before Appetite has eaten his fill.
Never let Sir Surfeit sit at your table;
Have no faith in him, for he is lecherous, and a fastidious eater,
And his guts are always greedy for gourmet dishes.
Make this your daily diet, and I'll wager my ears   270
Dr Physic's furred hoods will be sold to buy food,
And his cloak of Calabrian fur, with all its clasps of gold;[19]
And he'll be glad, by God, to give up medicine,
And learn to labour on the land, for sweet life's sake:
For many such quacks are murderers, may God forgive them.
Their drinks make men die much sooner than Destiny does!'
  Said Piers, 'By St Paul, these are profitable words!

But away with you now, if you wish, and the best of luck
                                                    with you.
You have read us a lovely lesson, may the Lord reward you!'
    'Good God be my witness,' said Hunger, 'I'm not going yet –   280
Not till I've had today's dinner, and some drink as well!'
    'I've not so much as a penny to purchase you pullets,
Nor geese nor grunters; I have only two green cheeses,
A few curds, and some cream, and an oaten cake,
And two bean-and-bran loaves that I baked for my children.
And I swear by my soul, I have no salt bacon,
Or eggs, by Christ, to cook-up for you into collops.
I have parsley, and pot-herbs, and plenty of greens,
A cow and a calf, and a cart-mare
To drag my dung afield while the drought lasts.   290
That is all I have to live on, until Lammas-time;
Though by then, I hope, I shall have my field's harvest in;
And then I'll dish up such a dinner as I'd dearly like to.'
Then all the poor people came with peasecods,
And brought beans in their laps, and baked apples,
And chibols, and chervil, and loads of ripe cherries,
And presented them to Piers for Hunger's placation.
    And Hunger ate all up fast, and asked for more.
Then the poor folk were afraid, and fed Hunger faster,
With plenty of green leeks and peas, in hope to polish him off.   300
By now it was nearly harvest-time, and new corn came
                                                    to market;
So the folk were happier, and fed Hunger finely,
And gave him good ale such as Glutton loved, until Hunger
                                                    grew sleepy.
    Then Waster would work no longer, but went wandering off;
And the beggars refused any bread that had bean-flour in it;
They called for high-class wheat of one kind or another,
And could not be persuaded to sample small beer,
But only the best and the brownest in the borough.
    Landless labourers who must live by their hands
Would not deign to dine on day-old greens;   310
No penny-ale would please them, nor a piece of bacon,
But only fresh meat or fish, either baked or fried –
And steaming hot, at that, lest a chill harm their stomachs.

And without the highest of wages they would all grumble,
Bewailing the day whereon they were born to be workmen,
Coming at last to cry out against Cato's advice:
> *Paupertatis onus patienter ferre memento.*
> (Remember to bear with forbearance the burden of your
>   poverty.)[20]

They grew angry with God, and grumbled at Reason,
And cursed the King and his Council too,
For laying down laws that harassed labourers.[21]
Yet when Hunger had the upper hand, *he* kept them quiet;   320
They made no strife with *his* statutes – his looks were too stern!
   But I warn all you workmen – earn while you may,
For Hunger is making haste, and will soon be here.
He shall awaken with the waters, for chastening wasters.[22]
Before five years have passed, there shall be a great famine,
Through floods and foul weather the fruits of the earth shall fail.
For so Saturn has foreseen, and sent you this warning:
When you see the Sun stand awry, and two monks' heads
                                    beside him,
And a maiden has mastery, multiplied by eight,
Then Death shall withdraw, and Dearth be your judge,   330
And Dawes the Ditcher shall die of hunger
Unless God in His great goodness grants us a truce.

Truth heard tell of all this, and he sent word to Piers
To go back to his ox-team, and till the soil;
And he granted Piers a pardon from both punishment and guilt,[1]
For him and for his heirs for ever more,
So long as he stayed at home and ploughed his soil.
And whoever might help him to plough, or to sow or to plant,
Or in any other activity useful to Piers,
Truth granted him too a pardon like that for the ploughman.

    The kings and cavaliers who took care of Holy Church,
And righteously ruled the people in their realms,   10
Had pardon enough to pass easily through Purgatory,
And be with patriarchs and prophets in Paradise.

    Truly blessèd bishops, who lived by their duty,
Learnèd in both kinds of law,[2] and preaching them to laymen,
And who did as much as they might to amend all sinners,
Were peers of the Apostles (so Piers's pardon showed),
And on Doomsday should sit upon God's high dais.

    Merchants were granted marginally many years' indulgence,
But none from both guilt *and* punishment – that, no Pope
                          could provide:
Because they do not hold by Holy Days, as Holy Church teaches,   20
And because they swear 'By my soul' and 'So help me God',
Oaths taken against their conscience, only to sell their goods.

    Still, under his personal signet, Truth sent them a letter
Telling them to buy up boldly what goods they found best:
Then sell all the stuff again, and save the profit
To endow hospitals, and help the poor in health,
And promptly to put right all unrepaired roadways
And to rebuild all broken-down bridges,
And give poor men's daughters their dowries or their
                          convent dues,
For paupers and prisoners to provide food,   30
And give scholars their schooling, or set them to a trade,

And assist and endow the Religious Orders.
'Then I myself shall send you St Michael, my Archangel,
That no devil, when you die, shall bring you dread or harm;
Do this, and he shall save you from all despair,
And bring your souls in safety to my saints in bliss.'
    This made the merchants happy – many wept for joy,
And praised Piers Ploughman for procuring this Bull.
    The lawyers had least indulgence, who make pleas for
                                   Meed the Maiden;
For the Psalter offers no salvation to such as take bribes,   40
Especially against the innocent and inexperienced:
    Munera super innocentem non accipies.
    (Thou shalt not take reward against the innocent.)[3]
The pleaders should take pains with their pleas for such people,
And princes and prelates should pay them for their trouble:
    A regibus et principibus erit merces eorum.
    (From princes and prelates shall their payment be.)[4]
But many a judge or juror would do more for Old Jack
Than they would do for love of God – and do not you doubt it!
But the speaker who speaks unsparingly on behalf of the poor man
Who is innocent, or of the needy, and oppresses no one,
But comforts them in calamity, without coveting gifts,
And explains for love of Our Lord the law he has learned:
No devil shall do him a jot of harm on his death-bed,   50
But he and his soul shall be safe, as the Psalter bears witness:
    Qui facit haec, non movebitur in aeternum.
    (He that doth these things shall never be moved.)[5]
    One cannot buy water or wind, or wisdom, or fire;
These four the Father of Heaven gave in common to all
                                    earthly folk;
They are Truth's treasures, intended for all honest men,
And cannot wax or wane without God's own will.
    When lawyers draw near their deaths, and want indulgences,
Très petit [6] is their pardon, before their departure,
If they ever took pay from poor men for their pleading.
All you legists and lawyers, learn this true lesson
(Or if it is false, the fault is St Matthew's, not mine,   60
For I have it on his authority, and the proverb is his):

Quaecumque vultis ut faciant vobis homines, et vos facite eis.
   (All things whatsoever ye would that men should do to
      you, do ye even so to them.)[7]
But all labourers alive, who live by their hands,
And have honestly earned whatever they receive,
And who live in love, and lawfully, with lowly hearts,
Theirs is the same absolution that I send to Piers.
   But cadgers and beggars have no part in my Bull,
Unless the cause was honest that induced them to beg.
For they who beg and beseech without being in need,
Are as false as the Fiend, and defraud the true poor,
And also beguile one to give against his will: 70
For if he knew they were not in need, he would give to others
Who were in real hardship, and so lend help to the poorest.
Cato, and the Clerk of the Stories,[8] both inculcate this:
Cui des, videto, 'Take care whom you give to,' says Cato;
And the Stories also teach us the bestowing of alms:
   Sit eleemosyna tua in manu tua, donec studes cui des.
   (Let your alms remain in your hand till you know who
      receives them.)
   But St Gregory was a good man, and he bade us give
Alms to any that asked, for love of Him who gives all:
   Non eligas cui misereraris, ne forte praetereas illum qui meretur
      accipere. Quia incertum est pro quo Deo magis placeas.
   (Do not choose upon whom you will have compassion, lest
      perhaps you pass over the man who really deserves your
      gift. For it is uncertain on whose behalf you will better
      please God.)[9]
   One never knows who is worthy, but God always knows
                                             who is needy;
The treachery is the taker's, if there *is* betrayal afoot;
To give is to repay God and prepare for one's grave,   80
But he who begs is a borrower, and brings debts on himself:
Beggars, I say, are all borrowers, and their bailsman is
                                             God Almighty,
Who alone can repay the debt, with interest added.
   Quare non dedisti pecuniam meam ad mensam, ut ego veniens
      cum usuris utique exegissem illam?

(Wherefore then gavest not thou my money into the bank, that
at my coming I might have required my own with usury?)[10]
Therefore beseech not, you beggars, unless in utter abjection;
For whoever has enough to buy bread, as the Bible bears witness,
Even if that is all he has, has riches enough –

> *Satis dives est qui non indiget pane.*

(He is rich enough who is not poor in bread.)[11]
Let your solace be the steadfast reading of saints' lives,
Since the Book forbids begging, and blames it thus:

> *Junior fui, etenim senui; et non vidi justum derelictum, nec semen*
> *ejus quaerens panem.*

(I have been young, and now am old; yet have I not seen
the righteous forsaken, nor his seed begging bread.)[12]
You beggars live in no love, and keep no law:
Many of you do not marry the women who are your mates,   90
But whinny like wild horses, and mount, and set to work;
And the babies that are born are flagrant bastards.
Then you break their bones or their backs, in childhood,
And falsely beg with your offspring for ever after.
There are more mis-shapen folk among you beggars
Than among any other sort of men that walk Middle Earth;
And those who lead this kind of life shall loathe the day
They were ever made man, when the time of their death is come.
But old grey-haired grandads, grown weak or disabled,
Or women who are with child, and cannot work,   100
And the blind, the bedridden, or the broken-limbed,
Or lepers or the like: if they lowlily bear their afflictions,
They have pardons as plenary as the Ploughman himself.
For love of their lowly hearts, their Lord has granted them
Their penance and their purgatory here upon Earth.
Then a priest said, 'Piers, let me read your pardon;
I will construe its clauses into clear English.'
And Piers, at the priest's request, unfolded his pardon;
And I, behind them both, could read the whole Bull.
It was all in only two lines, not a letter more.   110
And the two lines read thus, with Truth's attestation:

> *Et qui bona egerunt, ibunt in vitam aeternam;*
> *Qui vero mala, in ignem aeternum.*

(The righteous shall go into life eternal,
   But the unrighteous into everlasting fire.)[13]
Said the priest, then, 'By St Peter! I can find no pardon here,
But only, "Do well, and deserve well, and God will save your soul;
Do evil, and deserve evil, and dare hope no other
Than that after your death-day the Devil shall have it." '
  And Piers, in pure fury, tore the pardon in two,
    And said: '*Si ambulavero in medio umbrae mortis,*
     Non timebo mala; quoniam tu mecum es.
   (Yea, though I walk through the valley of the shadow
    of death,
    I will fear no evil, for thou art with me.)[14]
I shall cease from my sowing, and toil and sweat no more,
And nevermore be so busy about the joy of my belly.
Prayers and penitence shall henceforth replace my plough;
I will weep instead of sleeping. And what though I lack
                        wheaten bread? 120
King David ate his bread in dolour and penance,
By what the Psalter says; and so did many others.
Love God loyally, and your livelihood will not lack:
    Fuerunt mihi lacrymae meae panes die et nocte.
   (My tears have been my meat day and night.)[15]
  And unless St Luke is a liar, we are to live like birds,
And not be so busy abut this world's pleasures:
Ne soliciti sitis, he says in his Gospel,
   (Be not solicitous, saying what shall we drink?)[16]
And he teaches us by examples to instruct ourselves.
The wildfowl in the fields – who feeds them in winter?
They have no granaries to go to, yet God feeds them all.'
  The priest said to Piers, 'Why, Peter, it seems to me 130
You are not wholly illiterate. Where did you learn to read?'
  'Abstinence the Abbess taught me my ABC,
And Conscience came later, and schooled me in much more.'
  'Were you a priest, Piers, you might preach if you chose
Like a Doctor of Divinity with "The fool has said" as your text.'[17]
   'You graceless good-for-nothing! A great deal *you* know
                        of the Bible.
You have seldom looked, it would seem, at Solomon's proverbs
    Ejice derisorem, et exibit cum eo jurgium.'

(Cast out the scorner, and contention shall go out.)[18]
  Then Piers and the priest disputed with each other
Till the noise of their words awoke me. So I looked about,
And saw that the sun was now standing in the South,   140
And I, without meal or money, on the Malvern Hills.
Thus, wondering at my dream, I went on my way.
  This dream has made me ponder many times
Whether what I saw while sleeping might be truly so;
I have been inwardly pensive about Piers the Ploughman,
And what kind of pardon Piers had, that comforted people,
And how the priest impugned it with a pair of neat phrases.
But I have no relish for dream-reading – it is rarely true.
Cato and the Canon Lawyers counsel *Somnia ne cures*:
'Do not put faith in dreams, or in dream-divination.'   150
  Yet a certain book of the Bible bears witness
How Daniel divined the dreams of a king
Whom clerks and scholars call Nebuchadnezzar.[19]
Daniel said, 'Sire, your dream signifies
That paladins of Media and Persia shall come to split
                                                  your kingdom,
And lesser lordlings partition the land among them.'
And as Daniel divined, so indeed it befell –
The king lost his kingdom, and lesser lords took it.
  And Joseph dreamed a marvel – how the moon and the sun
And the eleven stars all made obeisance to him.   160
Jacob gave this judgment of Joseph's dream:
'Fair son,' said his father, 'this means that in time of famine,
I myself, and my other sons, will seek your help.'
  It befell as his father said, in the days of Pharaoh,
When Joseph was Justice over the land of Egypt,
That indeed his father and family came to him for aid.[20]
  All this makes me more thoughtful about my dream,
And the priest's proof that no pardon could match Do-Well,
His decision that Do-Well surpassed indulgences,
Biennial or triennial Masses, or Bishops' Bulls,[21]   170
And how Do-Well on Doomsday will be honoured with dignity
Surpassing all the pardons of St Peter's Church.
  Now, the Pope has power to grant people
Pardon, to pass into Heaven without doing penance;

This is our belief, and all learned men teach it:

> *Quodcumque ligaveris super terram, erit ligatum et in coelis.*
> (Whatsoever thou shalt bind on earth shall be bound in
> heaven.)[22]

So I loyally believe (the Lord forbid otherwise!)
That pardons and penances and prayers do save
Even souls that have sinned in seven deadly ways.
But to trust those triennials, I truly think,
Is certainly not so safe for the soul as Do-Well is.   180
Therefore I recommend to all you with riches on Earth,
Who trust in your treasure and the buying of triennials:
Do not be any bolder to break the Ten Commandments.
In especial, you masters of men, and mayors and judges,
Who hold this world's wealth and are thought to be wise,
And can purchase your pardons and Papal Bulls:
On that dreadful Doomsday when the dead shall rise up
And all come before Christ to render their accounts,
Your doom will depend on what you did day by day –
How you lived your life on Earth, and kept God's laws.   190
Then a pack full of pardons and Provincial's letters
Affirming you confrater in all the Four Orders,[23]
And your double indulgences – unless Do-Well stands by you,
I value your patents and pardons at a dried pea-pod.

  All Christians, therefore, I counsel: Pray to Christ
And to Mary His Mother as our mediator,
That God shall give us grace, before we go hence,
To do such deeds while we are down on Earth
That after our dying day Do-Well shall declare
On the Day of Doom, that we did as he ordained.   200

Passus 8

Thus robed in my russet I roamed about
All that summer season, seeking Do-Well;
And often I would ask of the folk I met
If anyone knew where Do-Well's lodging was,
And asked many more what sort of man he might be.
But wherever I went, not one could tell me –
Low and high alike – where the fellow lived . . .

   It fell out, one Friday, that I met two friars,
Masters of the Minorites,[1] and men of great intellect.
I gave them courteous greetings, as good manners teach,   10
And begged them, by God's mercy, before they proceeded,
If they had come across, in their travels, any country or quarter
Where Do-Well was dwelling, would they divulge it.
For they, of all walkers on Earth, are the most widely travelled,
Knowing countries and courts and all kinds of places,
From the palaces of princes to poor men's cottages,
And should know where Do-Well – and Do-Evil – both dwell.
   Said the Minorites, 'Why, that man dwells among us;
And he always has done, and I hope always will.'
   '*Contra!*'[2] said I, like a clerk, and commenced my disputation.   20
'The Scriptures say *septies in die cadit justus*:[3]
Seven times in a day the righteous man sins.
And whosoever sins,' I said, 'does evil, it seems to me;
But Do-Well and Do-Evil cannot dwell together.
Ergo, Do-Well is not always among you friars;
He must at times be elsewhere, as the people's teacher.'
   Said the friar, 'My son, I shall explain to you
The sinning of a just man seven times a day.
I shall expound it plainly, by means of a parable.
Imagine a man in a boat, amidst open water: 30
The wind, and the waves, and the boat swaying,
May make the man fall, and get up again, many times;
For however strongly he stands, a move makes him stumble.

And yet he is safe and sound, and so he needs to be:
For unless he stood up soon, and snatched the helm,
The boat would be overturned by the wind and water,
And his life be lost by his own laziness.
    Even so it is with all men on Earth:
The water, which dips and swells, is like this world;
The wealth of his world is like the great waves   40
That wallow about with the winds and weathers.
The boat is like our body, by nature so frail
That by force of the fickle world, the flesh, and the Devil,
The righteous man himself sins seven times a day.
    Yet his sins are not deadly; he is defended by Do-Well –
That is, by charity, our chief champion against sin;
He gives man strength to stand, and steers man's soul,
So that though your body may bow like a boat on the water,
Your soul is safe – unless of your own free will
You do fall to deadly sin, and so drown your soul: 50
God will not save your soul if you squander it.
For He gives you a constant gift by which to guard yourself –
Wisdom and Free-Will – in which all creatures share,
Though they be birds of the air, or beasts or fishes.
But since man has most of these, then he is most
To blame if he makes bad use of them, and disobeys Do-Well.'
    'I am too stupid,' said I, 'to understand your meaning;
But if I may live and reflect, I shall learn better.'
'I commend you, then, to Christ, who died on the Cross.'
'And may the same,' said I, 'save *you* from misfortune,   60
And give you grace in this world to be good men.'
    So I wandered widely, always walking alone,
And came to a wild waste-land beside a wood.
The blissful songs of the birds made me bide there;
So I lingered a little under a lime-tree in a glade,
To listen to the lyrics of the lovesome birds;
And the minstrelsy from their mouths made me fall asleep,
And there came to me then the most marvellous dream
That ever was dreamed by anyone, I think, in this world.
    It seemed that a tall man, one very much like myself,   70
Came and called me by my Christian name.
'Who are you?' I asked him, 'How do you know my name?'

'You are well aware of that, and no one better!'
'I really ought to know you?' 'I am Thought,
Who has followed you for years. Have you never seen me before?'
'It is likely, if you are Thought, you could let me know
Where Do-Well's dwelling is, and describe it to me.'
    'Do-Well, Do-Better, and a third called Do-Best,
Are three fair virtues, to be found not far away.
Whoever is trustworthy of tongue and of his two hands,   80
Earning his living from his own land or labour,
Whose tally is trustworthy, and who takes only his due,
Who is not drunken or disdainful: *he* knows Do-Well.
Do-Better does all this, but he does much more:
He is lowly as a lamb, and of likeable speech,
And assists all men according to their needs;
He has burst all the money-bags and boundaries
That once belonged to Earl Avarice and his heirs,
Has made himself friends with the money of Mammon;[4]
Has enrolled as a Religious, and re-translated the Bible,   90
And preaches now to the people on the words of St Paul:
        Libenter enim suffertis insipientes; cum sitis ipsi sapientes.
        (Ye suffer fools gladly, seeing ye yourselves are wise.)[5]
Allow those of little wisdom to live among you,
And gladly do them good, since God so commands.
    Do-Best is placed above both, and bears a bishop's crozier,
With a hook on one end to haul men out of Hell,
And a spike at the staff's other end, to strike down the wicked
Who lie in wait to work evil upon Do-Well.
Do-Well and Do-Better have determined between them
To crown a man to be king and control them both,
So that if Do-Well or Do-Better should injure Do-Best,   100
That King shall come and cast him into irons;
And unless Do-Best begs him off, he shall lie there forever.
    Thus Do-Well and Do-Better, and Do-Best for a third,
Have crowned a man to be King and protect *them all*,
And rule the realm by their threefold reason,
And only accordingly as these three shall advise.'
    I thanked Thought then for teaching me all this.
'But your lesson leaves me unsatisfied; I long to learn
How Do-Well, Do-Better, and Do-Best may act among men.'

'Only Reason[6] can instruct you where those three are.   110
I know of nobody else among those now living.'
   Thus for three days, Thought and I went on together,
Discussing Do-Well one day after another;
Till we ran quite unawares across Reason.
He was long and lean, and like no other man;
Neither pride nor poverty showed in his apparel;
So grave his manner, and so sweet his countenance,
I dared not moot any matter to move him to argument,
But begged Thought to be my go-between
And introduce the topic that might test his wits –   120
The difference, namely, between Do-Well, Do-Better
                                        and Do-Best.
   With this intention, then, Thought spoke these words:
'Here is Long Will who, if you could tell him, would ask
Where in this country are Do-Well, Do-Better and Do-Best;
He would also learn whether they are men or women:
For his desire is to do as these three direct.'

Said Reason, 'Sir Do-Well's dwelling is not a day's
journey hence,
In a castle constructed by Nature[1] from four kinds of thing:
It is made of earth intermingled with air,
And with fire and water wondrously conjoined.[2]
And Nature has cunningly enclosed within this castle
A leman whom he loves no less than himself.
Anima[3] is her name, and Envy abhors her:
He's a proud prancer from France, called the Prince of
this World,[4]
And would lure her away to him with his wiles, if he could.
   Nature of course knows this well, and keeps her the closer,   10
Defended by Sir Do-Well, who is Duke of the Marches.[5]
Do-Better is her damsel, Sir Do-Well's daughter,
Who serves the lady loyally both early and late.
Do-Best is above them both, and ranks with bishops;
His commands are unquestioned, and he rules the whole castle;
Lady Anima too is controlled by his teaching.
   Now, the Constable of the castle, and Captain of the Watch,
Is called Sir Insight,[6] a wise knight certainly.
He has five fine sons by his first wife:
Sir See-Well and Sir Say-Well and Sir Hear-Well the Courteous,   20
With Sir Work-Well-with-your-Hands (a strong, active man)
And Sir Godfrey Go-Well – all very great lords.
So these five are assigned to safeguard Lady Anima
Until Nature comes or sends for her to keep her safe for ever.'
   'What kind of character is this Nature? Can you tell me?'
'A conceiver and creator of all kinds of things;
The father and fashioner of all that was ever formed.
For he is the great God that had no beginning,
The Lord of life and light as of bliss and pain.
The angels, and all that live, are at his command;   30
But Man is the creature most like him, in image and quality.

It was at Nature's word that the animals issued forth:
> *Dixit, et facta sunt.*
> (He commanded, and they were created.)[7]
But when he made Man, in his own image,
And Eve out of Adam's rib, the act was "immediate";[8]
For, though singular himself, he said "Let *us* make",
As who would say, "More must be used than my word alone;
My might must help, and not my speech merely."
  If a lord must write letters, but lacks parchment,
Or, however fine his hand, if he has no pen:
For all his lordship, his letter, I believe, will go unwritten.   40
And it seems that God is the same, as we see in the Bible;
For where it says *Dixit, et facta sunt,*
He must work through His Word, and reveal His wisdom;
And in this manner Man was made, through power of
                                        Almighty God,
By His word and by His handiwork, for life everlasting.
For He gave him a soul from the Holy Spirit in Heaven,
And of His great grace granted bliss to him
In life everlasting, and to his lineage after him.
  This castle that Nature created is called Flesh;
And the meaning of that is Man made with a soul
By the word and the workmanship, acting as one,   50
And by the might, of God's majesty. Thus was Man made.
Conscience,[9] and *all* mental qualities, are enclosed in this castle,
For love of Lady Anima, whose name is Life;
She may move as she likes throughout all Man's body,
But her home is the heart, her haven of rest.
The home of Insight is the head, but he rules the heart:
What Anima likes or loathes, he allows – or not –
For, next to God's grace, her greatest friend is Insight.
  Much misery will befall the man who misuses Insight,
As it might be those gluttonous gobblers whose god is their belly: 60
> *Quorum deus venter est.*[10]
Because they serve Satan, he shall have their souls,
For those who lead sinful lives have souls like his;
And all who lead good lives are like God Almighty.
> *Qui manet in caritate in Deo manet.*
> (He that dwelleth in love dwelleth in God and God in him.)[11]

Alas, that drink should undo those whom God bought so dearly,
And force Him to forsake those whom He framed in His likeness!

Amen dico vobis, nescio vos.

(Verily I say unto you, I know you not.)

Et alibi: et dimisi eos secundum desideria eorum.

(And elsewhere it is written, So I gave them up unto their
      own hearts' lust.)[12]

But fools whose insight fails them . . . I feel that Holy Church
Should furnish the needs of such fools, and of fatherless children,
And of widows without skill wherewith to earn a living,
And mad men, and young girls who maybe are helpless:
All these lack insight, and are in need of instruction.   70

I might make a long speech about this matter,
And find a flock of proofs in the Four Doctors;[13]
And that I do not lie in my allegations, St Luke bears witness.[14]

Godfathers and godmothers who see their godchildren
In misery or misfortune, and have means to relieve them,
Shall do penance in Purgatory if they provide no help:
They owe more to the infant still unlearned in God's Law
Than giving him a name, of which he knows nothing!
No Christian creature need ever cry at men's gates,
Nor lack bread or bouillon, if priests behaved as they should.   80
No Jew would let another Jew be a jabbering beggar,
Not for all the wealth in the world, were he able to help him.

Alas that one Christian creature should be unkind to another,
When Jews − whom we judge to be just like Judas −
Will all help each other if need arises!
Why will not we Christians as kindly share Christ's goodness
As Jews? − who are thus our exemplars; shame to us all!
I fear all Christians in common shall pay for such unkindness.
Then the bishops will be blamed for the beggars' plight:
It's to act worse than Judas, to give money to a jester   90
And bid the beggar be off because his clothes are tattered.

*Proditor est prelatus cum Juda, qui patrimonium Christi minus
      distribuit.*

(That prelate who distributes too little of Christ's
      patrimony, is a traitor like Judas.)

*Et alibi: Perniciosus dispensator est, qui res pauperum Christi
      inutiliter consumit.*

(And elsewhere it is written, He is an evil bursar, who
    unprofitably scatters the property of Christ's poor.)[15]
Such a man does not do well, nor dreads God Almighty,
Nor savours the proverbs of Solomon, who says in his wisdom,
    Initium sapientiae timor Domini.
    (The fear of the Lord is the beginning of wisdom.)[16]
He who dreads God, does well; he who dreads Him from love,
And not for fear of punishment, therefore does better;
And he does best who withdraws, by night and day,
From needlessly spending speech or expending time:
    Qui offendit in uno, in omnibus est reus.
    (For whosoever shall keep the whole Law, and yet offend
    in one point, he is guilty of all.)[17]
Waste of time (God knows this is true)
Is that thing on Earth most hated by those in Heaven;
And second is waste of speech, that sprouting of God's grace,   100
God's gleeman, and a game played in Heaven.
Our faithful Father could not wish His fiddle untuned,
Nor his gleeman a good-for-nothing who goes round the taverns!
All honest, exact men who are eager to work,
Our Lord will love – and allow them (come hell or high water)
Grace to go labour and gain their livings:
    Inquirentes autem dominum non minuentur omni bono.
    (They that seek the Lord shall not want any good thing.)[18]
To live truly wedded in this world is Do-Well also,
For the married must work and earn wages and keep the
                            world alive.
From this kind of folk come all who are called Confessors –
And kings and cavaliers and Kaisers and countrymen,   110
And maidens and martyrs: all descended from one man
Whose wife was made as a means to help his work.
So wedlock was established with common people,
First by the father's will and the advice of friends,
Then by the assent of the two spouses themselves.
Such was wedlock's foundation, and God Himself was its founder,
And its Heaven is here on Earth, with Himself as its witness.[19]
But all false faithless folk such as thieves and liars,
The wasters and the wicked – out of wedlock, I think,
They were conceived, in a cursed time, as Cain was by Eve.[20]   120

Of such sinful wretches the Psalter makes mention:
> *Ecce parturit injustitiam: concepit dolorem, et peperit iniquitatem.*
> (Behold, he travaileth with iniquity, and hath conceived
> mischief and brought forth falsehood.)[21]

And all who are counted Cain's offspring come to evil ends;
For God sent a message to Seth by an angel, and said,
"My will is that your issue wed with your issue only,
And that your kin shall not couple nor marry with those of Cain."[22]

Yet some, against that speech from our Saviour in Heaven,
Did couple Cain's offspring with the kin of Seth,
Till God grew angry at their deeds, and gave this judgment:
"That I ever made Man, now makes Me sorry" —
> *Delebo, inquit, hominem . . . poenitet enim me fecisse eos.*
> (The Lord said, I will destroy men . . . for it repenteth Me
> that I have made them.)[23]

So anon He came to Noah, and bade him not delay: 130
"Go now, and build a boat of boards and timbers.
Yourself and your three sons, and your wives also,
Must hasten aboard that boat, and abide in it
For a full forty days, when the Flood will have washed
Clean away the accursed blood that Cain has begotten.
And animals now alive shall also damn the day
That ever the accursed Cain came to this earth,
And shall die for his misdeeds, by dale and hill,
Even the flying wildfowl, like all other flesh —
Except only a couple of each kind of creature   140
That shall be saved in the shelter of your shingled ship."[24]

Thus was ancestral sin paid-for by Cain's descendants;
And, for their forefather's sake, those folk must suffer.
In one regard, I find, the Gospel goes against this:
> *Filius non portabit iniquitatem patris, et pater non portabit*
> *iniquitatem filii.*
> (The son shall not bear the iniquity of the father, neither
> shall the father bear the iniquity of the son.)[25]

But I feel that if the father is a fraud and a villain,
The son will to some extent inherit his father's stain.
Graft an apple on an elder-tree, and if your apple grows sweet
I shall marvel very much — and far more if a scoundrel
Can beget any boy but will grow up like him

And have some smack of his father. One seldom sees otherwise: 150
    Numquid colligunt de spinis uvas, aut de tribulis ficus?
    (Do men gather grapes of thorns, or figs of thistles?)[26]
And thus, through accursed Cain, sorrow first came upon Earth –
And all because they wedded in ways God's will forbade.
Misery follows the marriage if children are thus married-off;
Yet nowadays I see some, to speak the truth,
Who marry thus monstrously for lust of money;
But the progeny of such pairings inherit as much pain
As the folk who died in the Flood, as I told you before.
Good men should marry good women, even if they lack goods:
Ego sum via et veritas,[27] says Christ, "and can advance anyone".
    What an uncomely coupling – or so, by Christ, *I* think –   160
It is, if a young girl is given to a feeble greybeard;
Or the wedding of a widow for her wealth's sake,
A woman too old to bear babies – except in her arms!
Since the pestilence, many a pair have been plighted together
Whose only offspring have been oaths and abuse,
Living joylessly in jealousy, and jangling in bed,
Breeding no babies but abuse and nagging.
If they did go off to Dunmow, they'd need the Devil's help
To afford them the flitch,[28] or they'd never fetch it home;
And unless they both swore lies, they would lose the bacon.   170
    Therefore I counsel all Christians: take no account of marrying
From the wish of wealth, or for well-off kindred.
Maidens and unmarried men should match themselves off,
And widows marry widowers in the same way.
Look to be wedded for love, and not for lands;
Then you will earn God's grace – and enough goods to live-on.
And every layman who lacks the power to live chastely,
Will be wise to wed, and avoid wickedness;
For lecherous delights are the lime-twigs of hell.
While you are young, and your weapon is eager,   180
Work it off within wedlock if you want an excuse:
    Dum sis vir fortis, ne des tua robora scortis;
    Scribitur in portis, meretrix est janua mortis.
    (While you are still a strong man, give not your strength to
      the whore;
    It is written upon the gates, *The harlot is Death's front door.*)[29]

When you have wedded, beware to use the right days only,
Unlike Adam and Eve when Cain was engendered.
For truly, at forbidden times,[30] between man and woman
There should be no sport in bed; and unless both are pure,
In life and in soul, and alike in perfect charity,
That same clandestine deed should be done by no one.
If they lead their lives thus, our Almighty Lord is pleased;   190
For he first created marriage, and He Himself ordained,

> *Propter fornicationem autem unusquisque suam uxorem habeat,*
> *et unaquaeque suum virum habeat.*

> (Nevertheless, to avoid fornication, let every man have his
> own wife, and let every woman have her own
> husband.)[31]

And those born of base unions will be mostly vagrants,
Fraudulent folk, foundlings, fakers and liars;
Graceless to get their living, or people's love,
They wander about, and waste whatever they can snatch.
In Do-Well's despite, they do evil, and serve the Devil;
And after their death-day they will dwell with him
Unless first God's grace is given them, to amend.

Do-Well, my friend, is to do as the Law demands;
Do-Better is to love both friend and foe, believe me;   200
But charity and cherishing to all, young or old,
To heal them and help, is Do-Best of all.
Do-Well is to fear God, and Do-Better is to suffer;
And, beyond both, Do-Best, who subdues rebellion
And that wicked self-will which spoils many good works
By driving Do-Well away through deadly sins.'

Now, Reason was wedded to one Dame Study,
A lady as lean in the face as in limbs and figure.
She was really enraged by what Reason had taught me;
Eyes wide with anger, she admonished him sternly.
'What a wise man you are, to speak words of wisdom
To flatterers and fools who are not fully sane!'
She condemned him and cursed him and told him to keep quiet
Rather than waste wise words upon the witless.
'In St Matthew it is said, "Do not scatter your pearls
Before swine"[1] – or such hogs as have haws to eat in plenty, 10
And only dribble on jewels: they would rather have draff
Than all the precious pierreries that grow in Paradise.[2]
And when I say "swine",' said she, 'I mean such as show by
their acts
That they better love land and earthly lordship,
Or riches and rents, and repose when they please,
Than all the sage precepts that Solomon ever spoke.

Insight and intelligence today are not worth a cress-leaf
Unless carded with covetousness, as clothiers comb wool.
Whoever can contrive deceits, and conspire to do wrong,
And lay snares for truth, from his seat on Settlement Days –[3]
Such crafty men are called into solemn councils, 20
And mislead lords with their lies, and blacken truth.

The blameless Job bears witness in his book
That wicked men wield all the wealth of this world;
They are lords in every land, who live outside the law:
    Quare ergo impii vivunt?. . . bene est omnibus, qui praevaricantur,
        et inique agunt?
    (Wherefore do the wicked live? . . . Wherefore are all they
        happy that deal very treacherously?)[4]
And the Psalter says the same of such as do evil:
    Ecce ipsi peccatores, et abundantes in saeculo, obtinuerunt divitias.
    (Behold, these are the ungodly, who prosper in this world;
        they increase in riches.)[5]

"Lo!" says this holy literature, "what lords these villains are!"
That man to whom God gives most, distributes least goods
                                    to others;
And the most unkind to common folk are those who
                              command most wealth:
   Quoniam quae perfecisti, destruxerunt: justus autem quid fecit?
   (For what thou hast accomplished, they have destroyed;
     and what hath the righteous done?)[6]
Harlots may have payment for their harlotry,   30
And jesters and jugglers and the jabberers of ballads;
   But he in whose mouth Holy Writ comes always,
He who can talk of Tobit and the Twelve Apostles,
Or preach about the pains that Pilate inflicted
On gentle Jesus Whom the Jews destroyed –
Little is he loved, who teaches such lessons;
He is daunted or disregarded, I declare by God Himself!
   And those who feign themselves fools, and live by
                                  false pretences –
Against the law of Our Land – and lie about themselves,
And spit and spew out the words of their foul speech,   40
And drink and drivel till the audience gapes at them,
And mock men, and make up tales about those who refuse
                               them money,
And know no more of minstrelsy, or of music to give
                                men pleasure,
Than Munday the Miller[7] knows of the Nine Muses:
But for their vile ribaldry, may God be my witness,
Never king or cavalier nor Canon of St Paul's
Would give them as gratuity or stipend even a groat!
   But merriment and ministrelsy among men are now
Mere bawdry, backbiting, and beastly stories;
Gluttony and Great Oaths adore such glee.   50
And if these clerks and laymen do discuss Christ,
When at table amid such amusements, when the minstrels
                              have paused,
It is only to tell a jest or two about the Trinity,
Or to bring out some bald opinion, with St Bernard as their source,
And prove their point with a *petitio principii*.
Thus they drivel at High Table about the Deity,

And gorge on God with their tongues, when their guts are full.
  The poor man may meanwhile call and lament at their gates,
Half dead from hunger or drought, or ashiver with cold;
No one asks him inside, to ease his pain; 60
He is howled at like a hound, and hurried away.
How little they love the Lord who allowed them their luxury,
If this is their way of sharing it with the needy:
If the humble had no more mercy than the rich have,
Every beggar would go to bed with an empty belly!
"God" is much in the gullets of such great masters,
But among humble men are His mercy and His works;
And so the Psalter says, as I have seen often:
  "Ecce audivimus eam in Ephrata: invenimus eam in campis silvae."
    (Lo, we heard of it at Ephratah; we found it in the fields of
      the wood.)[8]
The clergy, and men akin to them, converse easily about God,
And have Him much in their mouths: He is in common
                                                men's hearts. 70
  Friars and frauds have faked-up such questions
For the pleasure of proud men, since the time of the pestilence,
And preach at St Paul's[9] from pure envy of the clergy,
So that folk are neither confirmed in faith nor free in charity;
Nor are they sorry for their sins. So great has pride grown
Among the Religious, and in all the realm, both rich and poor,
That prayers have no power to halt the pestilence.
Yet not one of these worldly villains takes warning from others;
No dread of death reduces their pride,
Nor makes them profuse to the poor, as pure charity asks: 80
In gaiety and gluttony they themselves gulp down their wealth,
Breaking no bread for the beggar, as the Good Book teaches:
  Frange esurienti panem tuum.
    (Deal thy bread to the hungry, and . . . bring the poor that
      are cast out to thy house.)[10]
And the more they acquire and control, of capital and goods,
And gain the lordship of lands, the less they give away.
  Tobit tells us quite otherwise: take heed, you rich men,
How that book of the Bible bears witness of his words:
  *Si tibi sit copia, abundanter tribue; si autem exiguum, illud
    impertiri stude libenter.*

(If thou hast abundance, give alms accordingly: if thou have
    but a little, be not afraid to give according to that little.)[11]
Tobit means: if you have much, spend manfully;
If you cannot manage much, make that your guide;
For we have no letters-patent for how long we shall live.
Lords should love to hear such lessons as this,   90
And how they might maintain the greatest household
                            magnificently.
Not in the fashion of fiddlers and friars, who hunt-up feasts,
Making other men's houses theirs, and hating their own:
Unhappy is the hall when every day in the week
The lord and the lady like to eat elsewhere.
The rule is, today, for rich men to regale themselves alone,
In a private parlour (so escaping the poor),
Or in a chamber with a chimney – avoiding the chief hall
That was made for men to eat their meals in.
And all to spare the expending of what will be squandered by
                          an heir!   100
    I have heard men of high rank, who were eating at table,
Conversing as if they were clergy, about Christ and His powers,
And finding faults in the Father Who framed us all,
And complaining crabbedly against the clergy:
"Why should our Saviour suffer the Serpent to enter Eden,
There to beguile first Eve and afterwards Adam,
So that through his wily words they went to Hell,
And their seed, for their sin, must endure the same death?"
Your lore is fallacious here, such lords will argue,
"For by what you clergy can tell us of Christ's words in
                        the Gospels,   110
    Filius non portabit iniquitatem patris.
    (The son shall not bear the iniquity of the father.)[12]
So why should we, living now, because of what Adam did,
Be so rotted and ruined? Reason is against it –
    Unusquisque enim onus suum portabit.
    (For every man shall bear his own burden.)"[13]
Such are the motions moved by these masters in their glory,
So that men who muse much about them turn misbelievers.
    But Imagination hereafter shall answer them to good purpose.
In answer to such arguers, Augustine quotes this text:

Non plus sapere quam oportet sapere.

(Not to think of himself more highly than he ought to think.)[14]

Never, then, ask to know why God in His wisdom
Would allow the Devil to deceive His children;
But loyally believe in the lore of Holy Church,
Pray to God for pardon and the gift of repentance in this life,   120
And that by His mighty mercy you may cleanse your souls *here*.
All such who would learn the ways of the Lord Almighty,
I wish their eyes in their arse, and their finger in both!
I mean such men as wish to know what God's motive was,
In suffering Satan to lead His children astray,
Or Judas to betray Jesus to the Jews.
All was according to Thy will, O Lord, and worshipped be Thou,
And all shall be as Thou wilt, however we argue!
   And whoever has recourse to such quibblings, to cloud
                                                    men's minds,
About Do-Well and Do-Better, he deserves to go deaf.   130
Does this long lout really want to learn which is which,
Or lead the kind of life that belongs to Do-Well?
I will boldly go bail that *he* will never do better,
Even if Do-Best drags him on day after day.'
   When Reason understood the import of this oration,
He became so confused that he could not face her,
And withdrew to the room's end, as dumb as death:
Nor afterwards, for all my asking, and even kneeling before him,
Could I get from him one grain of his great wisdom.
He gave a little laugh, and looked with a bow towards Study,   140
As a sign that first I must ask for her forgiveness.
   So when I saw what he meant, I bowed to his wife,
And said, 'Madame, I ask mercy; I will be your man
So long as I live, to serve you early and late;
And I shall do all you wish, while my life endures,
If you will tell me truly what is Do-Well.'
   'Because of your meekness, my man,' said she, 'and your
                                                    mild speech,[15]
I will acquaint you with my cousin, whose name is Clerisy.[15]
He wedded a wife within these last six months;
She is called Scripture, and is kin to the Seven Arts.[16]   150
The two of them, I trust, since I myself taught them,

Will direct you to Do-Well; I dare promise you that.'
    Then my heart grew light as a lark's on a lovely morning;
I was merrier than a minstrel with money in his purse;
I enquired the quickest way to Clerisy's home,
And, since it was time I went, to be told some token.
    'Ask for the highway from here to the hamlet of Suffer-
Both-Weal-and-Woe, if you are willing to learn that;
Then ride on past Riches, and take no rest in that region,
For if it attracts you, you will never advance to Clerisy.   160
There is also a lovely lea-land called Lechery:
Leave it on your left side, by a mile or longer,
Till you come to a castle called Keep-your-mouth-clear
of-lying-and-loathsome-speech-and-lubricious-drinks.
There you will see Sobriety and Simplicity-of-Speech,
With whom all men are eager to display their wisdom;
And so you will come to Clerisy and his many skills.
Speak to him this password: that *I* first set him to school;
And I greet his wife warmly, since I wrote many works for her,
And set her to Solomon's proverbs, and the Gloss on the Psalms. 170
I left her skilled in Logic and in much other learning,
And in all the modes of Music I made her expert.
    It was I who first put Plato the poet to his book,
And first taught Aristotle and many others to argue.
I first got a grammar-book written for girls and boys,
And had them beaten with birches if they baulked at learning.
I contrived the tools for all kinds of crafts,
Such as carpenters and sculptors; I taught masons their compasses,
And the use of line and level, though now I see less clearly.
    Theology, though, has troubled me ten thousand times;   180
The more I muse upon it, the mistier it grows;
And the deeper I dare guess, the darker it seems:
It is certainly no science in which to play with subtleties,
And, if love were lacking, would be loathsome indeed.
But I love it the better because it sets love before all else;
And where love is the leader, grace is never lacking.
First learn to be loyal in love, if you look to Do-Well;
For Do-Better and Do-Best are both love's kinsfolk.
    In every other science, as I saw in Cato,

Qui simulat verbis, nec corde est fidus amicus,   190
Tu quoque fac simile, sic ars deluditur arte.
(If a man speaks false but fair, and is no true friend in his heart,
Do the same back to him – so art is deceived by art.)[17]
When flattered by some deceiver, do the same to him,
So false untruthful folk shall be fooled by you:
Such is the counsel that Cato teaches to clerks.
But theology, if you think, teaches otherwise;
Its counsel is contrary to Cato's words,
For it orders us to live as brothers, and pray for our enemies,
And love those who tell lies about us, and relieve their wants;
And to give back good for evil is God's own commandment:

Dum tempus habemus, operemur bonum ad omnes, maxime
autem ad domesticos fidei.

(As we have therefore opportunity, let us do good unto all
men, especially unto them who are of the household of
faith.)[18]

Thus Paul preached to the people, he who loved perfection: 200
To do good for the love of God, and give to whoever asked,
But especially to such as accept our own faith.
And Our Lord teaches us to love all who malign us or slander us;
And God has forbidden us to injure those who injure us:

Mihi vindicta: ego retribuam.

(Vengeance is mine; I will repay, saith the Lord.)[19]
Therefore, so long as you live, see that you love,
For no science under the sun can so heal the soul.

Now, astronomy is a difficult discipline, and the devil to learn;
And geometry and geomancy have confusing terminology:
If you wish to work in these two, you will not succeed quickly,
For sorcery is the chief study that these sciences entail.   210

There are many men, also, who makes use of strange devices,
Alchemical experiments for the deception of others:
If you desire to do well, have no dealings with these.
I myself conceived and set-out these sciences,
And was their first founder, in order to lead folk astray.

These things are all tokens that you must tell to Clerisy
and Scripture;

They will gladly teach you then the meaning of Do-Well.'
I said, 'Many thanks, madame,' and meekly took my leave,

And went at once on my way, with no more ado,
And could not rest until I came into Clerisy's presence.   220
I greeted that good man, as guided by Study,
And afterwards his wife, and was respectful to them,
And told them the tokens that I had been taught.
No man beneath the moon, since God made the world,
Was ever more friendlily welcomed and made warmly at ease,
Than certainly I myself was, as soon as Clerisy learned
How I had come from the house of Reason and of his wife
                                        Dame Study.
I told them truthfully that I had been sent to them
To learn about Do-Well, Do-Better, and Do-Best.
  'Do-Well,' said Clerisy, 'is a life among laymen, believing
                                        in Holy Church   230
And in all the articles of faith that are to be known.
That is, learned and unlearned alike must loyally believe
In that great God who was without beginning,
And in His steadfast Son Who saved mankind
From death and damnation and the Devil's power,
By the help of the Holy Ghost that proceeds from them both:
Three separate Persons, yet not plural in number,
For all are only one God, and each is Himself God:
        Deus Pater, Deus Filius, Deus Spiritus Sanctus:
God the Father, God the Son, God the Holy Ghost
                                        proceeding from both,
The Maker of mankind and of dumb animals.[20]   240
  St Augustine of old wrote books about this doctrine;
He first gave it form, to make us firm in faith.
On whose authority? That of all four Evangelists,
Who all confirm that Christ called Himself God:
      Qui videt me, videt et Patrem . . . Ego in Patre, et Pater in me est.
    (He that hath seen me hath seen the Father . . . I am in the
        Father, and the Father in me.)[21]
No clerk who followed Christ could ever explain this,
But thus the unlettered must believe if they long to do well;
For if no men had minds fine enough to question the Faith,
Or if it might be proved, no man would gain merit
                                        from believing it:

Fides non habet meritum, ubi humana ratio praebet experimentum.
 (Faith has no merit where human reason affords adequate
  proof.)[22]
So Do-Better is to suffer for your soul's health
All that the Bible bids, and is taught by Holy Church;   250
Which is, "Man, be mighty, for the sake of mercy,
To put into practice all that your words profess:
 Appare quod es, vel esto quod appares:[23]
As you seem in men's sight, so be in yourself.
Let nobody be beguiled by your outward bearing,
But be in your soul the same as you show yourself."
 Do-Best is to be bold to blame the guilty,
So long as you see *yourself* to be clean of soul;
But blame nobody, ever, if you are blameworthy yourself:
 Si culpare velis, culpabilis esse cavebis;
 Dogma tuum sordet cum te tua culpa remordet.   260
 (If others you wish to blame,
 Take care *you* have no cause for shame;
 Your dogmas are filthy and thin
 If your own crimes gnaw you within.)[24]
God in the Gospels grimly reproves
Those who find fault in others but do not feel their own:
 Quid autem vides festucam in oculo fratris tui; et trabem in oculo
  tuo non vides?
 (Why are you moved to condemn a mote in your brother's
  eye, since you are blind to the beam that is in your
  own?)[25]
 Ejice primum trabem de oculo tuo.
 (Thou hypocrite, first cast out the beam out of thine own
  eye.)[26]
For that stops you from seeing either great things or small.
 I advise every blind buzzard to better his soul:
Abbots, I mean, and priors, and all kinds of prelate,
And parsons, and parish priests, who should preach and instruct
All men to amend themselves with all their might:
All of you take this text as a warning; before you teach,   270
Be such as you say others must if they hope to be saved.
For *your* loss would not lose God's word; *that* works eternally,
And even if useless to others, might be useful to you.

But it certainly seems today, from a worldly standpoint,
That God's word is *not* at work, among learned or unlettered,
Unless in the manner that Mark has mentioned in his gospel:
    Caecus autem si caeco ducatum praestet, ambo in foveam cadunt.
    (If the blind lead the blind, both shall fall into the ditch.)[27]
Unlearned men may allege of you that the beam lies in *your* eyes,
And the mote of filth has fallen, by your fault, mainly,
Into all manner of men's eyes, you maledict priests.
The Bible bears witness what the Israelites had to bear,   280
Most bitterly buying the guilt of two bad priests,
Hophni and Phineas: for their avarice,
The Ark of the Covenant was miscarried, and Eli broke his neck.[28]
    Therefore, you "correctors", claw *this* in: correct yourselves first;
And then you may safely say, as David says in the Psalter,
    Existimasti inique quod ero tui similis: arguam te, et statuam
        contra faciem tuam.
    (Thou thoughtest wickedly that I am even such a one as
        thyself: but I will reprove thee, and set before thee the
        things that thou hast done.)[29]
Then such homespun scholars shall be ashamed to disparage
                              or grieve you,
Or carp as they carp now, calling you dumb dogs;
    Canes muti non valentes latrare.
    (They are all ignorant, they are all dumb dogs, they cannot
    bark.)[30]
They'll be anxious not to anger you by a word, or hinder
                            your activity;
They'll appear faster for your praying than for a pound in
                            gold nobles –
And all because of your holiness: hold *that* in your hearts.   290
    Among upright religious, this rule should be upheld.
St Gregory, that great scholar and good Pope,
Rehearses in his *Moralia* the rules for all religious orders,
And says, as a case in point, for them to follow suit,
"When the flood or the fresh water fail the fish,
They die of drought, lying upon dry land.
Just so," said Gregory, "a religious is spoiled,[31]
And suffocates and stinks, and steals alms from lords,
Who covets a life outside cloister or convent."

For if Heaven exists on earth, and ease for any soul,   300
For many causes I think it is in cloisters or convent schools.
No man comes into cloisters to quarrel or fight;
All is obedience there, and books, and imbibing of learning.
   He is scorned in school, if a scholar cannot learn;
Else, all is delight and love, and love of one another.
But the religious today is a rider, a roamer of streets,
The leading man on love-days, and a land-buyer,
A hustler on horseback from manor to manor,
An army of hounds at his arse, like an aristocrat.
And unless his lackey kneels when bringing his liquor,   310
He frowns at him, and asks him who taught him his manners.
The lords are ill-advised to shift land from their heirs
To religious who would not care if it rained on their altars!
   In many places they rule parishes, and are perfectly at ease,
But are pitiless to the poor; and pass that off as "charity".
They believe themselves barons, so broad are their lands.
   But a king shall arise and reform you Religious Orders,
And beat you – like Christ in the Bible – for breaking your Rule;[32]
And amend all ancresses and abbots and canons,
And put them to penance till their pristine state return.   320
And barons and earls shall beat them with "Blessed the man that
                    walketh not in the counsel of the ungodly."[33]
And their children shall shout at them and deride them shamefully
      Hi in curribus, et hi in equis.
   (Some trust in chariots, and some in horses, but we will
      remember the name of the Lord our God.
   They are brought down and fallen, but we are risen and
      stand upright.)[34]
   The friars in their fraters will find a key
To Constantine's coffers, which conceal the wealth
That Gregory's god-children have let go to waste.[35]
Then the Abbot of Abingdon,[36] and all his issue for ever,
Shall catch from that King's clout an incurable wound.
   That this will be so, search out – you who often study the Bible –
      Quomodo cessavit exactor, quievit tributum? Contrivit Dominus
      baculum impiorum, virgam dominantium.
   (How hath the oppressor ceased! The exactress of gold has
      ceased! The Lord hath broken the staff of the wicked, and
      the sceptre of the rulers.)[37]

But before that king shall come, Cain[38] shall awake,
And Do-Well shall strike him down, and destroy his power!'   330
'Then Do-Well and Do-Better,' said I, 'are knighthood and
                                                    kingship?'
Said Scripture, 'I do not scoff; but unless scriveners lie,
Neither knighthood nor kingship, by any text I know,
Has ever got one hair's-breadth nearer Heaven –
Nor, indeed, riches, nor the rule of lords.
St Paul proves it impossible for the rich to reach Heaven,[39]
And Solomon says that silver is the worst thing to love:
        Nihil iniquius quam amare pecuniam.[40]
Cato tells us not to covet more than our state requires:
        Dilige denarium, sed parce dilige formam!
        (Know the value of money, but value it little for itself.)[41]
Patriarchs and prophets and poets alike   340
Have warned us in their works not to wish for wealth,
And all praise poverty patiently borne. The Apostles bear witness
That the poor have by true right their heritage in Heaven,
Where rich men may claim *no* right but by grace and favour.'[42]
        '*Contra!*'[43] cried I. 'By Christ, I can rebut that
And prove you wrong by St Peter and St Paul.
The baptised shall be saved, both rich and poor.'[44]
        'Only if they are heathen, and at the point of death.
They may be saved thus, and that is part of our faith –
That even a non-Christian may in such cases christen heathens 350
Who, for their true belief when they take leave of life,
Shall inherit Heaven as surely as if they *had* been Christian.
But Christians cannot reach Heaven by Christianity alone,
For Christ confirmed the Law, by dying for Christians,
That whoever wishes and wills to rise up with Christ,
Should believe, and love, and fulfil the Law.
        Si cum Christo surrexistis.
        (If ye then be risen with Christ, seek those things which are
            above.)[45]
That is, Thou shalt love the Lord God above all,
And then all Christian creatures in common, each one another.
So, lacking love, do not believe yourself saved.
And unless we do love indeed, before Doomsday comes,   360
Bitter burdens shall be our hoards of silver,

Our mantles left for the moths while poor men went naked,
Our delight in wine and in wildfowl, while others went hungry.
For all Christian creatures should show kindness to each other –
And help the heathen too, in hope of their conversion.
God has told both high and low that no man must harm another;
He says, "You shall kill no creature created in My image,
Unless I send you a sign." That is, *non occides* –
Thou shalt not slay[46] – but suffer; and so all shall be well.
For "*Mihi vindicta; ego retribuam, dicit Dominus.*[47]
    (Vengeance is mine; I will repay, saith the Lord.)
"I shall punish in Purgatory or in the pits of Hell,   370
All Men's misdeeds, unless mercy restrains Me." '
  'This is a long lesson,' said I, 'but I am little the wiser;
Where Do-Well or Do-Better may be, you explain only darkly;
And you tell me many tales of what Theology teaches.
But that I was made a man, and my name entered
In the log-book of life[48] long before I was born,
Or else left unwritten for some sin, as the Scriptures bear witness –
    Nemo ascendit in coelum nisi qui descendit de coelo.
    (No man hath ascended up to heaven, but he that came
      down from heaven)[49] –
I believe this well,' said I, 'on Our Lord's word (no lecturer better).
For the sage Solomon, who taught sagacity,
Was given by God the grace of wisdom, and great wealth too,   380
To rule his realm and increase his riches.
He judged well and wisely, as is witnessed by the Scriptures.
Aristotle and he – who ever taught men better?
Masters who speak of God's mercy, when they teach men
                                  or preach to them,
Will use the words of these two, the wisest of their times:
Yet all Holy Church holds that both are in Hell![50]
  So if I should act as they did, in order to reach Heaven,
They who for all their wisdom and works now dwell
                              in damnation,
I should act most unwisely, despite all that you preach.
But, for many clever men, I do not marvel, truly,   390
If their souls are unacceptable and unpleasing to God.
For many men in this world have more set their hearts
Upon goods than on God; and they lack grace, therefore,

In their direst disaster, when death comes to them –
Like Solomon, and many such, who had great sagacity
But always acted unwisely, as Holy Writ proves.
So clever and sagacious men, and well-read scholars,
Themselves admit that their actions rarely accord with their
                                                    knowledge:
    Super cathedram Moysi sederunt Scribae et Pharisaei.
    (The scribes and the Pharisees sit in Moses' seat.)[51]
  I believe it will be, for many, as bad as in Noah's day,
When he built his boat out of boards and timbers: 400
Not one of the carpenters and workmen who toiled on it
                                                    was saved,
Only the birds and beasts and the blessed Noah himself,
With his wife and sons, and with their wives too;
Not one was saved, of all the workmen who toiled there.
God grant that things go otherwise for those who teach
                                                    the Gospels
And the faith of Holy Church, our harbour and God's house
                                                    of refuge,
In which we are shielded from shame, like the beasts in
                                                    Noah's ship,
Though all the men who made it were drowned amid the Flood.
The class this comment is aimed at are the priests with Cure
                                                    of Souls,
The carpenters that build Holy Church for Christ's own creatures:
    Homines, et jumenta salvabis, Domine:
    (O Lord, thou preservest man and beast.)[52]
On Doomsday shall come a deluge of death and fire together;
Therefore I counsel you clergy, carpenters of Holy Church,
Act as the Bible tells you, lest you too are excluded.
  I find that on Good Friday a felon was saved,
Who had lived all his life by lying and theft;
But because he confessed on the cross, and Christ absolved him,
He was sooner saved than St John the Baptist,
Or Adam, or Isaiah, or any of the prophets
Who had lain with Lucifer for many long years.[53]
A robber was ransomed, rather than all these,   420
Without penance in Purgatory, to perpetual bliss.
  What woman did worse than Mary Magdalene?

What man did worse than David, who devised Uriah's death?
Or Paul the Apostle, who was pitiless
In condemning many Christians to be killed?
Yet now they all sit like sovereigns among the saints in Heaven,
These whose works were the wickedest in the world, when
                                                    they lived;
  And those whose words were wise, who wrote many books
Of worth and wisdom, dwell now with damned souls.
I think that what Solomon says is true, and certain of us all: 430
    Sunt justi et sapientes, et opera eorum in manu Dei: et tamen
      nescit homo utrum amore, an odio dignus sit.
    (The righteous and the wise, and their works, are in the
      hand of God: no man knoweth either love or hatred by
      all that is before them.)[54]
Wise men, and of worthy life, and their works, are hidden
In the hands of Almighty God; only He knows the truth,
Whether a man will be applauded for his love and loyal works,
Or otherwise used for ill-will and the envy in his heart –
Being used according to his life; for by evil, men know good.
  How should we know what is white, if all things were black,
Or who good men are, if none were evil?
Let us live on, then, with bad men – few are good, I believe.
For *qant* OPORTET *vyent en place, yl ny ad que* PATI.
(When MUST is upon men, they may only ENDURE.)[55]
And may He Who can amend all, have mercy on us all.   440
God never spoke words more certain than when He said
                                                    nemo bonus –
    There is none good but one, that is, God.[56]
  Christ Himself commended clerisy only little,
For He said to St Peter, and to such as He loved,
    Ante praesides et reges stabitis propter me . . . Nolite praecogitare
      quid loquamini:
That is, though you come before kings and the clerks of the law,
Be not abashed, for I shall be in your mouths,
And give you wisdom at will, and the skill to confute
All those who argue against you and Christianity.[57]
David makes mention that he spoke among kings,
And none could overcome him by cunning speech.[58]
But wisdom and keen wits never won mastery   450

In a time of misfortune, without more grace from God.
   The doughtiest of the Doctors, the deepest expounder of
                                the Trinity,
Was ancient Augustine, the greatest of all four;[59]
And he said in a sermon that I once saw written,
   Ecce ipsi idioti rapiunt coelum, ubi nos sapientes in inferno
     mergimur.
    (Lo, the ignorant conquer Heaven swiftly, while we wise
     men are plunged into Hell.)
This means, for English men of mean rank or high,
That none are more readily ravished from right thinking
Than are subtle scholars who study many books;
And none sooner saved, nor of solider faith,
Than ploughmen and porters and poor common labourers.
Shoemakers and shepherds, and such unlettered wretches,   460
Can pierce with one Pater-noster the palace of Heaven;
And, when they depart, pass painlessly through Purgatory
Into the bliss of Paradise, for their pure faith,
Imperfect though their learning and lives were, here below.
   You must have come across scholars who have cursed the time
That ever their minds mastered more than *I believe in*
                         God the Father;
And many a parson has prized his pater-noster above all else.
I have seen examples myself, and so have many others,
That the lesser servants of lords seldom fall into arrears,
Unlike those who administer his estate, such as clerks and reeves. 470
In like manner, laymen and others with little learning
Seldom fall so far or so foully into sin
As the clerks of Holy Church, the keepers of Christ's treasure,
The souls of men to be saved, as God says in the Gospel:
   Ite vos in vineam meam.'
   (Go ye also into my vineyard.)[60]

Then Scripture grew scornful, and scolded me,
And said she thought little of me, and let me know it in Latin:
    '*Multi multa sciunt, et seipsos nesciunt.*'
    (Many who know many things are unmindful of themselves.)[1]
At these words I wept with grief and rage,
Till at last in a drowsy dudgeon I dropped asleep.
And there came to me then the most marvellous dream:
I was floated far away by the goddess Fortune,
Into the Land of Longing. There she brought me alone
To a mirror called Middle Earth, and made me look into it,
Saying, 'Herein you may see all sorts of wonders,
And your deepest desires – and attain them, perhaps.'   10
    Now, Fortune's followers were two fair damsels;
The elder of these ladies was called Lust-of-the-Flesh,
And Lust-of-the-Eyes was the other one's name;
And pursuant of this pair came Pride-of-Perfect-Living[2] –
Who bade me think lightly of Learning, but attend to my looks.
    Lust-of-the-Flesh laid her long arms round my neck,
And said, 'You are young and strong, and have many years
To live till old-age, and to love many ladies.
You may see in this mirror a multitude of pleasures,
That all your life long will give you delight.'   20
And the second said the same, 'And I will serve your wishes
Till you are a landed lord, and never leave
Your close companionship – so long as Fortune consents.'
And Fortune herself said, 'He shall find me his friend:
Folk who follow my wishes never fail to find happiness.'
    But a man called Old-Age stood by, and his aspect was heavy.
'Man, if you fall in with me, by St Mary in Heaven
You will find that Fortune fails you in your greatest need,
And Lust-of-the-Flesh will be altogether lost;
And bitterly then will you curse, both by day and by night,   30
That ever you even saw Lady Lust-of-the-Eyes,

Or that Pride-of-Perfect-Living brought you into such peril.'
But Recklessness appeared, all in rage: 'Bah! Pay no regard!
Follow after Fortune — you are still far from old:
Why start to stoop until your scalp starts to show?
Man proposes, said a poet called Plato,[3]
And God disposes — so let God do as He wishes.
If He himself will bear witness that it's well to follow Fortune,[4]
Then neither Lust-of-the-Flesh nor Lust-of-the-Eyes
Can bring you to *great* grief — nor beguile you against your will.'   40
    'Right! So long, cock!' cried Childishness, and carried me away
Till Lust-of-the-Flesh laid her rule upon all my doings.
Old-Age, and Holiness after him, cried, 'Alas,
That Reason should be ruined for the sake of will's revels!'[5]
    But Lust-of-the-Eyes was my consoler soon after,
And she followed me forty years, and five more on top of them;
Nor did I find delight in Do-Well or Do-Better;
I had no wish, believe me, to know anything about them.
Lust-of-the-Eyes lay more often in my mind
Than Do-Well or Do-Better among all my deeds.   50
And Lust-of-the-Eyes became my comforter often:
    'Have no heavy conscience about how you got your wealth;
Confess to some friar, as freely as you please.
For while Fortune is your friend, the friars will love you,
And embrace you in their brotherhood, and for your sake beg
Their Prior Provincial to obtain you a pardon;[6]
And they'll pray for you in person — if you've pennies enough.'
    Sed poena pecuniaria non sufficit pro spiritualibus delictis
    (Penance of money does not pay for spiritual trespasses),[7]
Yet I followed this wench's way, her words were so sweet,
Till my youth was over, and old-age fast approaching.
Then, Fortune became my foe, for all her fair promises,   60
And Poverty pursued me, and pushed me under;
And the friars seemed to fear me, they were so fleet-footed,
For all our first covenant — and this, because I refused
To be buried in *their* boneyard, but at my parish church.
For I had heard tell once how Conscience held
That by Nature a man should be buried where he had been
                                     christened,
And his grave be made in the ground on which he grew.

But the friars thought me a fool for saying this,
And liked me even less for my little speech.
I complained to my confessor, who thought himself cunning.   70
'For certain, friar,' said I, 'you are like those suitors
Who seek to wed widows only to have use of their wealth.
I declare by the Cross, you have never cared before
Where my body was buried, if you had my money about you.
It's a marvel to me, and to many others,
That your convent so covets to confess and bury people,[8]
Rather than baptise babies that want to be saved.'
Baptism and burial are both very necessary,
But baptism has far more merit, it seems to me;
A baptised man may, as masters of theology tell us,   80
Come at last to Heaven's courts, if he is contrite:
    Sola contritio delet peccatum
    (Only contrition can wipe out sin),[9]
But an unbaptised baby cannot be saved thus:
    Nisi quis renatus fuerit ex aqua
    (Except a man be born of water and of the Spirit, he cannot
      enter into the kingdom of God).[10]
Look and see, you lettered men, whether I lie or not!
   Then Loyalty looked at me, and saw me louring.
'Why do you frown so fiercely?' he said, and looked fixedly at me.
'I doubt if I dare,' said I, 'make this dream public.'
'Yes, by Peter and Paul, with their Epistles as proof!
    Non oderis fratres in corde tuo, sed publice argue illos.'
    (Thou shalt rebuke the brothers in public, not be their
      secret hater.)[11]
'But they will adduce the Scriptures against *me*, and quote:
    Nolite judicare.'
    (Judge not, that ye be not judged.)[12]
'What manner of use are morals that no man will uphold,
To stand against falsehood and faking? For the apostle said,   90
    Peccantes coram omnibus argue.
    (Them that sin, rebuke before all.)[13]
And also in the Psalter we find David saying,
    Existimasti inique quod ero tui similis: arguam te.
    (Thou thoughtest that I was altogether such an one as
      thyself: but I will reprove thee.)[14]

Laymen are allowed to lay the truth bare
If they are so inclined: the law grants it to all
Except parsons and priests and the prelates of Holy Church;
For it is not fitting that such folk should tell tales,
Even if the tales are true, and touch upon sin.[15]

But why should you worry, when all the world knows
                                                    them already,
To arraign with full rhetoric the friars' wrongdoings?
But never again be first to find and condemn the fault,
Howsoever evil; say nothing first; and be sorry if it is not
                                                    amended.   100
Nor must you publish any piece of private knowledge,
Whether to laud it from love, or belittle from envy:
      Parum lauda, vitupera parcius.'
      (Sparingly praise, more sparingly reprove.)[16]
'He speaks sense!' So said Scripture; and she skipped aloft,
                                                    and preached.
But the substance of her sermon, could laymen understand it,
Would be little loved by them, as I believe.
For this was the text on which she talked – and I took good heed.
'Many folk were called to a feast, and all the good food;
And when the whole press was present, the porter unbarred
                                                    the gate
And privately pulled in a few, and sent the rest packing!'[17]

Because of this troublous text, my heart trembled;   110
I was worked up with worry, and disputed within myself
Whether I were chosen or unchosen. I thought of Holy Church,
That admitted me at the font as one of God's elect;
Now, Christ called us all to come to him if we would:
Saracens and schismatics, and also the Jews –
      Omnes sitientes, venite ad aquas.
      (Every one that thirsteth come ye to the waters.)[18]
And he bade them, despite their sins, to suck from him safely,
And drink healing for their hurts, whosoever could use it.
'So all Christians may come,' said I, 'and claim to enter,
By the blood with which he bought us, and then by baptism:
      Qui crediderit, et baptizatus fuerit, salvus erit.
      (He that believeth and is baptised, shall be saved.)[19]
For even should a Christian wish to cast–off his christening,   120

A real such reneguing is against reason.
No serf may sign a contract, or sell his goods,
Without his lord's leave – no law allows that.
He may run himself into arrears, and stray from his field,
And recklessly roam about, a renegade wretch,
But Reason shall bring him to his reckoning, and rebuke
                                          him at last,
And Conscience present his account, and convict him of debt,
And put him in the prison of Purgatory, to burn;
Doomed there for his debts until Judgment Day –
Unless Contrition comes, and he calls before death,   130
With mouth or with mind, for mercy upon his misdeeds.'
   'What you say, is so!' said Scripture. 'No sin is so deep
That Mercy may not atone for it, and Meekness with her.
For both of them, as the books tell us, are above All God's deeds:
     Misericordia ejus super omnia opera ejus.'
   (His tender mercies are over all his works.)[20]
'Ah, bah to books!' cried one who had burst out of Hell:
Trajan[21] his name, and a true knight once, by a pope's testimony:
He had died and been damned to dwell in torment
As an unChristian creature. 'Scholars know for sure
That all the clerisy under Christ could not claw me from Hell,
But only love and loyal faith and my own just laws.   140
St Gregory knew this well, and he wanted my soul
To be saved, for he saw that my works had been worthy.
So when he had wept, and wished that I were given
Grace, his boon was granted – and without benefit of bead-telling;
And I was saved, as you see, without the singing of Masses;
Merely by love, by enlightenment, and by upright living,
I was brought out of bitter torment, when mere prayers would
                                          have been useless.'
   'See, all you lords,' said Loyalty, 'how good life saved a
                                          Roman emperor,
Though an unChristian creature, as the clergy find in their books.
Not by the prayers of a pope, but for pure righteousness,   150
Was that Saracen saved, as St Gregory bears witness.
You lords who guard the laws should remember this lesson:
Remember Trajan's righteousness, and deal righteously with
                                          the people.

This matter is a mystery to many of you men of Holy Church;
But in the Lives of the Saints you may learn more lavishly
                                              than from me.
Thus loyal love and righteous living
Pulled a Roman pagan from the pains of Hell.
Blessed be righteousness that so broke Hell's gate
And saved that Saracen from Satan and his power –
Which no clerisy could do, nor craft in Law.   160
Love and loyalty are a surer learning;
By them the Bible is blessed with hope of bliss and joy:
God wrought it and wrote it with His own finger,
And took it to Moses on the Mount, for all men to learn.'
'Law without love,' said Trajan, 'is worth less than a bean.
Every science under the sun, including the Seven Arts,[22]
Unless learned for love of Our Lord, is only time lost.'
'They are not for the making of money, or for a Master's degree,
But only for love of Our Lord, and to love the people better.
For what St John has said, is truly so: 170
    Qui non diligit, manet in morte.
    (He that loveth not his brother abideth in death.)[23]
   Believe me, the man without love is in living death.
John bade all manner of men, whether friends or enemies,
To love one another, and give as if to themselves:
Where nothing is given, there is no love; God knows that is true,
And commands all His creatures to conform themselves to love –
And especially to love poor people, and also one's enemy.
There is much merit in loving the man that hates us;
And if we give pleasure to the poor, their prayers may help us.
For our happiness and souls' health, Jesus Christ came
                                              from Heaven;
And, apparelled like a poor man, ever pursues us;   180
And in such likeness looks at us with loving countenance,
To discover the kindness of our hearts, and by the cast of our eyes
Whether we love earthly lords more than the Lord of bliss.
   And He exhorts us, through His evangelist, that when
                                              we hold feasts
We should not call our kinsmen to them, nor any kind of rich folk –
    Cum facis prandium, noli vocare amicos tuos . . .

(When thou makest a dinner or a supper, call not thy
    friends, nor thy brethren, neither thy kinsmen, nor thy
    rich neighbours)[24] –
But we should invite the unfortunate, the deformed, and the poor:
For your friends would return the feast, and fully repay you
Your feasting and fine gifts, as is all friends' custom.
But, "*I* shall pay for the poor," says Christ, "and requite the
                                          expense in full,
Of those who give meals or money to them, and love them
                                        for my sake."   190
For the best men may be poor, or beggars, while some may
                                        be wealthy.
We are all Christ's creatures, and enriched from His coffers,
Brothers of one blood, whether beggars or earls.
For from Christ's blood on Calvary, Christendom sprang,
And there we became blood-brothers, redeemed by one Body,
"As new-born babes",[25] and each of us nobly born,
Neither beggar nor bondsman among us, but those made by sin:
    Qui facit peccatum, servus est peccati.
    (Whosoever committeth sin is the servant of sin.)[26]
  In the Old Law, as Holy Writ lets us learn,
Man's name for all mankind was "Sons of men" –
All the issue of Adam and Eve until the God-Man died.   200
Then, after His resurrection, His name was Redeemer;
And we, rich or poor, became the brothers of Him that bought us.
Therefore let us love like fond brothers, and all men laugh
                                        together;
And, so far as each can afford, give freely where there is need,
And let all men help each other; for all must go hence.
    Alter alterius onera portate.
    (Bear ye one another's burdens.)[27]
Let us not use our belongings meanly, nor our skills either,
For no man knows how soon he will be left with neither.
So, do not disparage another – though he *does* know more Latin! –
Nor coarsely reprove your neighbour, for no-one lacks faults.
For whatever the clergy contend about christening and so forth,   210
Christ said to a courtesan at a communal banquet
That her faith had saved her, and absolved her from her sins.[28]
    True belief is a loyal helper, above logic and law;

To logic and law, in the Lives of the Saints,
Little applause is given, unless faith assists them.
Logic would need long to make-out a lesson from those lives,
And law is loth to love unless to get money.
Both logic and law – if he does not like lying,
I counsel every Christian, "Do not clasp them too tightly."
I find written certain phrases that are part of faith's teaching,   220
And have saved sinful men, as St John bears witness:

> *In qua mensura mensi fueritis, remetietur vobis.*
> (With what measure ye mete, it shall be measured to you
>   again.)[29]

And so let us learn love's law, as Our Lord taught,
And St Gregory said for the good of our souls:

> *Melius est scrutare scelera nostra, quam naturas rerum.*
> (It is better to research our evil deeds than the natures of
>   things.)

Why I make much of love, is mostly for the sake of the poor,
For it was in their likeness that Our Lord often let Himself
                                        be known.
For example, when He went to Emmaus, in Easter week,[30]
Cleophas could not recognise Him as Christ,
Because of His poor apparel and His pilgrim's clothing –
Not till He blessed and broke the bread that they ate.
It was by His works that they knew He was Jesus;   230
By His clothing they could not tell, nor by what His
                                        tongue declared.
All this is an example to us sinners here on Earth,
That we should be lowly and loving in our language,
Let our apparels not be proud, for we are all pilgrims;
And in the apparel of a poor man, or a pilgrim's likeness,
Many times has God been met among needy people,
Unrecognised by any man in the ranks of the rich.
St John and other saints were seen in poor clothing;
Like poor pilgrims they appealed for men's alms.
Jesus was born of a Jew's daughter, of gentle birth though she was, 240
And poor, though a pure maiden, and a poor man's wife.
Martha made huge complaints against Mary Magdalene;
And to Our Saviour Himself, she said as follows:

"Domine, non est tibi curae quod soror mea reliquit me solam
    ministrare?"
    (Lord, dost thou not care that my sister hath left me to
      serve alone?)[31]
And Our Lord quickly answered, and so pleased them both
(Both Martha and Mary, as St Matthew bears witness):[32]
    "Maria optimam partem elegit quae non auferetur ab ea."
    (Martha, Martha, thou art careful and troubled about many
      things . . . and Mary hath chosen that good part which
      shall not be taken away from her.)
Yet Our Lord had put poverty first, and praised it more highly.
All the wise men that ever were, for aught I can see,
Praise poverty as the best life, if patience goes with it,
And many times both better and more blessed than riches.
Though it is sour at first savouring, a sweetness follows;   250
Just as a walnut within its shell has a bitter husk,
But within both the shell and that bitter bark
Is a kernel both comforting and conducive to health:
So it is with poverty and penance patiently endured.
For they make a man's mind turn to God, with a great wish
To weep well and pray well – from which acts Mercy springs,
Of which Christ is the kernel that comforts the soul.
The poor man sleeps more soundly and securely,
For he has less dread of death, or of robbery in the darkness,
Than the rich man has – it stands to reason!   260
    Pauper ego ludo, dum tu dives meditaris.
    (I who am poor make merry, while you who are rich must
      ponder.)
For although Solomon said, as we see in the Bible,
    Mendicitatem, et divitias ne dederis mihi
    (Give me neither poverty nor riches; feed me with food
      convenient for me),[33]
One wiser than Solomon was bore witness and taught
That perfect poverty was to possess nothing:
The life that God likes most, as Luke bears witness:
    Si vis perfectus esse, vende quae habes, et da pauperibus.
    (If thou wilt be perfect, go and sell that thou hast, and give
      to the poor.)[34]
This means that all men living beneath the moon,

Who would reach pure perfection, must forsake possessions –
Or sell them, as the Book says, and give the silver
To beggars that go beseeching goods for the love of God.
  For no man ever lacked a meal if he served Almighty God: 270
    Non vidi justum derelictum, nec semen ejus quaerens panem.
    (I have not seen the righteous forsaken, nor his seed
      begging bread.)[35]
Thus David says in the Psalter; such as have the will
To serve God in good measure, no hardship grieves them:
    Nihil impossibile volenti
    (Nothing is impossible to him who has the will),[36]
Nor will they ever lack livelihood, nor linen and wool:
    Inquirentes autem Dominum non minuenter omni bono
    (They that seek the Lord shall not want any good thing).[37]
So if priests were perfect they would take no pay
For masses or for matins, nor their meals from usurers,
Nor kirtle nor coat, though they should die of cold;
For if they did their duty they would say like David in the Psalter,
    Judica me, Deus, et discerne causam meam.
    (Judge me, O God, and plead my cause against an ungodly
      nation.)[38]
Trust in the Lord[39] says to priests who have no spending-silver
That if they toil truly, and trust in God Almighty,
They shall never lack livelihood, nor wool nor linen.   280
And the title by which they take orders attests their advancement,
So they need not take silver for the masses that they sing:
It is his part, who made them priests, to pay their wages –
Or the bishop's who ordained them – if they deserve any.
  Never yet did the king knight a man who had not the wealth
Befitting his title, or else he found the wealth himself;
He is a careworn knight, and of a caitiff king's dubbing,
Who has no land or rich lineage or lauded prowess.
And I say the same is true of all such priests
As have neither learning nor lineage, but only a tonsure   290
And a priest's title, a trifle, to live-on in time of trouble:
I think they count more on their shaven crowns to get
Curacies or livings than on learning or known purity of life.
I wonder why and wherefore, then, the bishop
Will ordain such priests, or let them betray the laity.

A charter is challengeable before a Chief Justice:
If the language is false Latin, the Law will impugn it –
Or if it is illuminated between the lines, or has parts left out:
The scrivener who thus bescrawls documents is thought scatty.
So is the priest scatty, by God, who misreads the Gospel,   300
Or makes a mistake in his Mass or Matins.

> *Quicumque . . . offendat autem in uno, factus est omnium reus.*
> (For whosoever shall keep the whole law, and yet offend in
>   one point, he is guilty of all.)[40]

David also, in the Psalter, speaks to those who skip texts:

> *Psallite Deo nostro, psallite: psallite Regi nostro, psallite.*
> *Quoniam Rex omnis terrae Deus: psallite sapienter.*
> (Sing praises to God, sing praises; sing praises unto our
>   King, sing praises. For God is the King of all the earth:
>   sing ye praises with understanding.)[41]

That bishop is guilty in God's eyes, I give my word,
Who ordains knights in His Order that *without* understanding
Sing or read psalms or say the Mass of the Day.
Nor is either ever blameless, bishop or priest,
For each is indicted by the rule, *ignorantia*
Non excusat episcopos nec idiotic priests:
Ignorance excuses neither bishops nor priests for incapability.
This look at unlettered priests had led me away from the praise
Of poverty, which in patient men is more perfect than wealth.'   310
Much more, so I dreamed, did someone dispute with me.
Then I saw other things in my sleep; and first I saw Nature.[42]
By my own name he called me, and bade me be heedful
To gather wisdom from the wonders of this world.
To a mountain called Middle Earth (such was my dream)
He fetched me forth, to learn from examples
Of creatures of all kinds, to love my Creator.
I saw the Sun; and the sea and the sand beside it,
And where the birds and the beasts went about with their mates;
Wild crawlers in the woods, and wonderful birds   320
With feathers flecked in fifty colours.
Man and *his* mate, also, I might see,
In poverty and plenty, in peace and war,
And in mirth and misery at the same moment;
And how some loved Meed the Maiden and hated Mercy.

I saw how rigidly Reason ruled the beasts
In eating and drinking and engendering their species.
For after their sexual season, they no longer consorted
As when they had ridden in rutting-time; but right afterwards,
Males would mingle with males alone, at morning   330
And at evening alike, and keep away from females.
And no cow, or cowlike thing, once she had conceived,
Would bellow after the bull, nor the boar for the sow;
Nor would horse or hound or any other he-beast
Try to mount his mate in her months of pregnancy.

I beheld the birds in the bushes, building their nests,
Of which no man's wits would ever have built the simplest.
I wondered when and from whom the magpie had learned
To interwine the twigs in which she lays and breeds:
No weaver, I well know, could make it work,   340
And we should marvel at a mason who could make a model of it.

Yet I marvelled still more at how many other birds
Could so secretly hide and cover-up their clutch,
On moors and marshes, so that men should not find it –
And hid their eggs when they left them awhile,
For fear of other wild-fowl, or of prowling beasts.
And some birds trod their mates, and bred, in the trees,
And brought forth their brood so, above the ground;
And some birds bred through the beak, only by breathing,[43]
And some by cackling, I recorded, and the curious ways of
                                    the peacock.[44] 350
But much I marvelled what master so many had,
Who taught them to timber their houses so high in trees
That neither man nor beast could reach their nest.

Then again, I stared at the sea, and then at the stars,
And saw more wonders than I have space to describe.
I saw the flowers of the forest, with their fine colours,
Among the green grass growing so many-hued,
And thought how strange that some smelt sweet, others bitter;
But to describe all their kinds and colours would take too long.

Yet what most moved me and impressed my mind   360
Was that Reason ruled and regarded all these creatures –
All except Man and *his* mate: how many a time
Did Reason disregard *them*! And so I reproached

That same Reason himself, and said plainly to him,
'I wonder at you,' I said, 'with the name of being wise,
That you do not shield Man and his mate from their mishaps.'
    But Reason rebuked me, and said roundly, 'Never you mind
What I allow or do not; it is none of your business.
You make things better if you can; but I must bide my time.[45]
Long-suffering is a sovereign virtue, with a swift vengeance.   370
Who has more of it than God? No human, for sure!
God could amend in one moment all that is amiss,
But he forbears for the sake of a few; and all of us profit by it.
The Scriptures themselves teach men to suffer so:
       Subjecti igitur estote omni humanae creaturae propter Deum.
       (Submit yourselves to every ordinance of Man for the
           Lord's sake.)[46]
And Frenchmen and English freemen thus inform their children:
       Bele vertue est soffrance, mal dire est petyt veniance,
       Bien dire et bien soffrir, fait lui soffrant a bien venir.
       (Fair virtues lie in patient suffering,
           No more than small revenge in slandering;
           Soft answers turn away both parties' wrath,
           And bring the patient man to virtue's path.)
I would counsel you, accordingly, to control your tongue,
And do not attack others till you have taken a look at yourself.
No man beneath the moon can make his own nature;   380
If a man *could* remould himself to please other men,
Every man alive (believe me) would be blameless.
Besides, you will find few who are fond of hearing
Their ugly faults rehearsed for them, to their very faces.
    A wise and worthy king wrote these words in the Bible:
       De re quae te non molestat, noli certare.
       (Strive not in a matter that concernth thee not.)[47]
Be a man hideous or handsome, you have no right to judge
The face and form that God Himself framed;
For all that was done by him was done well, as the Scriptures
                                                                    witness:
       Viditque Deus cuncta quae fecerat: et erant valde bona.
       (And God saw every thing that he had made, and behold, it
           was very good.)[48]

And He bade every creature, after its kind, to increase and
                                         multiply,[49]
All to give pleasure to Man, who must suffer misery   390
From the temptations of the Flesh and of the Fiend as well.
For Man being made of flesh may not easily escape
From sometimes following the instincts of the flesh.
Cato is in accord – *nemo sine crimine vivit*.'
   (No man may live without misdemeanour.)
   My face coloured with crimson because of my shame,
And so I awoke; and great was my woe
That in my dream I had not managed to learn more.
I chid my lost chance, and began to tell myself,
'Now I know what Do-Well is, or by dear God I think so.'
And as I glanced up, I saw someone regarding me,   400
Who said, 'And what is it?' 'Why, surely, sir,' said I,
'To see much and suffer more must be Do-Well.'
   'If you had suffered in good sooth, although asleep,
You could have learned as much as Clerisy, and collected
                              more from Reason;
For Reason would have rightly explained what Clerisy ruled.
But because of your thrusting-in, they abandoned you here:
    Philosophus esses, si tacuisses.
   (You might be a philosopher – if you held your tongue.)[50]
So long as Adam said nothing, he had Paradise at command;
But when he argued about apples, and interfered
In the wisdom and will of God, he was barred from bliss.
So it was with Reason and you: you, with rude words,   410
Were praising and dispraising things beyond your purview;
He had no temptation to teach you more.
   Now, perhaps, Pride and Presumption will impeach you,
So that Clerisy will no longer care for your company.
No challenging or chiding will chasten a man so soon
As Shame will, that shows him his faults, and shapes him
                            towards better things.
For if some daft drunkard falls into a ditch,
Let him lie there, leave him till he feels like stirring;
For if Reason rebuked him at once, he would not regard it,
And for Clerisy's counsel would not give a cress-leaf: 420
To abuse or beat him at once would be sheer sin.

But when dire need and the fear of death get him upright,
And Shame scrapes the shite off his clothes, and he cleans his shins,
Then that daft drunkard knows what he has done wrong.'
　'You are speaking sense,' I said. 'I have often seen it.
Nothing can slap more smartly, or smell more sour,
Than Shame, wherever he shows himself – and so people shun him.
Was your motive for telling me this my rebuke of Reason?'
'Certainly that is so.' And he started to walk off.
But I rose fast to my feet, and followed after him,   430
Asking as a favour if I might know his name.

'I am Imagination, and I was never idle
Though I sit by myself in sickness and in health.
By my faith, I have followed you these forty-five winters,
And many times have moved you to remember your end,
And how many yester-years have gone, and how few remain
                                                    to you;
Of your wildness and wantonness when you were young –
To amend it in your middle age, ere your strength failed
In your *old* age, when one can ill endure
Poverty or hard penance or long praying.
      Si venerit in secunda vigilia, et si in tertia.
      (If he shall come in the second watch, or come in the third
          watch, and find them watching, blessed are those servants.)[1]
Amend yourself while you may – you have often been warned   10
By the power of the Plague, by poverty and anguish:
For with such bitter birch-rods God beats His dear children –
      Quem diligo, castigo.
      (Whom I love, I chastise.)[2]
And David says in the Psalter, of such as love Jesus,
      Virga tua et baculus tuus, ipsa me consolata sunt.
      (Thy rod and thy staff, they comfort me.)
Although you strike me with your staff, with your stick or
                                                    your rod,
It makes me the better pleased, for it amends my soul.[3]
Yet you mess about making poems when you might be
                                            reciting psalms
Or praying for those who provide your bread; there are plenty
                                            of books
To tell men what Do-Well is, and Do-Better and Do-Best,
And many a preacher, or pair of friars, to explain them.'
I well saw the truth of his speech; and a little to excuse myself,   20
I said, 'Cato, great clerk though he was, used to comfort his son,
Or amuse him at times, by making poems, as I do:

   Interpone tuis interdum gaudia curis.
   (Mingle, now and again,
    Some pleasures with your pain.)
And I have heard of holy men who sometimes
Would play, in many places, to perfect themselves.
But if there were anyone who would tell me
What Do-Well and Do-Better and Do-Best really are,
I would write no more works, but wend to Holy Church
And say my rosary except when eating or sleeping.'
   'St Paul, in an Epistle, explains Do-Well: 30
   Fides, spes, caritas . . . major autem horum est caritas.[4]
   Faith, Hope, and Charity, all of these are good,
And often save men's souls – but none sooner than Charity.
For doubtless a man does well to do as Loyalty teaches;
That is, if a man is married, to make his wife his love,
And live henceforth as the Law bids, for the rest of their lives.
   If you are a religious, do not go running
Away to Rome or Rochemadour; keep to your Rule,[5]
And hold to your obedience, the highway to Heaven.
If you are unmarried and maiden, and can maintain that state,
Stay so, seek no far saints, for your soul's health.   40
   For how did Lucifer come to lose High Heaven,
Or Solomon his wisdom, or Samson his strength?[6]
Job the Jew paid dearly for his joys,
And Aristotle, and others like Hippocrates and Virgil;
Alexander the all-conquering had a dismal end.[7]
Wealth and Mother-Wit were encumbrances to them all.
Felicia the Fair fell into disgrace;
And Rosamund so wretchedly misruled her life
That the beauty of her body was squandered in beastliness.[8]
I have read of many such, both men and women   50
Who would speak wise words, but whose works were the opposite:
   Sunt homines nequam bene de virtute loquentes.
   (There do exist bad men who are praisers of virtue.)[9]
   Just in this way, wealthy men will amass and be frugal,
For the men whom they hate most to administer it all in the end;
And, because they perceive and permit so many poor people,
Without loving them as Our Lord bade, they lose their souls too.
   Date, et dabitur vobis.
   (Give, and it shall be given unto you.)

So wealth and sharp wits will undo many people.[10]
Woe to him who wields them unless he uses them well:

> *Scientes et non facientes variis flagellis vapulabunt.*
> (They who know what is right, and do not perform it, are
> whipped with sundry scourges.)[11]

Sapience, the Bible says, makes a man's soul swell,

> *Sapientia inflat*
> (And wealth in the same way, unless it is rooted in worth),[12]

But the herb of Grace grows to relieve such griefs,   60
Yet Grace grows in no garden save among the humble:
Patience and Poverty are the plots in which it grows,
Among men of loyal life and holy living,
And only by gift of the Holy Ghost, as the Gospel tells us:

> *Spiritus ubi vult spirat.*
> (The wind bloweth where it listeth.)[13]

But informedness and intellect come from observation
                                          and teaching,
As the Book bears witness for bodies that can read:

> *Quod scimus loquimur, et quod vidimus testamur.*
> (We speak that we do know, and testify that we have seen.)[14]

From *that we do know* comes informedness, and acquaintance
                                          with Divinity;
And from *that we have seen*, and other things, arises intellect.
But Grace is a gift of God, and springs from great love;   70
Informedness does not know how it comes, nor intellect its ways:

> *Nescis unde veniat; aut quo vadat.*
> (Thou canst not tell whence it cometh and whither it goeth.)[15]

Yet learning is laudable, and intellect no less;
And clerisy in particular, since its root is love of Christ.
Moses gives evidence that God wrote to give people knowledge;
In the Old Law, as *Leviticus* tells us of the laws of the Jews,
Any woman caught in adultery, whether rich or poor,
Should be stricken with stones till she was stunned to death.[16]
But one woman, as we may read, was guilty of that act,
And Christ in His courtesy used clerisy to save her;[17]
From the characters that Christ wrote, the Jews grew conscious   80
That they were guiltier in God's eyes, and greatly more sinful,
Than the woman before them was; and shame drove them away.
Literacy and learning were that woman's deliverers.

And Holy Church is aware that Christ's writing acquitted her;
It makes clerisy a comfort to creatures that repent,
But to men under malediction, great misery at their end.

　　For bread could not become Christ's body, but for clerisy,
Which body is both blessing to the righteous
And death and damnation to those who die unabsolved.
As Christ's writing both comforted the woman and proved
　　　　　　　　　　　　　　　　　　　　culpable   90
The Jews who had judged her there, though Jesus would
　　　　　　　　　　　　　　　　　　　save her –

　　　Nolite judicare, ut non judicemini
　　　(Judge not, that ye be not judged)[18] –
Just so, my brothers, God's Body – unless received by the
　　　　　　　　　　　　　　　　　　　blameless –
Means damnation on Doomsday, as Christ's writing damned
　　　　　　　　　　　　　　　　　　　those Jews.[19]

Therefore I counsel you: for Christ's sake love clerisy;
Mother-Wit is akin to it, and both are close cousins
To Our Lord Himself, believe me. And so I say, *love them*;
For we may use them as mirrors, to amend our faults,
And as leaders for learned and laymen alike.

　　So never look askance at logic, nor its laws and customs,
Nor contradict clerisy. That is my counsel for ever.   100
No man may see if his eyes are missing,
And scholarship would be blind if there were no books.
Men made those books, but God was their master,
And the Holy Spirit their instructor, to say what they should write.
And just as sight serves a man to see his own high-street,
So literacy leads the unlearned to reason.
A blind man in a battle may bear weapons to fight with,
But has no hope of hitting an enemy with his axe:
No more has a man with Mother-Wit but untaught,
To come (for all his natural cleverness) to Christianity and
　　　　　　　　　　　　　　　　　　　salvation.   110
Christendom is Christ's treasure-chest, and scholars keep its keys;
They unlock it when they like, and dispense to laymen
God's mercy for misdeeds – if those men ask for it
Humbly, with good hearts, and as a gift of grace.

Under the old Law, Levites looked after the Ark of the
                                     Covenant;
None but Levites were allowed to lay hands on that coffer,
Except priests and their sons, or patriarchs or prophets.[20]
Saul, for an unpriestly sacrifice, ended in sorrow,
And his sons were also punished for that sin;[21]
And many more un–Levitical men   120
Who went before the Ark in reverence and worship
And laid hands on it to lift it, lost their lives for the act.[22]
I counsel, then, all creatures *Do not despise clerisy*,
Nor think lightly of the learned, whatever their lapses:
Respect the worth of their words, for they witness truth.
Do not meddle much with them, in case you make them angry,
Lest strife should stir us up to strike one another;
     Nolite tangere christos meos.
     (Touch not mine anointed.)[23]
For clerisy, under Christ in Heaven, keeps us safe;
And every knight that there is, was made knight by clerisy.
     Mother–Wit comes from all kinds of experiences,   130
Of birds and beasts and of tests both true and false.
Our ancestors in olden days used to record
The strange things they saw, and teach them to their sons;
And they held it a high science, to have knowledge of such things.
But no soul was ever saved by all that science,
Nor brought by books into eternal bliss;
Their science was only a series of sundry observations.
So patriarchs and prophets disapproved of their science,
And said their so-called words of wisdom were but folly –
And compared with Christian philosophy, a contemptible thing. 140
     Sapientia enim hujus mundi stultitia est apud Deum.
     (For the wisdom of this world is foolishness with God.)[24]
For they knew that the high Holy Ghost would split Heaven
                                    asunder,
And Love leap out upon our low Earth,
And a clean virgin catch it, and clerks find it:
     Pastores loquebantur ad invicem.
     (The shepherds said one to another, Let us now go even
        unto Bethlehem.)[25]
Not rich men, be it noted, nor men of mere cleverness,

Nor unlettered lords, but the most learned men alive:
    Ecce Magi ab Oriente.
    (Behold, there came wise men from the East.)[26]
So if any friar was found there, I'll give you five shillings!
Nor was that boy born in a beggarly cottage,
But in the abode of the richest burgess in Bethlehem:[27]
    Quia non erat eis locus in diversorio; et pauper non habet diversorium.
    (Because there was no room for them in the inn; and a
      poor man has no inn.)[28]
  To peasants and poets there appeared an angel
That bade them go to Bethlehem and honour God's birth,   150
And sang a song of solace – *Gloria in excelsis Deo!*[29]
While the rich men lay routing in their beds of rest,
There shone before the shepherds a vision of Heaven.
  Wise Men were aware of this, and came with their gifts,
And paid humble homage to Him Who was almighty.
  I have told you all this because I took good heed
Of how you contradicted Clerisy with crabbed words,
And said the unlettered were likelier to be saved than the learned,
The educated and intellectual among us Christians.
You spoke the truth about some; but see in what way: 160
  Take two strong men, and throw them into the Thames,
Both naked as needles, and nothing to choose between them
Save that one is skilful at swimming and diving,
The other inexperienced in the sport, and unable to swim.
Which of those two in the Thames, do you think, has more
                             to fear?
He who has never dived, and knows nothing of swimming,
Or the swimmer who is safe, and proceeds as he wishes
While his fellow floats along where the flood carries him,
In great dread of drowning, since he never dived or swam?'
'He who is unable to swim, I should imagine.'   170
'Obvious, is it not? And it stands to reason
That learned men are more able to climb out
Of sin, and be saved, even though they sin often,
Than the unlearned are – if the learned so wish.
If the lettered man is intelligent, he knows what sin is,
And how contrition even without confession may comfort
                              the soul;

As you may see in the Psalter – in more psalms than one –
Contrition is commended for the carrying-off of sin:

    Beati, quorum remissae sunt iniquitates: et quorum tecta sunt peccata.
    (Blessed is he whose transgression is forgiven, whose sin is
       covered.)[30]

This comforts all who can read, and keeps off despair,
In which flood the Fiend most fiercely tests a man.   180
But the unlettered lies powerless and waits for Lent,
Having no contrition before confession (and then he can say
                      very little),
And then believing and leaning on all his confessor has him learn.
And *he* will be a parson or a parish priest, and perhaps
Unable to instruct lay-folk, as Luke bears witness:

    Caecus autem si caeco ducatum praestet, ambo in foveam cadunt.
    (If the blind lead the blind, both shall fall into the ditch.)[31]
    The man who must wade with such leaders was marked
                      out for woe!

Well may boys bless those who set them to their books,
So that, living with literature, they may save life and soul!
Dominus pars hereditatis meae is a cheerful text
(The Lord is the portion of my inheritance)
That has robbed Tyburn Tree of scores of tough thieves.   190
They hoist unlettered thieves high, but see how the lettered
                      are saved![32]

That thief who obtained God's grace on Good Friday, as you say,
Did so by confessing his faith to Christ on the Cross, and
                    acknowledging guilt,
And by asking grace from God – Who is ready to grant it
To them that biddably beseech it and are bent on amendment.
But though that thief reached Heaven, he has less high joy there
Than St John and other saints, who served God better:
Just as if some man gives me a meal, and seats me in the midst
                    of the hall-floor,
And I have more than enough to eat, but not so much honour
As those that sit at the side-tables, with the seigneurs of that hall, 200
But sit like a beggar, with no table, by myself on the ground:
So it fared with that felon who was saved on Good Friday;
He sits neither with St John nor with Simon, nor with Jude,

Nor with the Virgins, nor with the Martyrs and Confessors
                                                 and Widows,
But is served sitting on the floor by himself.
For he that has once been a thief is forever at risk
From the Law, that has the last word whether he lives or dies:
       De peccato propitiato, noli esse sine metu.
       (Concerning propitiation, be not without fear to add sin
           unto sin.)[33]
Should a saint and such a thief be served together?
It is neither right nor reason to reward them alike.
Just as the true knight Trajan was no tenant of *deep* hell,   210
So that Our Lord had him easily out, so I think of the thief
                                                 in heaven –
That he is in the lowest level, if our beliefs are true,
And lolls there lubberly by the law of Holy Church;
       Quia tu reddes unicuique juxta opera sua.
       (Thou renderest to every man according to his works.)[34]
   And why one thief on the cross would confess himself
                                                 Christian,
Rather than the other thief: were you to ask that,
All the clergy of Christendom could not clear up the mystery.
       Quare placuit, quia voluit.
       (Whatsoever the Lord pleased, that did he . . .)[35]
And so I say to you that seek for "why",
And that reasoned with Reason, and almost rebuked him,
About the flowers of the forest, and their fine colours,
And where those colours come from, so clear and bright;   220
And that asked about birds and beasts and their breeding-habits
(Why some breed low down, some aloft), and looked for
                                                 an answer;
And are astonished at stones and at stars (are you not?),
And at how all birds and beasts have such able brains:
   Neither Clerisy nor Mother-Wit, but only Nature,
Can ever know all causes; no other creature.
He is the magpie's patron, and puts into its mind
That it is best to build and breed where the thorn is thickest.
It is he who found the pea-fowl their fashion of mating,
He who taught Adam to know his private parts,   230
And showed him and Eve how to hide them in leaves.

Unlettered men often ask of their learned masters
Why Adam did not first hide his mouth, which ate the apple,
Rather than his body, down low: thus laymen ask the learned,
But only Nature knows why, and no scholar at all.

   Now, from birds and beasts, by men in olden times,
Examples and parables were produced, as the poets tell:
For instance, the most beautiful birds are the foulest breeders,
And the feeblest fliers of all that fly or swim –
Namely, the peacock and peahen, who stand for the proud
                             and rich;   240
For the peacock, when pursued, cannot rise up high,
And because of its trailing tail it is soon overtaken.
Its flesh is foul to eat, and its feet are ugly,
And its voice is revolting, and vile to hear.

   The rich man resembles it, if he hoards his riches
Unshared until he dies, like a trailing tail of sorrow;
For as the peacock's pen-feathers impede its flight,
So does possession of pence and pounds impede
All who hold on to them until Death's hand pulls their quills.
And though the rich man may repent then, and rue the day   250
That he ever gathered such great wealth, and gave so little of it;
And though he may cry to Christ, and no doubt in keen longing,
His appeal, in Our Lord's ears, will be like a magpie's chatter;
And when his corpse comes to the clay for burial,
I think it will spread its vile odour through all the
                            surrounding earth,
And envenom with its evil all others that lie there.
The peacock's feet, as I find in the fables, mean
Executors and false friends, who do not fulfil his will
As it was written, though they bore witness that they would.
The poet[36] explains that the peacock is admired for his feathers,   260
And the rich man revered only by reason of his wealth.

   Though the lark is a far lighter bird, its voice is far lovelier,
And it is far and away more swift of wing than the peacock –
And its flesh manifoldly fatter and sweeter;
So the lark is likened to men of the lower classes;
The great scholar Aristotle tells of such interpretations,
And his *Logic* draws lessons from the littlest of birds.[37]
And whether he is saved or not, is known to no scholar;

Nor of Socrates nor of Solomon are there scriptures to tell that.
But God is so good that I hope, since he gave them wisdom   270
With which to teach us folk (and lead us towards salvation
All the better for their books), and we are bound to beseech
God in His grace to give their souls rest;
For men now learned would be unlearned had they lacked
                                          those men's books.'
    'All these clergy,' quoth I, 'who believe in Christ,
Say in their sermons that neither Saracens nor Jews,
Nor any other creature in Christ's likeness, will be saved
                                          without christening.'
    'Not so,' said Imagination, and frowned somewhat,
Saying, '*Justus vix salvabitur in die judicii*
    (The righteous scarcely shall be saved on Doomsday).[38]
Ergo salvabitur – "Therefore he *shall* be saved." ' Then he
                                          stopped speaking Latin.
'Trajan was a true knight, although never baptised,   280
And he is saved, so the books say, and his soul is in Heaven.
For there is baptism by water and baptism by shedding of blood,
And baptism by fire: this is firm belief –
    Advenit ignis divinus, non comburens, sed illuminans.
    (The divine fire comes not to burn but to illuminate.)[39]
A true man, who has never trespassed nor transgressed his
                                          own law,
But lives as that law teaches, and believes there is no better
(And if there were, he would adopt it), and who dies in this
                                          outlook:
Surely no God of truth could reject a truth of this kind?
And whether that be so or be not so, such belief is mighty in truth,
And a hope hangs therefrom that such faith may have its reward.
    For *Deus dicitur quasi dans vitam aeternam suis, hoc est, fidelibus*
    (It is said that God gives eternal life to His own, that is, to
        the faithful),
    Et alibi
    (And we find elsewhere),[40]
    Si ambulavero in medio umbrae mortis
    (Yea, though I walk through the valley of the shadow of
        death, I will fear no evil).
And the gloss upon that text grants a great reward to truth.'   290

He added, 'Wisdom and reason were once thought treasure
           enough
To keep a commonwealth safe; they considered these
           properties best,
And the cause of much comfort and courage.' And at once
           he vanished.

Passus 13

With this I awoke, well-nigh out of my wits;
And, as a fellow free to do so, forth I went roaming
In the manner of a mendicant, for many years.
Many a time I thought much about my dream.
First, how Fortune had failed me in my greatest need,
And how Old Age had menaced me should we ever meet;
And how the Friars follow after rich folk,
And put little price upon poor people;
And how no corpse could lie in their graveyard, nor be buried
                              in their crypt,
Unless when alive he had left them money or helped settle
                               their debts;   10
And how covetousness has overcome the priests, and all clergy;
And how the unlettered are led (unless Our Lord helps them)
By such incompetent clergy to incurable agonies;
And how Imagination had told me in my dream
About Nature and His knowledge, and His kindness to animals,
And how loving He is to all animals of land or water;
He leaves nothing alive forsaken, whether small or big;
Even the creeping creatures were created by Nature.
I thought then how Imagination had said, 'The righteous
                            scarcely shall be saved,'
And of when he had said so, and how suddenly he vanished.   20
Once I lay thinking for a long time, and at last slept;
And, as Christ willed, Conscience appeared, to give me comfort,
And invited me to come to his castle and dine there with Clerisy.
And because Conscience mentioned Clerisy, I came the
                            more readily.
I met there a Master of Divinity – not then knowing more
                            about him –
Who made low and loving obeisance to Lady Scripture.
Conscience was well acquainted with this cleric,
So they washed and wiped their hands, and went in to dinner.

Now, Patience was outside that palace, in pilgrim's clothes,
Begging his food like a hermit, as holy charity.   30
Conscience called him in, and said courteously,
'Welcome, good man! Go and wash, and we shall sit down soon.'
   The Master, as most important, was made seated first;
Then Clerisy and Conscience; and Patience came last.
Patience and I were both put away from that party,
And seated by ourselves at a side-table.
Conscience called for the food, and Scripture came in
And served them swiftly with many sorts of dish –
Such as Augustine, and Ambrose, and all four Evangelists:
   Edentes et bibentes quae apud illos sunt.
   (Eating and drinking such things as they give.)[1]
But neither the Master nor his manservant ate such honest meat,   40
Only the richest stews, ratatouilles, and ragoûts:
From ill-gotten gains, they were used to good living.
Yet their sauce was too sour, and their seasoning ill-ground
In a mortar called Post Mortem, which holds much future
                                          pain for them
Unless they sing Masses for souls, and weep salt tears:[2]
   Vos qui peccata hominum comeditis, nisi pro eis lacrimas et orationes
   effunderitis, ea quae in deliciis comeditis, in tormentis evomitis.
   (You who feast upon the sins of men, unless for their sake
      you pour out tears and prayers, those things that now
      you eat among pleasures you shall vomit up among
      torments.)[3]
   Then Conscience very courteously requested Scripture
To bring some bread for both Patience and me.
She set a sour loaf before us, and said, '*Do penance,*'
And drew us a draught of a drink called *Long-endure.*
I said, 'Yes! As long as I live, and my body lasts out!'   50
Said Patience, 'This is proper service! No prince fares better!'
   Then she brought us a mess of other meat, of
                  'Have-mercy-upon-me-O-God'.[4]
   Then she brought us 'Blessed-is-he',[5] made by
                  'Blessed-is-the-man'[6]
And 'Whose-sin-is-covered',[7] in a dish
Of covert confession, 'I-said-I-will-confess-my-transgressions-
                  to-the-Lord'.[8]

'Bring Patience his special pittance,' said Conscience privately.
And Patience's pittance was 'For-this-shall-every-one-that-is-godly-
          pray-unto-thee-in-a-time-when-thou-mayst-be-found'.[9]
And Conscience encouraged us, and recounted cheerful things:
      '*Cor contritum et humiliatum, Deus, non despicies.*'
      (A broken and a contrite heart, O God, thou wilt not
          despise.)[10]
And Patience was proud of such proper service,
And he was mirthful over his meal; but I mourned throughout   60
Because that Divine on the high dais drank wine so fast –
      Vae qui potentes estis ad bibendum vinum
      (Woe unto them that are mighty to drink wine) – [11]
And devoured so many different dishes, ragoûts and puddings,
Tripes, wild-boar's brawn, eggs fried in butter . . .
Then I said to myself – but so that Patience could hear it –
'It is not four days since this fellow, in front of the Dean
                                                          of St Paul's,
Preached about the privations of Paul the Apostle
From fasting and cold and from flogging with scourges:
      *Ter virgis caesus sum . . . a Judaeis quinquies quadragenas, una
      minus, accepi.*
      (Thrice was I beaten with rods . . . Of the Jews five times I
      received forty stripes save one.)[12]
But there is one phrase that they forget when such friars
                                                          preach so,
One that Paul in his Epistle told to all people,
      Periculis in falsis fratribus:
      In perils among false brethren.[13]
The Scriptures bid us beware – but I will not write it here   70
In English, in case it is too often repeated,
And grieves good men; but grammarians shall read it:
      *Unusquisque a fratre se custodiat; quia, ut dicitur, periculum est
      in falsis fratribus.*
      (Let each of you be on guard against a friar; for it is said
      that there is danger in false friars.)[14]
I know of no fellow who, as a friar, spoke before folk in English
And took *that* for his text, and taught it without sophistry!
They preach that penance is a profit to the soul,
And what agonies Christ endured on behalf of Man;

But this glutton of God, with his gross face,
Has no pity on the poor, and practises evil.
He does not practise what he preaches,' I said to Patience;
And I wished with all my heart and will   80
That the dishes and plates placed before that preacher
Were molten lead in his middle, and Mahound among them!
'I shall approach,' I said, 'this piss-pot with his puffed-out belly,
To explain what that penance *is*, that he preached-of earlier.'
But Patience had seen my intention, and signalled me to silence:
'You will see soon enough, when he can stuff no more,
He'll do *his* penance in his paunch, and burp when he speaks;
And his guts will gurgle, and he'll go gapy-faced;
For he's drunk so deeply that he'll soon start discoursing,
And prove by the *Gluttons' Apocalypse* and the passion of
St Aurea,[15]   90
That bacon and brawn and hash and blanquette of chicken
Are neither fish nor flesh, but penitential food.
Then indeed he will talk about his "trinities", and make
his companion testify
What is found in a frail after a friar has fed;
And unless his first words are lies, nevermore believe me!
That will be the time to take and question this "master"
Whether Do-Well and Do-Better and Do-Best mean "penance".'
So I sat still, as Patience said. And soon this Master,
As rubicund as a rose, rubbed his cheeks,
Coughed, and began to converse; and Conscience listened,   100
And told him of the trinity we sought. He looked towards us.
'What is Do-Well, sir doctor?' said I. 'Is it doing penance?'
'Do-Well?' said this Divine, and took his cup, and drank:
'It is to do all you can to avoid harming others.'
'Then, by this day, sir doctor, you are not Do-Well's man;
You *have* harmed us two, by eating-up the hashes
And the puddings, and plenty more, of which *we* had no piece!
If the sick fare so in your infirmary, I find it amazing
If quarrelling is not their *caritas*, and the very choirboys complain!
I would permute my penance with yours though I *am*
pursuing Do-Well.'   110
But Conscience, with a courteous countenance,
Appeared to ask Patience to pray my silence,

And himself said, 'Sir Master, if you do not mind,
What *are* Do-Well and Do-Better? You Divines know such things.'
'Do-Well is to do what the clergy say is your duty,
And Do-Better is he that teaches, and toils to teach others,
And Do-Best is to do oneself all that one teaches and preaches.

> *Qui autem fecerit et docuerit . . . hic magnus vocabitur in regno*
> *coelorum.'*

>> (Whosoever shall do and teach . . . shall be called great in
>> the kingdom of heaven.)[16]

'Now, Clerisy,' said Conscience, 'give us *your* account of
                                                    Do-Well.'
'I have seven sons,' said Clerisy, 'who serve in a castle
Where the Lord of Life lives and teaches them of Do-Well.   120
But till I see those seven reconciled with myself,
I am unwilling to explain it to any man.
For a certain Piers Ploughman has impugned us all,
And set all sciences at a crumb's worth, save only love.
And he takes no texts to maintain his opinion
Except *Love thy Lord* and *Lord, who shall abide in thy tabernacle?*[17]
He says that Do-Well and Do-Better are both infinite;
Which infinites, with faith's help, will find Do-Best;
And Do-Best will save Man's soul. Thus says Piers Ploughman.'
'I know nothing of that,' said Conscience, 'but I know Piers well;   130
I am certain that *he* will say nothing against Scripture,
So let this question pass until Piers comes to explain it in practice.
Patience has been in many places, and perhaps knows
What no clerk could tell us, for Christ bears witness:

> *Patientes vincunt:* "The patient conquer." '

'Since you wish it, I will,' said Patience, 'if no one objects.
Disce,' said he, '*Doce*, and *Dilige inimicos*;
Disce is Do-Well, *Doce* is Do-Better, and *Dilige* is Do-Best.
To learn is Do-Well; To teach is Do-Better; and Do-Best is
                                          To love your enemies.
This I learned from a lady called Caritas, whom I loved.
"In word and in deed," she said, "and with all your heart's will,   140
So long as you live you must faithfully love your soul;
Thus you will learn to love, for the love of Our Lord in Heaven,
Your enemy as much as yourself, in every way.
Cast coals upon his head, with your kindly speech;

With both words and deeds, try to win his love,
Surround him so with love that he *must* smile on you –
And if such beating does not break him, may he go blind!
   But it would be foolish to treat your friend in such a fashion;
For a friend who is truly fond of you covets little of yours.
Instinctive affection asks to own nothing but speech,   150
With half-a-line limned in Latin, *ex vi transitionis*."
    (From the power of passing over.)
Bound fast within these words, I bear Do-Well about with me,
As a sign of that Saturday which started the Calendar,
And the wisdom of the Wednesday in the week that followed;
And the middle of the moon gives might to both.
While I have it, I am welcome wherever I go.[18]
Undo it, then, let this Doctor decide if it holds Do-Well;
For by Him who made me, no lack of money,
No misfortune or calamity, no evil of men's tongues,
No cold or care, or the company of thieves,   160
Neither heat nor hail, nor any fiend from Hell,
Nor fire nor flood, nor fear of an enemy,
May at any time trouble you, if you take *that* with you:
    Timor non est in caritate.
    (There is no fear in love.)[19]
And also, as I hope to be saved, for only your asking
There's no emperor, empress, earl or king or baron,
Pope or patriarch, but by power of pure reason
You may master them, and all men, through the might of
                         this riddle –
Not by witchcraft, but by wisdom. And if you yourself wish
You may make the King and the Queen, and the whole
                        commonwealth too,
Give you all that they can give, as their best guardian;   170
And as you decide, so shall they do, for the rest of their days:
    Patientes vincunt.'
    (The patient conquer.)
   'This is only a diddle,' said the Doctor, 'a minstrel's deceit.
All the wisdom in the world, all the might of great war-lords,
Cannot patch-up a peace between the Pope and his enemies,
Or contrive a truce between two Christian Kings,
That shall please both the peoples.' Then he pushed away the table,

And took Clerisy and Conscience into conclave, as it were,
Saying Patience should push-off – 'since pilgrims are fine liars'.
   But Conscience cried aloud, and yet courteously,
'Farewell, my friends!', and spoke fair to Clerisy,   180
'If God gives me grace; I will go along with this man,
A pilgrim beside Patience, till experience teaches me more.'
   'What?' said Clerisy to Conscience, 'Are you covetous now
Of gold, or New Year's gifts? Do you want to guess riddles?
I could bring you a Bible, say a book of the Old Law,
And instruct you, if you wished, in the tiniest detail –
Which Patience the Pilgrim could never do properly.'
   'No, by Christ,' said Conscience to Clerisy, 'though may
                                              God reward you.
For all that Patience promises, I feel little pride;
But the earnest intent of the man, and of these other people,   190
Has so moved my spirit that I mourn for my sins.
A man's meaning to do good may never be wholly bought,
For an honest intention is more precious than any treasure.
Was not Mary Magdalen given more for a box of ointment [20]
Than Zacchaeus, though he said *Dimidium bonorum
   meorum, Domine, do pauperibus?* [21]
   (Lord, the half of my goods I give to the poor.)
And the poor widow more for her pair of mites
Than all of the others who offered-up into the Treasury?' [22]
So Conscience courteously took congé, first of the Friar;
After which he said softly in Clerisy's ear,
'By Our Lord, as I hope to live, I should sooner like   200
To own perfect patience than half of your pack of books!'
   But Clerisy would take no congé of Conscience.
He said very soberly, 'You will see the time
When you are wearied-out with walking, and want my advice.'
'That may well turn out true,' said Conscience, 'but I take
                                            God to witness,
Were Patience our sharing-partner, and personal friend of us both,
We three could put right every woe in the world;
We could make peace between all kings and countries,
And turn to the true faith, to one single creed,
The Syrians and the Saracens and the Jews themselves.'   210
'This is certainly so,' said Clerisy, 'and I see what you mean;

But I shall dwell where I do, and perform my duty
Of confirming the faith of infants and such partly-taught folk,
Till Patience has put you to the test, and made you perfect.'[23]
    So Conscience went forth with Patience, and they lived
                                                    as pilgrims,
And Patience, like all pilgrims, had victuals in his pack –
Sobriety, simple speech, and steadfast faith –
To comfort him and Conscience when they should come
To the hungry countries of Unkindness and Covetousness.
    As they went their way, and spoke of Do-Well,   220
They met with a man who seemed to me a minstrel.
Patience approached him first, and prayed him tell
To Conscience his calling, and the country he was seeking.
    'I am a minstrel, and my name is *Activa Vita*;[24]
I abhor an idle man, for Active Life is my name.
If you want to know, I'm a waferer, and work for many lords;
But they furnish me with few robes or furred gowns.
Could I lie to make people laugh, I should latch on
To mantles and money among the lords' minstrels;[25]
But I play neither tabor nor trumpet, and cannot tell romances,   230
Or harp or fiddle or fart in tune at feasts,
Or tell jokes, or juggle, or pipe a jig,
Nor tumble, neither, nor dance, nor sing to the gittern.
So I get no good gifts from those great lords,
For all the bread I bake, except a blessing on Sunday
When the priest tells the people to say their Pater-noster
For Piers the Ploughman and all who help him prosper –
Of whom I, Active Life, am one, since I hate idleness;
For all true toilers and tillers of the soil,
    From Michaelmas to Michaelmas, I make wafer-cakes.   240
Beggars and cadgers beseech my bread,
And fakers and friars and other very bald folk.
I provide bread for the Pope, and fodder for his palfrey,
And (God's my guarantee) he never gave me
Either prebend or parsonage, did the Pope;
Only a pardon and a piece of lead with a pair of heads on it![26]
If I'd a clerk, who could write for me, I'd convey a petition
That he send me, under his seal, a salve against the Plague,

And his blessing, and some Bulls to get rid of boils:

> *In nomine meo daemonia ejicient . . . super aegros manus*
> *imponent, et bene habebunt.*

> (In my name shall they cast out devils . . . they shall lay
> hands on the sick, and they shall recover.)[27]

Then I'd make pastry for the people *prestissimo*,   250
And be busy and obedient to find bread and drink
For the Pope and all his people if I found that his pardon
Could cure a man, as I consider it should.
For since the Pope has the powers that St Peter himself had,
It seems certain to me he has that little pot full of salve:

> *Petrus autem dixit: Argentum et aurum non est mihi: quod*
> *autem habeo, hoc tibi do: In nomine Jesu Christi Nazareni,*
> *surge, et ambula.*

> (Then Peter said, Silver and gold have I none; but such as I
> have give I thee: In the name of Jesus Christ of Nazareth
> rise up and walk.)[28]

But if he may not work miracles, then man's unworthiness
To receive God's grace is the cause, not the Pope's guilt.
No blessing can benefit us till we amend our behaviour,
Nor any man's Mass make peace among Christian people
Till pride is entirely uprooted – when people lack bread!   260
Before I make bread out of meal, I must sweat hard for it;
And before the crowd has corn enough, I see many cold mornings;
So before my wafers are baked, I have bothers enough.
All London, I believe, loves my wafers,
And grumbles at not getting them. Not long ago
They were a downcast crowd when no cart came to town
With baked bread from Stratford.[29] How the beggars wept!
And the workmen were scared for a while – they will long
                                                    remember it.
This happened in our drought-days, the dry April
Of one thousand three hundred twice thirty and ten: 270
My wafers were not many when Chichester was mayor.'[30]
I took careful note, by Christ, and so did Conscience,
Of Haukyn the Active Man, and of his dress.
His coat is of Christendom, in Holy Church's cut,
But is marked in many places with all kinds of mess:
Here a patch of pride, and a patch here of bragging;

Scorn here, scoffing there, here uncouth behaviour –
In deportment as in apparel, a proud man in public,
To seem other than he is, or has, in heart or appearance,
Wishing all men to believe that he is what he is not.   280
Therefore he boasts and brags, with many brazen oaths,
Ignoring all reproof from anyone living.
He seems a law unto himself, in all men's sight –
None like him, a nonpareil, none so pope-holy,
As if habited like a hermit, but of his own Order,
A Religious with no Rule or obedience to Reason,
Disparaging the learnèd and the unlettered alike,
Laying claim to a loyal life, but in his heart a liar.

His inward or outward mind, his imagination and scheming,
Are all for his body's benefit, and his bad reputation.   290
He interferes everywhere in what are not his affairs,
Meaning men to think *his* mind better than their own –
For his craft and cunning, the wisest of clerks,
And the strongest horse-bestrider, and the sturdiest-thewed,
And the loveliest to look at, and most loyal to his word,
None so holy as he, nor with purer habits,
Nor with finer features, nor so well-formed and strong;
The subtlest singer, the most skilful with his hands,
And the most lavish lender, even if he loses by it.
But if he does give to the needy, he blazons it abroad;   300
And though poorly provided in both purse and coffer,
He is lordly as a lion in both looks and speech;
Boldest of beggars, and a beggarly boaster,
In farmstead or tavern to tell tall stories,
Describing, and swearing true, such things as he never saw,
Declaring and bragging about deeds he never did –
And of anything he truly did, he will take testimony and oath:
'Look, now, if you don't believe me, if you think I'm a liar,
Ask So-and-So or Such-and-Such, and *they'll* tell you
What I suffered, what I saw, all the stuff I once had,   310
How clever I was, the things I could do, what kin I come of . . .'
All that he wished men to know of his words or doings
Was to impress other people, and praise himself.
  Si adhuc hominibus placerem, Christi servus non essem.
    Et alibi: *Nemo potest duobus dominis servire.*

(If I yet pleased men, I should not be the servant of Christ.
    And elsewhere: No man can serve two masters.)[31]
'By Christ, Haukyn,' said Conscience, 'your best coat
Shows many marks and spots – you must wash it.'
    'Yes, if anybody bothers to look at the back or the front,
Inside it or outside, or either left or right,
He will find many furrows and many foul spots.'
    He turned quickly about, and I was able to see
That his coat was filthier by far than at first it had seemed.   320
It was all spattered with anger and with wicked ill-will,
With envy and with evil speech that instigates fights,
With lying, malicious laughter, and loose angry speech
That would repeat whatever ill he knew of anyone,
To backbite people and to wish them bad luck.
Whatever he heard about Will, he would tell it to Walt,
And what he learned from Walt would go back to Will,
So that friends were turned into foes by his false tongue:
'By the might of the mouth, if not by male strength,
I am often avenged – for otherwise, inwardly,   330
I should gnaw away at myself like a shepherd's shear.'
Evil, accursed men! *Cujus maledictione os plenum est . . .*
    Et alibi: Filii hominum, dentes eorum . . .
    (His mouth is full of cursing and deceit and fraud . . .
        And elsewhere: The sons of men whose teeth are spears
        and arrows, and their tongue a sharp sword.)[32]
    'I love no man alive for very long,
And I tell such tales that no one trusts me.
If a man overmasters me I am seized with such melancholy
That I catch internal cramp or a cardiac pain,
Or an anguishing ague, or it may be a fever,
That is with me a twelvemonth, till I come to despise
All Christian modes of medicine, and my trust goes to witches:
I claim that no doctor can cure, nor Christ Himself,
Like the shoemaker of Southwark or Dame Emma of
                                Shoreditch![33]   340
I grumble that God's word never yet got me cured;
My best chances and chief cures came from magic charms.'
    Considered yet more carefully, his coat was smeared
With a liking for lechery, and a lustful roving eye;

For to every miss he met, he made a sign
Suggesting that they should sin – and would sometimes taste her
About the mouth, and begin to grope her down below,
Till both of them were well aroused. Then to work they went,
On fast-days, Fridays, or forbidden nights,
In Lent or out of Lent – all times were alike;   350
That sort of work, with them, was never out of season.
Till, both tired out, they would tell funny stories,
And laugh and joke about lecherous lovers,
And (even in old age) talk of harlotry and of whoredom.

    Then Patience perceived that parts of Haukyn's coat
Were eroded by avarice and unnatural grasping;
Goods, rather than God, had got *this* fellow's love,
And he planned perpetually how to profit
From false measures, false weights, and false witness.
He loaned for lust of the pledge; and he loathed fair dealing,   360
Always awaiting some way to deceive.
He mixed up his merchandise to make a good display –
'But the worst was underneath – I've cunning ways, eh?
If someone had a servant, or perhaps an animal,
More valuable than mine, I would plan many tricks
For securing that same; I set all my wits to work
And even – for want of a better way – would steal it,
Or privately strip his purse, or pick his locks.
By night and by day I was always busy
Getting guilefully together such goods as I have.   370

    Should I go to plough, I would shave my ground so short
That I would filch a foot or a furrow at least,
And so narrow my next-door neighbour's land.
And if I reaped, would reach over (or tell my reapers to)
And seize by the sickle what I had never sown.
Should a borrower be wishful to buy more time,
He must give me private presents, or a fixed down-payment,
So that whether he wished or not, I would make more profit.
To my own kith and kin I was close with my money.
Those who made offers for my merchandise, I abused   380
Unless they proposed to pay me a penny or two
More than the stuff was worth; and still I would swear
That it cost me more than they offered, and I added many oaths.

On holidays, at Holy Church, when I heard Mass,
God knows I never tried to pray in earnest
For mercy on my misdeeds; I felt more sorrow,
Believe me, for bad bargains than for bodily sins,
Even had I done deadly ones; I dreaded them less
Than when I lent money and thought it lost, or it was long
                                        in repaying.
So even if I *could* show kindness, to help a fellow-Christian,   390
My heart was hung-up on the hardest avarice.
If I sent my servants overseas to Bruges,
Or my apprentices to Prussia, to seek my profit
By making exchanges or sales of merchandise or money,
Nothing could make me happy in the meantime:
Neither Mass nor Matins, nor amusement of any sort,
Nor any penance performed, nor Pater-noster said,
But my mind was on my goods, and in mortal fear,
Rather than on God's grace and His great mercies.'
    Ubi enim est thesaurus tuus, ibi est et cor tuum.
    (For where your treasure is, there will your heart be also.)[34]
    This glutton's garments were also soiled with great oaths,   400
And filthily beslobbered by foul and false speech —
Such as needless and idle use of the name of God,
By which he had sworn a swarm of times, till sweat came
                                        through his coat.
He had devoured more food and drink than nature could endure:
'Yes, and gone sick many a time because of my surfeiting.
Then I *was* put in dread of dying in deadly sin.'
Then he would drop into despair, and doubt his salvation —
A form of Sloth so stark, no skill can cure it,
And no mercy amend such a man who dies thus.
    What may the branches of sloth be, that bring men to despair?   410
When a man does not mourn his misdeeds, or feel sorry;
When he performs badly the penance his priest lays on him,
Does no deeds of charity, feels no dread of sin,
Lives contrary to religion, and holds to no law.
For him, all days are holidays or high feast-days;
And all he is willing to hear are the harlotries of buffoons.
When people converse about Christ, and cleanness of soul,
He grows angry indeed, and demands only jollity.

Penance and the poor, and the pangs of saints,
He hates to hear about – and all who discuss them.   420
These are the branches (beware them!) that bring men to despair.
    You lords and ladies, you lieutenants of Holy Church,
Who feed wise fools and flatterers and liars,
And love to listen to them when they make you laugh,
        Vae vobis qui ridetis nunc: quia lugebitis et flebitis.
        (Woe unto you that laugh now! for ye shall mourn and
            weep.)[35]
You give them food and fees, and refuse poor people:
On the day of your death, I deeply fear,
These three kinds of creature will cause you great sorrow:
        Consentientes et agentes pari poena punientur.
        (Assenters to evil shall bear the same penalties as those who
            commit it.)[36]
Patriarchs and prophets, and preachers of God's word,
By means of their sermons, save men's souls from Hell;
Just so, flatterers and fools are the Fiend's disciples,   430
Whose tales entice men to ribald talk and sin.
Priests learned in Holy Writ should let their lords know
What David said of such men, as the Psalter shows:
        *Non habitabit in medio domus meae qui facit superbiam; qui
            loquitur iniqua, non direxit in conspectu oculorum meorum.*
        (He shall not dwell in the midst of my house, that acts
            proudly; he who speaks iniquities shall not tarry in my
            sight.)[37]
No harlequin should have audience in the halls or chambers
Where wise men may be (God's word is my witness),
Nor any self-admiring man be allowed among lords.
    Clergy and cavaliers welcome the king's minstrels,
And for love of their liege-lord listen to them at banquets.
Much more, then, should the rich, it seems to me,
Call beggars to be their guests, who are *God's* minstrels.   440
Christ Himself says, as St John bears witness,
        Qui vos spernit, me spernit.
        (He that despiseth you, despiseth me.)[38]
So I recommend to you rich men, when you hold revels,
That you solace your souls with such minstrels as *these*:
A poor man, instead of a so-called wit, seated at your High Table;

A learned, to give you lessons of Our Lord's Passion,
That saved your souls from their enemy Satan,
And to fiddle for you, without flattery, the Ballad of Good Friday!
A blind man, or a bedridden woman, in place of your buffoon,
Who shall cry to Our Lord for largesse, and laud you to *Him*.
Such minstrels as these three might make you laugh wholesomely, 450
And, when you die the death, give you comforts indeed
Who listened to them when living, and loved to hear them.
These would solace your soul, which you would see grow
Into strong hope, for having so acted towards saints of worth.
But flatterers and fools, with filthy words,
Lead those that love them to Lucifer's feast,
And a lament called *Lasciviousness*, sung to Lucifer's fiddle.

   Thus had Haukyn the Active Man made his coat filthy,
Till Conscience courteously called him to account
For why he had not washed it, or wiped a brush over it.   460

Passus 14

'I have only one whole suit,' said Haukyn, 'and am hardly
to blame

If it is soiled and seldom clean, for I sleep in it at night;
Also, at home I have a wife, and have servants and children,
Who many times muck it up, my protests notwithstanding!
    Uxorem duxi et ideo non possum venire.
    (I have married a wife, and therefore cannot come.)[1]
It has been lathered in Lent, and out of Lent, too,
With the soap of sickness, that sinks very deep in,
And with loss of belongings, that made me loth to offend
Either God or any good man, had I grace to avoid it.
The priest also heard me confess, and gave me for my sins
The penitence of patience and providing for the poor –   10
And of keeping my coat clean if I wished to stay Christian.
Yet I never could, by Christ, keep it clean for an hour;
For I soiled it with lewd looks or with worthless talk;
Or with wickedness of word or of deed or the will of my heart,
I have filthily befouled it, from morn till eve.'
    'I will acquaint you,' said Conscience, 'with the making of
an act of contrition

That will scrape your coat free from all sorts of smut.
Take *Cordis contritio,* contrition of the heart:[2]
Do-Well shall wash it and wring it through a wise confessor.
Take *Oris confessio,* oral confession:
Do-Better shall boil it and beat it as bright as scarlet,
And engrain it with good-will, and with God's grace to
amend you;   20

Then send you to sacramental penance – Do-Best – to sew-up
its rents.

    Satisfactio Do-Best: Do-Best is sacramental penance.
No mist will ever mar it again, nor moth nibble it,
Nor fiends nor false men befoul it so long as you live;
No herald nor harper shall have a finer garment

Than Haukyn the Active Man may, if he follows my teaching.
No minstrel shall be made more of, among rich or poor,
Than the wife of Haukyn the waferer, with his *activa vita*.'
'I shall present you with your paste, even when no plough
                                        stirs,' said Patience.
'And with flour to feed folk with, for the good of their souls,
Even when no grain grows in the fields, nor grapes on the vines.   30
All that live and look for a living, I will supply,
And none shall have less than enough of what he needs.
Men should not be too busy about their livelihood:

> *Ne soliciti sitis . . . patientes vincunt . . . '*
> (Take no thought for your life, what ye shall eat . . . the
> patient conquer . . .)[3]

   Then Haukyn laughed a little, and lightly swore:
'By our Lord, to rely on you, I believe, would bring small comfort!'
'Not so!' said Patience, *with* patience; and he took from his pack
Some victuals of great value to every kind of creature.
'Lo! Here is livelihood enough, if our beliefs are true!
God lent no creature life without means of livelihood –
Whereof, or wherefore, or whereby, to live.   40
Consider the wild worm, under the wet earth,
Fish that live in the floods, and the cricket in the fire;
The curlew, by consuming air, has the cleanest flesh of all birds;
And cattle live on grass and grain and green roots.
The meaning is that all men might in like manner
Live by loyal faith and love – as Christ bore witness:

> *Quodcumque petieritis Patrem in nomine meo, hoc faciam.*
> (Whatsoever ye shall ask the Father in my name, that will
> I do.)[4]

And elsewhere

> *Non in solo pane vivit homo, sed in omni verbo quod procedit de
> ore Dei.'*
> (Man shall not live by bread alone, but by every word that
> proceedeth out of the mouth of God.)[5]

Now I looked at this provender that Patience so praised,
And perceived that it was a piece of *Pater-noster* – 'Thy will
                                        be done.'
'Take it, Haukyn,' said Patience, 'and have some when you
                                        are hungry,

Or when you are clumsy with cold, or clemmed with drought.   50
Manacles shall not make you grieve, nor magnates' anger,
Nor prison nor pain, for – *the patient conquer.*
Be sober in your behaviour with both eye and tongue,
In eating and in handling, and in all your five senses,
And you will not care about corn, or cloth of wool or linen,
Nor for drink nor for death, but die as God wills,
By hunger or heat or however He chooses.
For if you live by His lore, the shorter your life, the better:
    Si quis amat Christum, mundum non diligit istum.[6]
    (He who loves the King of Kings
    Takes no delight in earthly things.)
It was by His breath that beasts grew, and wandered abroad: 60
    Dixit et facta sunt.
    (He commanded, and they were created.)[7]
And therefore through His breath must beasts and men live,
As Holy Scripture substantiates when men say grace:
    Aperis tu manum tuam, et imples omne animal benedictione.
    (Thou openest thy hand, and satisfiest the desire of every
       living thing.)[8]
  We find that for forty winters folk lived without husbandry,
And a flood sprang up out of the flint, for the folk and
                       beasts to drink;[9]
And in Elijah's time Heaven's floodgates were closed,
And no rain ran down (so we read in the books);[10]
Yet the Tribes lived so, many winters, without either bread
                       or tillage.
There were seven men that slept, says the book, for seven
                       hundred winters,
Living without food or liquid, yet waking at last.[11]
And if all men lived in moderation, famine would cease   70
Among Christian creatures, if Christ's words are true.
Dearth causes unkindness among Christian people,
And overplenty brings pride among poor and rich;
But moderation has such merit, no man can overprice it.
For the sins and the sorrows that the Sodomites suffered
Rose from bread in abundance and unabated sloth:
    Otiositas et abundantia panis peccatum turpissimum nutrivit.
    (Fullness of bread and abundance of idleness bred up that
       vilest of sins.)[12]

Because they were immoderate in their eating and drinking,
And did that deadly sin that the Devil rejoiced at,
For their vile vices, vengeance fell on them;
And both of their cities sank into Hell.[13]   80

   Let us temper our tastes, then, and take faith for our shield;
For through faith comes contrition, as Conscience knows well,
Which drives off deadly sin and reduces it to venial.
And though a man were mute, contrition might save him
And bring his soul to bliss, if Faith bore witness
That while he lived he believed in the lore of Holy Church.
So contrition, faith, and conscience, are correctly Do-Well –
The surgeons for deadly sin when spoken shrift fails.

   But oral confession is more excellent for the inwardly contrite,
For that slays any sin, howsoever deadly.   90
By confession to a cleric, all sins are killed,
But contrition can do no more than cut them down to venial.
Thus David in the Psalter says, "Blessed whose sin is covered."[14]
But satisfaction seeks out sin's root, and both slays and expels it,
And annihilates deadly sin as if it had never existed;
The sin leaves no scar or soreness, but seems a healed wound.'

   'Where does Charity live?' said Haukyn. 'For I never looked
                                                       yet, in my life,
On any man who had met him, for all my wide wandering.'

   'With perfect truth, and poverty of spirit, and a patient tongue;
There dwells Charity, the chief of God's chamberlains!'   100
'So, is patient poverty,' said Haukyn, 'more pleasing to Our Lord
Than riches rightfully gained, and reasonably spent?'

   'Come, now, but quis est ille? Quick – laudabimus eum!'
(First find me such a man, then we'll praise the fellow!)
'You may teach men how to use riches till the end of the world;
But I never ran across a rich man who, when he reckoned
That the day of his death was near, was not sorely in dread,
Or who, in that last reckoning, was not in arrears rather
                                                     than credit.

The poor man dares to plead, and to prove by pure reason,
His right to Our Lord's lenience; he claims by Law,
From that just Judge, the joys he never had.   110
He says, "Look at the birds and beasts, debarred from
                                                  Heaven's bliss,

And the wild worms in the woods: You anguish them in winter,
And make them, with famine, almost meek and mild;
But then you send them summer, their sovereign joy,
The Heaven's–bliss of the beasts both tame and wild.
So beggars, like the beasts, wait to be comforted,
They who have lived all their lives in languishing want."
Unless God sent them sometime *some* kind of pleasure –
Either here on Earth or elsewhere, nature would not bear it;
What man was ever made with no means towards joy?   120

   The angels who are now in Hell, had joy at one time;
Dives lived among dainties and *la dolce vita*[15] –
As really, we know by reason, do *all* rich men;
And their ladies also live lives of pleasure.

   To Man's Mother-wit, God's will may seem strange,
That He gives many men their thank-money before they
                          have earned it –
For thus it is that He treats the rich; and I think it worth pity
That they have their reward, and their Heaven as it were,
                          here on Earth,
In luxury of life, without labouring bodily,
But are disavowed when they die – as David says in the Psalter: 130
    Dormierunt somnium suum, et nihil invenerunt.
    (They have slept their sleep, and all the men of wealth have
       found nothing in their hands.)[16]
And in another psalm too!
    Velut somnium surgente, Domine, in civitate tua, imaginem
      ipsorum ad nihilum redige.
    (As a dream when one awaketh, so shalt thou make their
      image to vanish out of the city.)[17]
Alas that riches should wrench and rob man's souls
From the love of Our Lord, at their late end!
Servants who take their salaries in advance are always needy;
He seldom dies out of debt, who has not earned his dinner
By first doing his full day's work and duty.

   When a workman has finished his work, one may see exactly
What that work is worth, and what he has earned:
Take no fee beforehand, for fear your work is refused.
So I say to all you rich folk, you do wrong to expect   140
Your Heaven here below and in the hereafter too,

Like a servant with prepaid salary, who claims it a second time,
As if he had nothing, but must have his hire now.
It must not be, you rich men, unless Matthew lies in God's face:
    De deliciis ad delicias, difficile est transire.
    (From delights to delights is a difficult passage.)[18]
  Yet if you rich are not ruthless, but reward the poor well,
And live as God's law teaches, acting justly towards all,
Christ in His courtesy will comfort you at your ending,
And reward with double riches those of ruthful heart.
As a servant with prepaid salary who has served well
May, before he is relieved, receive extra rewards –   150
Say, a coat on top of his contract – so Christ will give Heaven
To both prosperous and poor who show pity in their lives;
All who do their duty well shall have double pay for their toil –
Forgiveness here for their sins, and hereafter Heaven's bliss.
  But the holy saints say in their books that it is seldom seen
That God rewards a rich man with double repose.
For the rich make high merriment with their meals and clothes,
As in May there is high merriment among wild beasts;
And their high spirits stay as long as Summer does.
But beggars have no bread to their supper even about
                                  Midsummer;   160
And Winter is even worse, for they walk wet-footed,
Always thirsty and hungry, and abused so foully,
And so despised by the prosperous, it is piteous to hear.
Lord, send them their Summer, and some kind of pleasure –
Heaven when they go hence – who have known such want here!
For You might have made all men equal in means,
And quick-witted and wise, had Your wish been so.
Then pity the prosperous who give Your prisoners nothing;
For all the goods You gave them, ingratitude comes from many;
But, God, in Your goodness, give them grace to reform.   170
No dearth is dire to them, nor drought, nor flood,
Nor heat nor hail, so long as they have their health;
And of all they might want or wish, in this world they lack
                                      nothing.
  But the poor people, Lord, Your prisoners in the pit of
                                      misfortune:
Comfort those creatures, who are so careworn

By dearth and drought all their days here below –
Woeful in winter, for want of clothing;
Seldom, even in Summer, supping well:
Comfort the careworn, Christ, in Your Kingdom;
For how You comfort all creatures, the clergy bear witness: 180
    Si revertamini et quiescatis, salvi eritis.
    (In returning and rest shall ye be saved.)[19]
Thus, courteously incarnate, Jesus Christ said
To robbers and reavers, to rich and to poor.
You taught them, Lord, to take baptism in the name of the Trinity,
And grow clean, through that christening, from all kinds of sin;
And if it befell through our folly we should later fall into sin,
Confessing and acknowledging it, and craving Your mercy,
Would redeem us as often as any man might wish.
But if Apollyon counter-pleaded, and punished our conscience,
You would rapidly take our Reprieve for that wretch to see:
    Pateat . . . per Passionem Domini. . .
    (Be it known that by the Passion of Our Lord . . .)[20]
And so drive off the Devil and demonstrate our ransom.   190
But poverty must be the parchment of which this Patent is made,
And pure patience too, and perfect faith.
From pomp and pride, this parchment falls away,
And indeed from all except the poor in spirit:
All else is idle, that ever we wrote on it –
Pater-nosters and penances, and pilgrimages to Rome;
Unless our expense and spending spring from right motives,
All our labour is lost. See how men have their names cut
On friary windows, when the foundation of the act is false.[21]
All Christians should hold wealth in common, none covetous
                                          for himself.   200

   There are seven sins that continually assail us,
And the Fiend follows them all, and makes efforts to help them –
And it is with riches that that Wretch most readily traps men.
For where riches reign, reverence is found,
Which is pleasing to the pride of both rich and poor.
The rich man is reverenced by reason of his riches,
And the poor man is pushed back – though perhaps he has more
Of wit and wisdom in him – which are far and away better
Than riches or royalty, and reach Heaven oftener.

For the rich owe great reckonings, and walk really slowly   210
The highway to Heaven, for their riches hinder them:
> *Dives difficile intrabit in regnum coelorum.*
>   (A rich man shall hardly enter into the Kingdom of
>   Heaven.)[22]
There, the poor press ahead of the rich, with packs on their backs:
> *Opera enim illorum sequuntur illos*
>   (And their works do follow them),[23]
And blatantly and boldly, as beggars do, they ask
Perpetual bliss for their poverty and patience.
> *Beati pauperes spiritu: quoniam ipsorum est regnum coelorum.*
>   (Blessed are the poor in spirit: for theirs is the kingdom of
>   Heaven.)[24]
  But Pride reigns in riches rather than in poverty,
And his mansion is in the master more often than in the man;
For Pride has no power over patient poverty,
Nor may any of the Seven Sins stay long with it,
Nor have power over poverty if patience attend it:
The poor man is always prompt in pleasing the rich man,   220
And obedient to his bidding, for the sake of his bits of bread.
But obedience and boastfulness do constant battle,
And each hates the other in all human life.
  If Wrath wrestles with the poor man, Wrath comes off worse;
If they take a quarrel to Court, the poor man pleads quietly,
For loud and abusive language would lose his case.
So his looks are lowly, and he lets his speech be likeable,
Who must ask other men for meal or for money.
  If Gluttony grapples with poor men, he gains the less,
For their earnings do not run to buying rich food,   230
And gluttony for even good ale makes them go to a cold bed,
With head all uncovered, and awkwardly twisted;
And, when they shift or stretch, only straw for sheeting.
So, for their gluttony and great sloth, they do grievous penance,
And cry *welladay* when they wake and weep for cold,
And sometimes for their sins; so they are never merry
Without some admixture of mourning, and misfortune as well.
If Cupidity tries to trip the poor man, he can hardly take hold,
And neither can ever take the other by the neck!
It is common knowledge that Cupidity has keen desires   240

And has hands and arms of huge extent,
While Poverty is a poor shrimp who must peer up to his navel;
And a boring bout it is, between long and short!
   If Avarice would injure the poor, he has little advantage;
For Poverty has only pockets to put his wealth in,
Whereas Avarice keeps his in cupboards and in coffers bound
                                    with iron –
And which is more easily rifled? There is less row
From a beggar's bag than from a coffer bound in iron!
   Lechery does not like the poor, for they give little silver,
Cannot dine on delicate food, nor drink wine often.   250
Broken reeds in brothels! – which would all break down
If they depended on poor men, and be un-pantiled!
   If Sloth pursues the poor man, and he serves God ill,
Then Adversity will teach him to think again,
That God is his highest helper, and no human being,
And his lackey (as Our Lord Himself said)[25] in the livery
                                    of Mankind.
And whether He helps him or not, He bears the sign of poverty,
And in such garb Our Saviour saved all Mankind.
Therefore poor men who are patient may expect and ask,
After their earthly ending, the bliss of Heaven's kingdom.   260
   Much more hardily may he ask who might, here on Earth,
Have enjoyed lands and lordship and the lusts of the flesh,
But for love of God left it all and lived like a beggar.
He is like a maiden who leaves her mother for a man's love;
Leaves her father and all her friends, and follows her mate:
Such a maiden is much to be loved by the man who weds her,
More than a maiden who was married through brokage,
By assent of several parties, and money to seal the bargain –
An agreement made for avarice, not by affection shared.
The first girl is like all folk who forsake their possessions   270
Purposing to be patient and make Poverty their mate
(That sib to God Himself, and to His saints.)'
   'God hear my oath!' said Haukyn. 'This is high praise
                                of poverty!
But what does patient poverty imply, exactly?'
    Paupertas, said Patience, '*est odibile bonum; remotio curarum,*
    possessio sine calumnia, donum Dei, sanitatis mater; absque

> *solicitudine semita, sapientiae temperatrix, negotium sine*
> *damno; incerta fortuna; absque solicitudine felicitas.'* [26]

'I cannot construe that,' said Haukyn. 'You must counsel me
in English.'

'In English,' said Patience, 'it is hard to explain in full;
Yet I will say something about it, within your understanding:
> Poverty is a hateable good, the removing of cares,
>   possession without cheating, a gift of God, the mother
>   of good health; a narrow footpath without anxiety; the
>   governess of wisdom, business without loss; doubtful
>   fate; happiness without worry.

Poverty is the prime object of Pride's hatred,
And anything abhorrent to Pride can only be good!   280
Conscience knows well that contrition brings comfort to men;
Though in itself a sorrow, it brings solace to the soul;
Just so, poverty is properly penance done with joy,
And produces in the body pure and spiritual health.
>   Therefore *paupertas est odibile bonum,*
As contrition is a comfort and a cure for souls.
Poverty seldom sits upon a sworn jury,
Nor are poor men enjoined as justices, to judge others,
Nor as mayors to lead other men, nor as ministers of the Crown;
Seldom is a poor man appointed to punish others:
>   *remotio curarum.*
Therefore poverty and poor men put in practice the
                                    commandment,   290
>   *Nolite judicare quemquam*
>   (Judge not, that ye be not judged).
And thirdly – rarely does a poor man grow rich, save by
                                    rightful heirship;
He does not win money with false weights or warrantless measures,
Nor borrow from folk near-by too much to pay back easily:
>   *possessio sine calumnia.*
Fourthly, it is a fortune by which the soul flourishes
In sobriety, far from all sin; and still there is more:
It makes the flesh forgo a great many foolish things,
With a corresponding comfort that this is Christ's own gift:
>   *donum Dei.*
Fifthly, it is mother of health, and a friend in all ordeals,

Leechcraft for all the land, a lover of cleanness:
 sanitatis mater.
Sixth, it is the Path of Peace – yes, even through Alton Pass[27] 300
Poverty might progress without peril from robbers.
For where poverty passes, peace follows after;
And your heart is the hardier, the less you have upon you.
Therefore Seneca says *paupertas est absque solicitudine semita,*[28]
And makes a man hardy of heart among a host of thieves:
 Cantabit pauper coram latrone viator.
 (The poor traveller will sing in the presence of the
  highwayman.)
Seventh, it is wisdom's well, and few words come from it;
For lords praise it little, nor listen to its opinion;
It turns its tongue towards Truth, and desires no treasure:
 Sapientia temperatrix.
Eighth, it is an honest labourer, unwilling to take more
Than well-deserved wages, in winter or in summer, 310
And in commerce cares nothing for loss, but for increase of charity:
 Negotium sine damno.
Ninth, it is sweet to the soul, far sweeter than sugar;
For poverty's proper bread is perfect patience,
And sobriety is a sweet drink, and sickness's best doctor.
This I learned from a lettered man, for love of Our Lord –
St Augustine said to be poor is a blessed life, without bother
For body or for soul: *absque solicitudine felicitas.*
Now may God, Who gives all good things, grant rest to the soul
Of the man who first wrote to teach us what poverty might mean!'
 'Alas!' said Haukyn the Active Man, 'that after my baptism 320
I did not die and get buried, for Do-Well's sake!
How hateful it is, to live and have to sin!
Yet sin pursues us for ever.' And he grew sorrowful,
And wept from watery eyes, and bewailed the times
That ever he did a deed that displeased dear God;
He sobbed and sighed often, and well-nigh swooned,
For having ever owned land or lordship, no matter how little,
Or more mastery over other men than over himself.
'God's my witness, I'm unworthy to wear *any* clothes,
Neither shirt nor shoes, except only, for shame's sake, 330
One rag to cover my carcass!' He cried aloud for mercy,
And wept and wailed. And with all this, I awoke.

Passus 15

Yet after my waking, it was still a long while
Before I had full knowledge and feeling of Do-Well.
My wits waxed and waned until I was crazy;
Few men approved my life, and many abused it,
Alleging that I was a losel, and loth to be humble
Towards lords and ladies or any of that lot –
Such as parsons in furred apparel, with pendants of silver.
To Sergeants-at-Law and such I never once said,
'God bless you, my lords!' nor did low obeisance.
And so, folk thought me a fool; and I raved in that folly   10
Till Reason took pity on me, and rocked me to sleep.

    Then I saw, as if by sorcery, a most subtle creature:
He had neither tongue nor teeth, but he told me where
                                       I was going,
And whence I came, and my character. I conjured him, at last,
If he were a creature of Christ, for Christ's love to tell me.

    'I *am* a creature of Christ, widely known as a Christian,
Even in Christ's Court itself, and as one of His kinsmen.
Neither Peter the Porter nor St Paul with his falchion[1]
Will defend its door against me, knock I never so late.
At midnight or midday my voice is known,   20
And every member of His Court makes me right welcome.'

    'What are you called in that Court, among Christ's people?'
'When I quicken Man's carcass, I am called *Anima*: Life.
When I am a wisher, a user of will, I am *Animus*: Soul.
Because I know and comprehend, I am called *Mens*: Mind.
When I make moan to God, my name is *Memoria*: Recollection.[2]
When I lay down decrees, and do as Truth teaches,
Then *Ratio* is my right name – or, in English, Reason.
When I perceive what men say, my first name is Sense –
Which means wisdom and understanding, the well-spring
                                of all skills.   30
When I claim or do not claim, buy or withdraw my custom,

Then I am called Conscience – God's clerk and notary.
When I love Our Lord truly, and all other men,
My name is Loyal–Love, or in Latin *Amor*.
When I flee from the flesh, and forsake the carcass,
I am inexpressible spirit, and *Spiritus* is my name.
Augustine and Isidore, the one as much as the other,
First found me these names; and it is for you to choose:
Call me what name you wish, now that you know them all.'

> *Anima pro diversis actionibus diversa nomina sortitur: dum*
> *vivificat corpus, anima est; dum vult, animus est; dum scit,*
> *mens est; dum recolit, memoria est. Dum judicat, ratio est;*
> *dum sentit, sensus est; dum amat, amor est; dum negat vel*
> *consentit, conscientia est: dum spirat, spiritus est.'*

> (According to its different functions, the soul receives
> different names: in animating the body, its name is Life;
> in exercising will, its name is Soul; in having
> knowledge, it is Mind; in recollecting, it is Memory. In
> judging, it is Reason; in feeling, it is Sense; in loving, it
> is Love; in denying or consenting, it is Conscience; in
> being the breath of life, it is Spirit.)[3]

'You must be a bishop,' I said, by way of a joke.   40
'For bishops, once being ordained, go by all sorts of names,
Such as *presul* and *pontifex* and *metropolitanus*,
> *Episcopus* and *pastor*, and piles of others.'[4]
'That is true,' he returned. 'Now I see your intention!
You need to know the reason for the many names they have –
And for mine too, I fancy, from the way you speak!'
'Yes, sir,' I said, 'so long as no one minds.
All science under the sun, and all subtle arts,
Were it possible, I would know and hold naturally within
                                                          my heart!'
'That proves you imperfect,' he said, 'and one of Pride's knights; 50
Such longings and lusts made Lucifer fall from Heaven:
> *Ascendam super altitudinem nubium, similis ero Altissimo.*
> (I will ascend above the heights of the clouds; I will be like
> the Most High.)[5]
It would be unnatural, and against all kinds of reason,
That any being should know all things, except Christ alone.
Solomon speaks against men such as you, and despises their minds.

He says, *Sicut qui mel multum comedit, non est ei bonum: sic
qui scrutator est majestatis, opprimetur a gloria.*
(It is not good to eat much honey; so for men to search
their own glory, is not glory.)[6]
Remade into English, this means, for men with their senses,
That the man who eats too much honey does a mischief to
his belly,
And the more a man hears of profitable matters,
Unless he acts upon them, he is doubly harmed.
"Blessed is he," says St Bernard, "who reads the Scriptures
And turns their words to deeds, to his utmost ability."[7]   60
The hunger to have and apprehend great knowledge
Pushed our first parents out of Paradise:
Scientiae appetitus hominem immortalitatis gloria spoliavit.
(The lust for knowledge despoiled Man of the glory of
immortality.)[8]
As honey is hard to digest, and harmful to the stomach,
So they who seek by reason to understand the roots
Of God and His great might, must forgo His grace.
For in such longing lie pride and lust of the flesh,
Against Christ's counsel, and all clerical teaching:
Non plus sapere quam oportet sapere.
(To know no more than is proper to know.)[9]
Your friars, and experts in the Faith, the lay-folks' preachers,
You are mooting inscrutable matters when you mention
the Trinity;
So that lay-folk lose their belief, all too often.   70
Better did the bulk of you Doctors abandon such teaching,
To teach men the Ten Commandments, and touch on
the Seven Deadly Sins,
And the branches that burgeon from them, and bring men to Hell;
And of how folk will dissipate on follies all five senses:
Friars, like other church-folk, go to foolish expense
On their convents, their clothing, and conceit in their learning —
More in pomp than in pure charity. The people know that's true;
I'm not lying, look you! You become lords' toadies,
Paying reverence to the rich with regard to their money:
Confundantur omnes qui adorant sculptilia.
(Confounded be all they that serve graven images.)[10]

And elsewhere:

> *Ut quid diligitis vanitatem, et quaeritis mendacium?*
> (How long will ye love vanity, and seek after lying?)[11]

Go to the gloss on that text, all you great scholars;   80
If I lie to you, in my illiteracy, lead me out to be burned![12]
For it seems to me you will forgo alms from no one,
Whether usurers or whores or grasping hucksters either;
You bow low to the lords who may load you with gold
(Against your Rule, and religion – I refer this to Jesus,
Who said to His disciples, *Ne sitis personarum acceptores*:[13]
> Thou shalt not respect persons, neither take a gift.)
I could write a long book about all this business;
But I shall recount (of those with cure of Christian souls),
For truth's sake, what the Fathers tell: take heed who wishes!

As holiness and high worth spring from Holy Church   90
Through religiously-living men who teach the Law of God:
Just so, out of Holy Church all evils arise
When an imperfect priesthood are the preachers and teachers.
We see a symbol of this on summer trees,
When some boughs bear leaves, but others are naked;
When boughs are thus bare, there must be badness at the roots.
Now, the parsons and priests and preachers of Holy Church
Are the roots of right belief, if they rule folk well;
And where those roots are rotten, reason requires
There shall be no flowers or fruits, nor fair green leaves.   100
So if you lettered men could leave your lust for rich clothing,
And be kind and courteous, as clerks should, in the use of
                                                         Christ's bounty,
And be truthful of tongue, and keep your tails chaste,
Loathing to hear lewd talk, and loth to accept
Tithes from dishonest earnings by tillage or trade:
Then laymen would be loth to neglect your teaching,
And they would reform wrongdoers, if *you* were exemplars
Instead of preaching and not practising – which is pure hypocrisy.
Hypocrisy in Latin[14] is likened to a dunghill
Concealed under snow, and with snakes inside it;   110
Or to a whitewashed wall, with filth underneath.
Many priests and preachers and prelates are like that:
You are whitewashed with fine words, and with clothing too;

But most unwinning are the words and the works that you hide.
  St John Chrysostom[15] speaks of clergy and priests:

    Sicut de templo omne bonum progreditur, sic de templo omne
      malum procedit.
    Si sacerdotium integrum fuerit, tota floret ecclesia; si autem
      corruptum fuerit, omnium fides marcida est.
    Si sacerdotium fuerit in peccatis, totus populus convertitur ad
      peccandum.
    Sicut cum videris arborem pallidam et marcidam, intelligis quod
      vitium habet in radice,
    Ita cum videris populum indisciplinatum et irreligiosum, sine
      dubio sacerdotium ejus non est sanum.

  (Just as all good proceeds from the Temple, so also from the
    Temple proceeds all that is evil.
  If the priesthood be uncorrupted, the whole Church will
    flourish; but if it be corrupt, all men's faith is enfeebled.
  If the priesthood be in the midst of sins, the whole people
    is directed towards sin.
  Just as when you see a tree to be yellow and withered, you
    understand that there is rottenness at its root,
  So when you see an undisciplined and irreligious populace,
    without doubt its priesthood is unsound.)

  If an ignorant man could correctly construe that Latin,
And identify the author, I should think it a wonder;
But how if many priests were to bear, not baselards and brooches,[16]
But a rosary in their hand and a book under their arm?
Sir John and Sir Geoffrey[17] wear silver girdles,   120
And a short-sword or a stiletto with studs of silver-gilt.
But the breviary should be their instrument for reciting the Office,
Which they're unwilling to say unless someone slips them silver!
Alas, you unlettered men, you lavish too much on priests!
Wise God would not allow it, were not all of it gained
Wickedly and with falsehood – and goes to wicked men
(Namely, imperfect priests, and preachers who are venal,
And executors and sub-deans, and summoners and sweethearts),
So that what was gained by guile, is degradingly spent:
Pimps and prostitutes get the profit of such goods;   130
And God's folk, in default of them, are enfeebled and perish.
  Some curates and clerics of the Church, close-fisted all their lives,

Let all the gold they leave go straight to good-for-nothings;
Or one such dies intestate, and then the Bishop enters,
And he and his men make merry with the money,
Saying, "He was a niggard, and he never had a halfpenny
For friend or foreigner – may the Fiend have his soul!
He kept a wretched household all his life long;
All that he saved and scrimped, we'll spend on pleasure!"
  Be he learned or illiterate, that man loth to spend,   140
That's the way his goods go, when he gives up the ghost.
But for good men, God knows, there is great mourning;
Men bemoan good meal-givers, and bear them in mind
With prayers and penances, in perfect charity.'
  'What is Charity?' I asked. And he said: 'A childlike thing:
    Nisi efficiamini sicut parvuli, non intrabitis in regnum coelorum.
    (Except ye be converted, and become as little children, ye
      shall not enter into the kingdom of Heaven.)[18]
Yet it is not infantile or foolish, but free and liberal good will.'
  'Where can one find such a friend, with so free a heart?
I have lived in this land, and my name is Long Will,
But I never found free-handed Charity before or behind me!
Men are often merciful to mendicants and poor people,   150
Or will lend if they believe their loan will be honestly repaid;
But Charity such as Paul praised as best, such as pleased
                              our Saviour –
    Non inflatur, non est ambitiosa, non quaerit quae sua sunt.
    (It is not puffed up, doth not behave itself unseemly,
      seeketh not her own.)[19]
I never saw such a man, so help me God,
As would not ask for his own, and also covet
Things that he did not need, and nab them if he could!
The clergy tells us that Christ can be found everywhere,
Though I certainly never saw Him, except mirrored in *me*:
    Per speculum in aenigmate; tunc enim facie ad faciem.
    (Through a glass darkly; but then face to face.)[20]
And by what I am told of Charity, I take it as truth
That he's not found where men fight, or haggle for bargains.'
  'Charity does not challenge or chaffer or claim;   160
He is as proud of a penny as if of a pound of gold,
As glad of a gown of grey homespun

As of a tunic from Tartary, or of choicest scarlet.[21]
He is glad with all who are glad, and is good to the wicked,
And believes and loves all whom Our Lord created.
He curses no creature, he does not continue in anger,
He does not like lying, or laughing men to scorn.
All that men say, he accepts, and receives with pleasure,
And mildly endures all manner of misfortunes;
He covets no earthly commodity, but bliss in the Kingdom
                                           of Heaven.'   170
   'He has no riches or rents, nor any rich friends?'
   'Of rents or of riches he makes no reckoning,
For no friend that finds him in need ever fails him.
Fiat-voluntas-tua, "Thy will be done", always finds him;
And he sups sparely on the soup of *Spera-in-Deo* –
                                           Trust-in-the-Lord.
He can portray the Pater-noster well, and paint it with Hail-
Marys.[22]
At whiles it is his wont to walk on pilgrimage
To where the poor lie in prison awaiting pardon;
He brings them no bread, but a much sweeter food,
And loves them as Our Lord bids, and looks to their welfare.   180
   When he is weary of this work, he will sometimes
Labour for a mile's length in a laundry;[23]
For eagerly he addresses himself to youth's errors,
And to pride and its appurtenances, and presses them together
And batters them upon his breast till they are beaten clean.
Then he lays into them a long time, labouring with groans
                                           of contrition,[24]
And with warm water from his eyes he afterwards washes them.
Yet he sings as he does so, and sometimes says, weeping,
   "*Cor contritum et humiliatum, Deus, non despicies.*" '
   (A broken and a contrite heart, O God, thou wilt not
      despise.)[25]
   'By Christ!' quoth I, 'I wish I knew him – no creature more so!'
'Without help from Piers the Ploughman, you will never see
                                           him in person.'   190
   'Cannot the clergy find him, the keepers of Holy Church?'
   'The clergy can know man only by works or words,
But Piers the Ploughman can penetrate more deeply

Into men's motives, and the reason why so many suffer:

> *Cum vidisset Jesus cogitationes eorum, dixit: Ut quid cogitatis*
> *mala in cordibus vestris?*

(And Jesus, knowing their thoughts, said, Wherefore think
  ye evil in your hearts?)[26]

For there are many proud-hearted men who are mild in
                                                their speech
And biddable in their bearing towards burgesses and lords,
Yet who, meeting poor people, have pepper in their noses,
And who lour like lions if someone belittles their doings.
There are beggars and bums one might take for beadsmen,
Looking meek as lambs, and of holy life-habit;   200
But it is more to get their meals in the easiest manner
Than for penance or self-perfection, that *these* assume poverty.

   Neither clerisy nor outward colour can reveal Charity to you,
Nor words, nor deeds, but only the knowledge of men's hearts;
And those are known to no clerk or other creature on Earth,
Except Piers the Ploughman alone: Peter, that is: Christ![27]

   The Lollards do not know Charity, nor do land-loping
                                                "hermits",[28]
Nor ancresses with alms-chests: all these are fakers.
Fie upon fakers and all who show them favour!
Charity is God's champion, though as gentle as a child;   210
He is the merriest of mouth when he sits at meals;
The love that lies in his heart makes him lively of speech
And as companionable and comforting as Christ Himself:

> *Nolite fieri, sicut hypocritae, tristes.*

(Be not, as the hypocrites, of a sad countenance.)[29]

For I have seen him sometimes in silks, sometimes in homespun,
In both grey wool and grey furs with golden trappings,
But all alike giving gladly to any who were needy.

   Edmund and Edward were each of them kings,[30]
But esteemed as saints since Charity dwelt with them.

   I have also seen him reading and singing in Church;
Riding, or running along in ragged clothes;   220
But I never beheld him cadging like a beggar.
He is readiest to walk in rich robes,
Cleanly clothed in cyprus or in Tartary-cloth,
Capped, and with crimped hair round a shaven crown.[31]

In a friars's frock he was at one time found,
But those days are far-off, in the time of St Francis;
He has been seldom seen since then in that Order.

He regards rich men highly, and accepts robes from them
If they live their lives honestly and without wile:

    Beatus est dives.

  (Blessed is the rich that is found without blemish, and hath
    not gone after gold).[32]

He comes often to the King's court, when the counsellors

                                           are honest;   230

But if Covetousness joins the Council, he will not come to it.
He seldom consorts with the King's court-jesters,
For they brawl and backbite and bear false witness.

In the Consistory, before the Commissary, he comes rarely,
For their law-suits are long-drawn-out, unless you use bribery;
And there they make and unmake marriages, for money;
What Christ and Conscience had closely conjoined,
Those Doctors of Law undo dishonestly.

Among archbishops and bishops and prelates of Holy Church,
He was at one time wont to remain,   240
And share-out Christ's patrimony piecemeal to poor people.
But Avarice keeps the keys now, and saves everything for

                                      his kinsmen,

His executors, and his servants – and some for the Bishops'

                                      children.

Now, I blame nobody; but – make us better, O Lord,
And give us grace, good God, to follow Charity!
For whoever may meet him, finds him hating such manners
As condemning and cursing and commending and boasting,
Fault-finding, flattering, frowning sternly,
Claiming and coveting and crying for more:

    In pace in idipsum dormiam, et requiescam.

  (I will lay me down in peace, and sleep.)[33]

All his living and livelihood is love under Christ's Passion;   250
He does not beg or beseech, nor borrows to repay;
He does mischief to no man, nor makes trouble with his mouth.

Among Christian men, such mildness should prevail;
In all kinds of anguish, they should have this at heart,
That whatsoever they have suffered, God suffered more for us:

He showed by example what we should do – take no vengeance
On foes that treat us falsely: that is Our Father's will.
It is obvious to all, that if God had not willed it,
Judas and the Jews could never have put Jesus on the Cross,
Nor have martyred Peter and Paul, nor have imprisoned them.   260
Christ suffered as an example that we should suffer too,
And said to such as will suffer that *the patient conquer.*
There are texts enough,' said Reason, 'and true examples to study,
In *Legenda Sanctorum*, the Lives of the Holy Saints,
Of the penances and poverty and pains that they endured,
In hunger and heat and in all kinds of hurt.
Saints Antony and Aegidius, and other Holy Fathers,[34]
Dwelt in the wilderness among wild beasts;
And monks and mendicants, men living alone
In caverns and cubby-holes, conversed rarely.   270
Neither Antony nor Aegidius, nor any hermit then,
Had leopards or lions to bring them food to live on,
But, we read in books, the birds of the air.
(Except that Aegidius summoned to his cell a hind,
And managed to live on the milk of that mild creature;
Yet he did not have her daily to reduce his hunger,
But only from time to time, as the book teaches and tells us.)
   Antony, every day at about noontime,
Had a bird that brought him bread, by which he lived;
And God, if that saint had a guest, gave enough for both.   280
   Paul, the primary hermit,[35] had so pleached himself in
As to be out of sight behind moss and leaves;
But the birds for many winters brought him food, none-the-less;
And finally he founded the Augustinian Friars' Order.
Paul the Apostle, after preaching, wove baskets,[36]
Earning with his hands what his hunger demanded.
Peter fished for his food, like his friend Andrew.[37]
They sold some, and they seethed some; and so they both lived.
Mary Magdalen lived on morning-dew and roots,[38]
But more upon remorse and on memories of Our Lord.   290
In a week I could not recount all the cases
Of those who for love of Our Lord lived thus for long years.
Neither leopard nor lion that prowled those lands,
Nor bear nor boar, nor other wild beast,

But fell at their feet and fondled them with their tails.
And could the creatures have spoken, by Christ I believe
They would have fed those folk before the birds did.
For all such courtesy as beasts can, they showed often to
                                        those recluses,
In licking them, and in lowliness, in the lands where they walked.
But God sent the fowls of the air with food, and not fierce beasts,   300
In emblem that meek men should be fed by mild creatures.
By this rule, righteous men should feed the religious,
And loyal believers bring food to men of holy life.
Then lords and ladies would loathe injustice,
Or taking too much money from their tenants,
When they found the very friars refusing their alms
And bidding them take it back whence it was borrowed.
For we are all God's fowls, and are forced to wait
Till other birds bring us that by which we live.
If you had broth and bread enough, and small beer to drink,   310
And a single dish of some sort to set beside them,
You Religious would eat right well – and so your own Rule says.

> *Nunquam rugiet onager cum habuerit herbam? aut mugiet bos*
> *cum ante praesepe plenum steterit?*
> (Doth the wild ass bray when he hath grass? or loweth the
> ox over his fodder? . . . The nature of the brute beasts
> condemns you, for among them ordinary food suffices;
> your sin proceeds from luxury.)[39]

If laymen knew Latin enough, they would look where
                                        their gifts went,
And consider for five or six days before
They signed their estates away to monks or canons.
Alas! You lords and ladies are ill-advised
To take from your heirs all that your ancestors left you,
And render it, in return for prayers, to the rich
Who are already endowed and enfeoffed to pray for others.

> Who today performs this prophecy, among living people –   320
> *Dispersit; dedit pauperibus*
> (He hath dispersed, he hath given to the poor)?[40]

If any people perform it, they are these "poor" friars!
For what they beg, all about, they spend on their buildings,
And some upon themselves and such as labour for them:

So they take from them that have, and give to those that have not!
  But you rich clergy and cavaliers and commoners
Are acting as I would be if I had a forest
Full of pleasant trees, but plotted and planned
How I might plant more in among the rest.
Just so you rich men give robes to clothe the rich,
And help those who help you, and give to those that have –   330
As if one filled a firkin with fresh river-water,
And went off with that water to widen the Thames!
You are really the same, you rich men, who give robes and food
And help to people who have as much as you have yourselves.
And the rich Religious should rather feed beggars
Than the rich burghers are bound to, as the Book teaches:

> *Quia sacrilegium est res pauperum non pauperibus dare. Item,
> peccatoribus dare, est daemonibus immolare. Item, Monache, si
> indiges et accipis, potius das quam accipis. Si autem non eges,
> et accipis, rapis. Porro, non indiget monachus, si habeat quod
> naturae sufficit.*

> (For it is sacrilege not to give to the poor what belongs to
> the poor. Also: *Giving presents to defaulters/Is laying gifts
> on devils' altars.* Also: O monk, if thou art needy, and
> takest gifts, thou givest more than thou takest. But if
> thou art not needy, to take gifts is to steal.

> Moreover: A monk is not poor if he has what suffices
> nature.)[41]

  Therefore I counsel all Christians to conform with Charity;
For charity, unchallengeably, discharges sin from the soul,
And many a prisoner from Purgatory, by means of prayer.
But there are faults in the folk who should guard the Faith;   340
Whereby lay folk are feebler, and less firm, in theirs.
As snide contains base alloy, yet looks like sterling,
And is marked as if from the Mint, but of frangible metal:
So we find many folk nowadays, fair of speech,
In tonsure and christening the King of Heaven's currency,
But the metal (man's soul) misalloyed with sin.
Both lettered and illiterate are now thus misalloyed,
So that no man now loves his neighbour or Our Lord.
Through wars and wickedness and immoderate weather
The weatherwise seaman and well-read scholar   350

Have lost their faith in the skies and philosophers' lore.
   Astrologers every day find their art fails them,
Who once could warn us of things that were to come.
Shipmen and shepherds, in charge of ships and sheep,
Could read in the clouds what weather was coming,
And were able to warn us of whirlwinds and storms.
The tillers who tended the soil could tell their masters,
From the seed they had sown, how much it was best to sell
Or to lend or to live-on: the land was so trustworthy.
But now the folk of both flood and field fail,   360
The shipmen and the shepherds and the tillers shilly-shally
Between one course and another, having no certain knowledge.
Astrologers also are at their wits' end,
For what they computed from the spheres comes out the contrary.
Grammar, the ground of all teaching, now baffles girls and boys;
Not one of our new learners today takes pains enough
To write correct verses or compose a competent letter;
Not one in a hundred can construe the Classics,
Nor read one letter of any language but Latin and English.
Look at any level of learning, you'll find Flim-flam in charge,   370
And his colleague Toady as an apt assistant:
I marvel at such matters among us all.
Doctors who study decretals, Masters of Divinity,
Men who should have mastered all manner of knowledge,
And be able to answer all arguments in quodlibets:
(I scarcely dare say it, for shame) if such men were examined,
They would fail in philosophy and physic both.[42]
Therefore I fear that officials of Holy Church
May also make omissions, in their Offices and Hours.
If they do make omissions (and I hope not), our faith will
                                       supply them;   380
For, as clergy at the feast of Corpus Christi counsel and sing,
Simple faith is sufficient to save the ignorant.[43]
   Therefore Saracens may be saved, and Scribes and Jews;
Alas, then, that our teachers teach otherwise than they live,
And by their lax lives make laymen guiltier towards God.
For Saracens own something similar to our faith;
For they believe in, and love, one Almighty God,
As we, both learned and lay, believe in one God.

But a man called Mohammed brought the men of Syria
Into dire disbelief; and he did it thus:[44]   390
He was formerly of our faith, but, failing for the Papacy,
He strayed into Syria, where by subtle devices
He tamed a turtle-dove, and at all times fed her;
And the corn that she always ate, he laid in his ear.
Now, when he preached to the people in the places he visited,
He would let this culver come and seek corn from his ear,
For it was to this end that he had taught and trained her;
And he made the folk fall to their knees, for he swore in
                                         his sermons
That the culver had come down from God in Heaven
As a messenger to Mohammed, for men's instruction.   400
Thus, by his wily wits and a white dove,
Mohammed led men to misbelief, and women too;
And learned and unlearned, there, still live by his laws.

   Now, since our Saviour let the Saracens be so beguiled
By a once-Christian cleric, accursed of soul . . .
But for dread of death I dare not tell the truth,
How the clergy of England feed a culver, called Covetousness,
And act so in Mohammed's manner that no man follows honesty.

   Anchorites and hermits and monks and friars
Are peers of the Apostles if they perfect their lives.   410
The Father of true faith would never wish that His ministers
Should take alms from tyrants that oppress true Christians,
But should do as Antony did, and Dominic and Francis,
And Benedict and Bernard, who had been their first teachers
Of how to live on little, in lowly houses, on loyal men's alms.[45]
Grace should grow like a green tree, through their good living;
And folk that have any form of sickness should find themselves
The better in body and soul for these men's beseeching God.
Their prayers and penances should pacify all
Who are at enmity, were these honest beadsmen: 420
    Petite, et dabitur vobis.
    (Ask, and it shall be given you.)[46]
Salt is a preservative, or so say housewives:
    Vos estis sal terrae.
    (Ye are the salt of the earth.)[47]
The heads of Holy Church, were they holy themselves,

Would be called by Christ "salt" for preserving Christian souls:
    Quod si sal evanuerit; in quo salietur?
   (But if the salt have lost his savour, wherewith shall it be
      salted?)[48]
For fresh meat or fish, with insufficient salt,
Is certainly insipid, whether seethed or baked.
So indeed is a man's soul, when set no good example
By those of Holy Church who should teach us the Highway,
And guide us, and go before us like good standard-bearers,
And by their own bravery embolden fallers-back.

   Eleven holy men converted all the world[49]   430
To the true faith; how much lighter a task it seems
If all manner of men (we have so many Masters
And priests and preachers, and a Pope as their head)
Became the salt that should save the souls of men!

  All England and Wales was at one time heathen,
Till Gregory appointed priests to come here and preach.
Augustine at Canterbury christened the King;[50]
And by miracles, as all men may read, converted that march-land
To Christ and Christendom and the honour of the Cross.
He baptised folk fast, and taught them the Faith   440
More through miracles than through much preaching,
As well through his works as through his holy words;
But he told them what baptism and faith were about.

  Cloth that comes straight from the loom cannot well be worn:
One must full it with one's feet, or in fulling-mills,
Wash it well in water, comb it with teasels;
Then, well tucked and tentered, it reaches the tailor's hands.
So a new-born baby, brought fresh from the womb,
Till christened in Christ's name, and confirmed by the Bishop,
Is a heathen still, and its soul is helpless to reach Heaven.   450
"Heathen" means "of the heath" or untilled land,
Like the wild beasts that thrive in the wider wilderness,
Rude and unreasoning, and running without restraint.

  You will remember how in St Matthew a certain man
                               planned a feast;
He fed his guests no deer-flesh or roast pheasants,
But on flesh of tame fowl that followed him when he whistled:
    Ecce, prandium meum paravi, tauri mei et altilia occisa sunt, et

omnia parata.
  (Behold, I have prepared my dinner: my oxen and my
    fatlings are killed, and all things are ready.)[51]
Also on calves' flesh he fed those folk that he loved,
For the calf betokens cleanness and keeping of the laws:[52]
As the cow feeds the calf on her milk until it becomes an ox,
So love and loyalty sustain true believers;   460
And maidens and mild men desire mercy and truth;
Just as the cow's calf covets sweet milk,
So must righteous men desire mercy and truth.
By the hand-fed fowls are meant those of God's folk
Who are loth to lose Him without learning by fables.
Just as capons in the courtyard come to men's whistle,
And follow the whistler for the sake of food,
So simple men without subtle reasoning –
May love and believe by example of the learnèd,
And wise men's works and words are their thought and belief.   470
And as fowls find their food by following a whistler,
So these hope to have Heaven by heeding the call of their pastors.
By the man who made the feast, Majesty is meant;
That is, God in His grace gives all men bliss:
Wonders and high winds are his warning whistles,
When He wishes to call us to come into His courtesy
And be fed and feasted for ever more.
    And who are those that excuse themselves? Parsons and priests,
The heads of Holy Church, who have all they want *here*,
And without trouble – taking their tithes from true men's toil.   480
They will be angry at my saying this, but as witnesses I call
Both Matthew and Mark, and the Psalm *Lord, remember David.*
        Ecce, audivimus eam in Ephrata.
    (Lo, we heard of it at Ephrata.)[53]
What Pope or prelate now performs what Christ bade?
        Euntes in mundum universum, praedicate Evangelium.
    (Go ye into all the world, and preach the Gospel to every
        creature.)[54]
Alas that men should remain, who believe in Mohammed,
While the Pope ordains so many prelates to preach
As Bishop of Nazareth, of Nineveh, of Naphtali or of Damascus![55]
Let them work as Christ wishes, if they want such titles,

And be true pastors, and preach the Passion of Jesus,
As He Himself said, and so live and die –

   Bonus pastor animam suam dat pro ovibus suis.

   (The good shepherd giveth his life for the sheep.)[56]

He said this for the salvation of Saracens and the like,   490
For unChristian as well as Christian he meant the words

   Ite vos in vineam meam.

   (Go ye also into the vineyard.)[57]

And since the Saracens and Scribes and Jews
Share a little of our belief, the lighter (surely) the task
Of whoever should try to convert them, and teach them the Trinity.

   Quaerite, et invenietis.

   (Seek and ye shall find.)[58]

   It arouses one's pity to read how the righteous lived,
Mortifying their flesh and forsaking their desires;
And, far from their kith and kin, they went poorly clad,
And barely bedded, conscience their only book,
And rejoicing in the Rood as their only riches:

   Mihi autem absit gloriari nisi in cruce Domini.

   (God forbid I should glory, save in the Cross of our Lord.)[59]

Then there was plenty and peace among poor and rich;   500
But now it rouses pity to read how the red gold-piece
Is reverenced more than the Rood, and received with more

                                                    worship

Than Christ's Cross which overcame death and deadly sin.
   And now there is war and woe; and the reason why
Is covetousness for that cross on the gold crown-piece;
Both the rich and the religious honour the rood
That is graven on groats and on gold nobles.
For coveting that cross, the clergy of Holy Church
Shall be tumbled as the Templars[60] were – the time is coming fast.
Have you not heard, you wise men, how these men honoured   510
Treasure more than truth? I dare not tell all the facts,
But Reason and Rightful Judgment condemned that

                                    Religious Order.

Just so, you clergy, they shall quickly condemn your covetousness,
And doom the "Church's Dowry",[61] and dispose your pride:

   Deposuit potentes de sede, et exaltavit humiles.

   (He hath put down the mighty from their seats, and

exalted them of low degree.)[62]

　If knighthood and native intelligence and the nation's conscience
Are loyal allies, then believe well, you Bishops,
You shall soon lose for ever your lordships over lands,
And live like Levites, as Our Lord teaches,

　　Per decimas et primitias.

　　(By your tithes and heave offerings.)[63]

　When Constantine, of his courtesy, gave Holy Kirk endowments
Of lands and labourers and lordships and rents,   520
An angel was heard to cry, in the air above Rome,
"The Church's dowry has today drunk poison,
And all who hold Peter's power are poisoned by it."[64]
Would there might be a medicine to amend those prelates
Who should pray for peace, but whose possessions prevent them!
Take their lands from them, you lords, let them live upon tithes.
If possessions are a poison, causing imperfect lives,
Better unburden them, on behalf of Holy Church,
And purge them of that poison before fresh perils befall us.

　If the priesthood were perfect, all the people would reform,   530
Who conflict with Christ's law, and hold Christendom
　　　　　　　　　　　　　　　　　　　　　in contempt.
For the paynims all pray to, and perfectly believe in,
The great and holy God, and His grace is their prayer,
Though they make their appeals to Mohammed, as their
　　　　　　　　　　　　　　　　　　　　intermediary.
Thus those folk have true faith, but a false intermediary;
And this is a pity for the pious, who are part of God's Kingdom,
And perilous to the Pope and the prelates that he makes –
Those who bear the names of Bishop of Bethlehem or Babylon.[65]

　When the High King of Heaven sent His Son to Earth,
He performed many miracles for Mankind's conversion,   540
As examples by which men should see that by sober reason
No man might be saved, but only by mercy and grace,
And by penance and pain, and by perfect belief.
He became man, born of a maiden, our great Metropolitan
　　　　　　　　　　　　　　　　　　　　Bishop;[66]
He baptised, and bishoped, with the blood of His heart,
All who would willingly believe Him within their conscience.
Many a saint since then has suffered death

To affirm the Faith, in countries far and wide:
They have died in India, Alexandria, Armenia, and Spain,
Dying dreadful deaths for their Faith's sake.   550
For the saving of Faith, St Thomas accepted martyrdom;
Because he loved Christ, he died among Christian traitors,[67]
To keep the rights of God's Kingdom, and of all Christian realms.
Holy Church is highly honoured by his dying;
He is a pattern to all prelates, a polished mirror,
And especially to such as have "Sees" in Syria,
But career about in *this* country, consecrating altars,
And creep-in among local curates to hear confessions –
                              against God's Law:
> *Si intraveris in segetem amici tui, franges spicas, et manu conteres:*
> *falce autem non metes.*

   (When thou comest into the standing corn of thy
      neighbour . . . thou shalt not move a sickle.)[68]
In Rome there were many men martyred for love of Christ,
Before Christianity came there, or the Cross was honoured.   560
   Every Bishop who bears a crozier is bound by that symbol
To proceed through his province, that his people may see him,
And to tell them and teach them true belief in the Trinity,
And feed them with spiritual food, and find for the poor:
Isaiah speaks of *your* sort, and so does Hosea;
They say none should be a bishop but he who gives
Both spiritual food and bodily, where those boons are needed:
> *In domo mea non est panis, neque vestimentum: nolite constituere*
> *me principem populi.*

   (In my house is neither bread nor clothing: make me not a
      ruler of the people.)[69]
And Hosea says, for such as are sick or feeble,
> *Inferte omnem decimam in horreum, et sit cibus in domo mea.*

   (Bring ye all the tithes into the storehouse, that there may
      be meat in my house.)[70]
Let us Christian creatures, who believe in Christ's Cross,
Hold firm in our faith – God forbid otherwise! –   570
And have clergy to keep us in it, *and* those who come after us.
   The Jews live under a true Law, that the Lord God Himself
                                             laid down
In stone, that it should be steadfast, and stand forever:

Dilige Deum et proximum.[71]

"Love God and love your neighbour" is Jewish Law to perfection,
And God gave it to Moses to teach men till Messiah should come.
Jews still live by that Law, and believe it the best.
Yet they could see that Christ, Christendom's founder,
Was a pure prophet, and that many people were saved by Him
From all sorts of sickness. They saw this often,
And other miracles and marvels: meals were given by Him,   580
From two loaves and five fishes, to five thousand people.[72]
By those meals, men should have seen that Messiah's look
                                        was on Him.
Likewise, He raised-up Lazarus, who had lain in the tomb
Dead, under a stone, and stank: in a strong voice He called him,

> *Lazare, veni foras.*

> (Lazarus, come forth.)[73]

And the dead man stood and strode where the Jews could see him.
Yet they said and swore it was by sorcery Christ did it;
And they set-about to destroy Him — and destroyed themselves,
For by His patience their power was brought to precisely nothing.

> *Patientes vincunt.*

> (The patient conquer.)

Daniel had predicted their undoing. He said,

> *Cum Sanctus Sanctorum veniat, cessabit unctio vestra.*

> (When the Holy of Holy comes, your anointment shall
> cease.)[74]

Yet those wicked ones still believe He was a pseudo-prophet,   590
And His teaching untrue; they contemn it all,
And believe their Redeemer to be unborn still,
Whether Moses again, or Messiah. Thus their Masters prophesy.
  But the Pharisees and Saracens and Scribes and Greeks
Are folk of one faith in that they worship God the Father;
And since, then, the Saracens and the Jews also
Recognise the first clause of our Creed:

> *Credo in Deum Patrem Omnipotentem.*

> (I believe in God the Father Almighty.)

The prelates of unChristian provinces should strive if possible
To make them learn, little by little,

> *Et in Jesum Christum filium*

(And in Jesus Christ His only Son),
Until they could spell out *et in spiritum sanctum*   600
    (and in the Holy Ghost),
And read and remember "in the remission of sins",
Until "the resurrection of the body, and life everlasting. Amen." '

Passus 16

'A happy fate befall you,' I said, 'for your fine sermon;
On account of Haukyn the Active Man, I shall always love you.
And yet I am still anxious about the meaning of Charity.'
    'Truly to tell,' said Reason, 'it is a *tree*, of great virtue.
Mercy is the name of its root, the stem of it is Pity;
Its leaves are the loyal words of the law of Holy Church;
Its blossoms are biddable speech and benignant looks.
The perfect tree is called Patience or Poverty of Spirit;
And, through God and the work of good men, it grows fruit
                                                called Charity.'
    'To see this tree, I would travel two thousand miles;   10
And to eat my fill of that fruit, forsake all other food.
Lord! Can I learn of *no one* the land where it grows?'
    'It grows in a garden that God Himself planted,
For the root of that stem is in the midst of Man's body,
And his heart is the humus that nourishes it.
Free-Will is the lessee of that land
From Piers the Ploughman, to hoe it and pull out weeds.'
'*Piers Ploughman!*' I cried; and for pure joy
At hearing his name again, into a swoon I fell,
And lay a long while in a lonely dream; till at last it seemed   20
That Piers the Ploughman was showing me all that place,
And bidding me take note of the tree from top to bottom.
Three props were supporting it, as I soon perceived.
    'Piers,' I said, 'I pray you, what are these props for?'
'Why, in case of windy weather,' said he, 'to keep it from falling:
        Cum ceciderit justus, non collidetur: quia Dominus supponit
            manum suam.
        (Though [a good man] fall, he shall not be utterly cast
            down, for the Lord upholdeth him with his hand.)*[1]*
For in budding-time the blooms would wither, but for those props:
The world is an ill wind for them who wish Truth,
For Covetousness comes on that wind, and creeps among the leaves

And for all its fair appearance gnaws away near the fruit.
So I push him down with the first prop – the power of God
the Father.   30
And the Flesh is a fierce wind; and in flowering time,
With lewdness and lust, it blows so loud
That it foments flirting looks and foul speech,
And the wicked works of the worms of sin
That bite-down the blossoms to the bare leaves.
So I set-to with the second staff – the wisdom of God the Father.
Namely, the Passion and power of the Prince Jesus.
And by prayer and by penance, and with that Passion in mind,
I save the tree till I see it ripen, and to some extent fruited.
But then the foul Fiend plots to destroy my fruit,   40
With all the wiles that he knows: he will shake the root of the tree,
Or hurl up at the harvest some hateful neighbours,
Or breach-of-the-peace backbiters, brawlers and quarrellers;
Or he lays a ladder up against it, with rungs of lies,
And sometimes filches my flowers before my very eyes.
But my lieutenant, who looks after the tree by my leave –
Free-Will – can for a while resist the Fiend:
    Qui autem dixerit contra Spiritum sanctum, non remittetur
    (Whosoever speaketh against the Holy Ghost, it shall
        not be forgiven him),
    Hoc est idem: qui peccat per liberum arbitrium non repugnat
    (And in like manner, [he speaks against the Holy Ghost]
        that sins of his free will, and resists not).[2]
But when the Fiend and the Flesh, in fellowship with the World,
Threaten furtively behind me to filch my fruit away,
Then Free-Will goes to work with the third prop,   50
And brings down the Devil by dint of pure grace
And help of the Holy Ghost; and so we have won.'
    'Happy fate befall you, Piers,' I said, 'for so well describing
The power of those props, and their particular virtues.
But I still have thriving thoughts about those three posts:
Of what wood are they, and where did they grow?
For all are of the same length, and none larger than others:
All have the same degree of girth and of greenness.
And it seems to me they must have grown from one root.'[3]
    'Certainly what you have said may well be so.   60

I will tell you in a nutshell what this tree implies.
The ground in which it grows is called Goodness;
And as for the tree itself – I have told you it betokens the Trinity.'
And he shot me such a sharp look, I felt I should not
Enquire any more about that; but I gently asked him
To let me know more of the fruit that lay luscious on the boughs.
'On the lowest boughs, here within reach when I wish,
Is Marriage – a most juicy fruit, I may say.
Closer to the crown is a grafting of Cailloux pears, called
                                        Continence;
And topmost, the tree's purest fruit, and most natural,   70
Maidenhead, equal of the angels, and earliest to ripen,
Sweet without swelling-up, and never souring.'[4]
    Then I prayed Piers to pluck me an apple, if he would,
So that I could ascertain what sort of taste they had.
He cast something up at the tree's crown, and the tree
                                        began crying;
He wagged the branch called widowhood, and again it wept;
But when he meddled with Marriage, it made such a din,
And wailed so woefully when he shook it, that I pitied it.
For whenever fruits fell down, there was the Fiend,
Eager to gather them up, both big and small –   80
Adam, and Abraham, and Isaiah the Prophet,
Samson, and Samuel, and St John the Baptist –
And bore them off bodily, with nobody to stop him,
And made a hoard of holy men in the Marches of Hell,[5]
Where dread and darkness are, and the Devil is master.
    Then Piers, in pure anger, picked up the prop
Called Son, by the Father's will and by grace of the Holy Spirit,
And hit out heedlessly at the Devil's hind-quarters,
To recapture from that wretch the fruits of his robbery.
    Then the Holy Ghost began speaking through Gabriel's mouth   90
To a maiden called Mary, of great meekness;
He said that one Jesus, a Judge's son, must sojurn in her bower
Till in *plenitudo temporis*, the fullness of time,[6]
Piers Ploughman's fruit had flowered and fully ripened.
Then Jesus should joust for that fruit, and judgment of arms
Should fix who should take the fruit, the Fiend or himself.
    The maiden meekly assented to this message,

And humbly said to him that she was God's handmaid,
Without sin, and willing to do as he wished.

    Ecce ancilla Domini; fiat mihi secundum verbum tuum.
  (Behold the handmaid of the Lord; be it unto me according
    to Thy word.)[7]

Then God was in her womb for forty weeks,   100
Till He was born from her flesh, a child fit to fight
And defeat the Fiend even before time was ripe.
But Piers the Ploughman[8] understood the plenary time,
And taught Him the art of healing, so as to save His life
Were He wounded by the enemy, and to work His own cure.
Piers made Him assay His skill upon sick people,
Till He was a perfect practitioner in any kind of peril.
And He sought-out the sick, and the sinful too,
And he cured the sick and the sinful, the crooked or blind,
And converted common whores to a clean life;   110

    Non est opus medicus valentibus, sed male habentibus.
  (They that be whole need not a physician, but they that are
    sick.)[9]

The dumb, and those with dysentery, and doomed lepers:
He often healed such people, and thought little of His powers –
Save when He lifted up Lazarus, who had lain in the grave
Four days dead, and arose living, and walked.
Then when He put forth His power, He was dispirited,
And wept water from His eyes, and was seen by many.[10]
Some that saw that sight said at the time
That He was Life's Healer, and Lord of High Heaven.
The Jews judged differently, and alleged by their laws
That He worked miracles by witchcraft, with the Devil's help: 120

    Daemonium habet, et insanit.
  (He hath a devil, and is mad.)[11]

  'Then you are serfs,' said Jesus, 'and your sons also,
And Satan is your saviour, as yourselves have borne witness.
I have saved you yourselves, and your offspring also,
Your bodies, and your beasts, and have cured blind men,
And fed you with two fishes and five loaves,
And left basketsful of broken meat to be borne-off by
                         whoever wished.'
Then He abused the Jews boldly, and threatened to beat them,

And laid into them with a lash, and threw low the tables
Of those who traded in the Temple and trafficked in money;[12]
And He said to all that stood there, so that everyone heard,   130
'I shall overturn this Temple and destroy it utterly,
And in three days re-erect it anew,
In every respect of the same size, or bigger,
As ever it was, and as wide; so I would have you
Call this a place of prayer and of perfection:[13]

    Domus mea domus orationis vocabitur.'

   (My house shall be called the house of prayer.)[14]
Envy and ill-will imbued the Jews;
They cast-about and contrived to kill Him if they could;
And day by day they bided their time,
Till one Friday, a little before the Feast of the Passover.
He had made His Maundy[15] after the meal on Thursday   140
When, sitting at supper, He said these words:
'I am betrayed by one of you, who shall bitterly rue the day
That he sold his Saviour for silver, or at all.'[16]

   Judas questioned this judgment, but Jesus told him
The man was indeed himself, saying, 'Thou hast said.'
Then that wicked man went out, and met with the Jews,
And told them a token by which to recognise Jesus
(A token which to this day is too much used) –
A kiss from a friendly countenance, with unkindness at heart;
Which is how it was with Judas when he betrayed Jesus.   150
'Hail, Rabbi,' said that wretch, and went right up to Him,
And kissed Him, to have Him caught and killed by the Jews.

   Then Jesus said to Judas, and the Jews also,
'I find falsity in your fair speech,
Guile in your glad face, and gall in your laughter.
You shall be made a mirror, to deceive many men;
But your wickedness, and the worst fate, will fall upon *you*:[17]

   *Necesse est enim ut veniant scandala: verumtamen vae homini
     illi, per quem scandalum venit.*

   (It must needs be that offences come; but woe to that man
     by whom the offence cometh.)[18]
But though I am treacherously taken, by intent of you all,[19]
Leave my apostles in peace, peacefully to depart.'

   Thus was He taken after twilight on that Thursday,   160

By Judas and the Jews. Jesus was His name,
Who on the Friday following, for the sake of mankind,
Jousted in Jerusalem, a joy to us all.
On the Cross on Calvary, Christ gave battle
Against Death and the Devil, and destroyed the power of Hell;
Dying, He undid Death, and made day out of night.[20]

   With this I awoke, and wiped my eyes,
And peered and stared all around for Piers the Ploughman;
Eastward and Westward I eagerly searched for him,
And set out as if insane, to search around the countryside   170
For Piers the Ploughman. I sought in many places,
Till on a Mid-Lent Sunday I met with a man
As hoary as a hawthorn; his name was Abraham.
At once I asked him where he had come from,
And where he lived, and whither he was bound.

   The old fellow said, 'I am Faith, I tell you no falsehood,
And a herald-of-arms in the house of Abraham.
I am seeking someone I have seen only once,
A bold knight-bachelor, whom I knew by his blazon.'
'What *is* the boy's blazon, God bless you?' I asked.   180
'Three persons in one body, all equal in height,
In majesty, and in might, and in all other measures.
What one does, all do, and each of his own accord.
The first has might and majesty, and made all things;
Pater is his proper name, this person being the Father.
Filius, the Son of that Sire, is the second, called Truth;
Warden of his sire's wisdom, he is without beginning.
The third has for name Holy Ghost, Himself a person,
The light of all that has life by land or water,
The comforter of all creatures, from whom comes all bliss.   190
A lord who lays claim to lordship needs three things:
Power, a path by which to prove that power,
And his servant's also, and what both suffer.[21]
Thus God Who could have no beginning unless it seemed
                       good to Him,
Sent forth His Son as a servant for a while,
To be busy here until the birth of children –
That is, the children of Charity, with Holy Church for mother.
Patriarchs and prophets and apostles were those children,

Also Christ and Christendom and the Christian Holy Church.
The meaning of this is that men must believe in one God,   200
Who, wherever He fashioned or favoured, took the form of
                                              three Persons.
Mankind itself is a sign that this is so in truth;
Wedlock and widowhood, with virginity named first,
In token of the Trinity, had their root in one man.
Adam, father of us all, had Eve spring from him;
And the issue that they had, sprang from them both,
And each is the other's joy, in three separate persons,
On Earth as in Heaven, yet with only one nature.
Thus mankind, and manhood, with marriage their source,
Betoken the Trinity, and true belief.   210
    Marriage is mighty, and multiplies the Earth,
And truly betokens, if I dare talk so,
The Father of Heaven, Who first framed all things.
The Son (if I dare say so) is a symbol of widowhood –
    Deus meus, Deus meus, ut quid dereliquisti me?
    (My God! My God! why hast thou forsaken me?)[22]
The Creator had become the creature, to know both kinds
                                              of being;
And as widows would not exist if wedlock did not,
No more could God become man except by means of a mother.
And if widowhood without wedlock is a contradiction,
So a sterile marriage is scarcely to be praised:
    Maledictus homo qui non reliquit semen in Israel.
    (Cursed is the man who has not left seed in Israel.)[23]
So mankind's perfection proceeds from three persons in unity,   220
Man and his mate and their legitimate offspring
(Though Jesus Christ in Heaven was engendered by one
                                              gender only.)[24]
The Father puts forth the Son, and free-will springs from both,
As also the Holy Ghost does, yet all are but one God:
    Spiritus procedens a Patre et Filio.
    (The Holy Ghost proceeding from Father and Son.)
Thus I saw Him one summer, as I sat in my porch.[25]
I rose up and did Him reverence, and greeted Him right fairly;
Yet it seemed that I saw and received three men.
I washed and wiped their feet, and afterwards they ate

Calves' flesh and cakebread; and they could read my mind.
Sure tokens passed between us, and I am free to tell them.   230
   First, He tested me to see if I loved better
Him or Isaac my heir, whom He ordered me to kill.[26]
Thus He grew aware of my will; and he will praise me for it,
And my son too; I am certain of that, in my soul.
For His sake I circumcised my son Ishmael;
And I myself too, and all the males of my household,
Bled for love of that Lord, and hope of His blessing.[27]
My faith and fealty are firm in this belief;
For He Himself has promised me, and all my issue,
Land and lordship and eternal life.[28]   240
Yet to me and to my issue he granted still more:
Mercy upon our misdeeds, as many times as we ask it:
      *Sicut locutus est ad patres nostros, Abraham, et semini ejus in
      saecula.*
      (As he spoke to our fathers, to Abraham, and to his seed for
      ever.)[29]
Then He sent me a message to say I should make sacrifice,
And worship Him with both bread and wine.[30]
He called me a foundation-stone of His faith, for the saving
                                                          of His people,
And to defend from the Fiend all those who followed me.
Thus I have been His herald, both on Earth and in Hell,
Where I comforted many of the careworn that await His coming.[31]
And this is why I seek Him; for I recently heard say
That somebody baptised him, John Baptist by name –   250
Who to patriarchs and prophets and other people in that darkness
Has said that he saw here the Salvation of us all:
      Ecce agnus Dei, ecce qui tollit peccatum mundi.'
      (Behold the Lamb of God, which taketh away the sin of the
      world.)[32]
   I wondered at his words, and at the width of his garments;
For in his bosom he bore something that he continually blessed.
I looked at the overlap, and saw that a leper lay there
Among patriarchs and prophets in great pleasure.
'Why are you waiting? What do you want?' he asked.
'I should like to learn what you have in your lap.'
So he let me see, saying, 'Lo!' 'Lord have mercy!' said I.

'That is a present of great price! What Prince is it for?'   260
'It is a precious present; but the Devil has appropriated it —
And me into the bargain; no pledge can buy us back,
Nor anybody go bail to bring us out of his power,
Nor any mainprise procure our release from his pound,
Till He of whom I tell (and Christ is His name)
Shall some day deliver us from the Devil's power
By offering a better pledge for us than we could be worth:
That is, life for life. Else, these will lie for ever
Lounging in my lap until such a lord comes for us.'

   'Alas,' I said, 'that sin should hinder so long   270
The might of God's mercy, that has power to amend us all!'
And I wept at his words. Then at once I saw someone else,
Rapidly running in our direction.
I enquired of him what he was called, and whence he came,
And where he was going; and he willingly told me.

He said, 'I am Spes, or Hope; and I seek a knight
Who gave me a commandment upon Mount Sinai
With which to rule all realms. Here *is* that writ.'
'Is it sealed?' I said. 'Can one see the script?'
And Hope said, 'No; I seek Him in whose charge the seal is,
That shows Christendom, and Christ hanging on the Cross.[1]
And when my writ is so sealed, I know for a certainty
That the lordship of Lucifer shall last no longer.'
'Let us see this letter,' I said, 'and learn that law.'
So he pulled out his patent – a piece of hard rock   10
Whereon there were written only eight words, and a comment:
    '*Diliges Dominum Deum, et proximum tuum sicut teipsum.*'
    (Thou shalt love the Lord thy God, and thy neighbour as
       thyself.)[2]
This truly was all the text, for I took a good look;
But the gloss was gorgeously written in gold ink:
    '*In his duobus mandatis universa lex pendet, et prophetae.*'
    (On these two commandments hang all the Law and the
       Prophets.)[3]
'Are these,' I asked, 'your Lord's only laws?' 'Believe me, they are.
And whoever lives by those laws, I will attest
That the Devil shall not daunt him nor Death affright his soul.
For though I say it myself, I have saved with this charm
Many score thousands of men, and of women too.'
   'He is telling the truth,' said the herald, 'as I myself can testify.
Look: here in my lap are some who believed in those laws: 20
Joshua, and Judith, and Judas Maccabaeus;
Oh, and sixty thousand besides, whom you do not see here.'
'Your words are wonderful. But which of you is truer?
Belief in whom is likelier for the life of the soul?
Abraham says that he saw the Holy Trinity,
Three separate Persons, distinct from each other
And all only one God. This is Abraham's teaching,

And has saved those who believed, and were sorry for their sins:
He cannot count them all, but he carries some in his lap.
Then I do not see the need for starting a new law,   30
Since the first is sufficient for salvation and Heaven.

    Yet here comes Hope, who claims to have found that law;
And he tells us nothing of the Trinity that gave him the statute
"Believe in, and love, one Lord God Almighty,
And love, as you love yourself, all other people."

    The man who walks with one staff is better off,
It seems to us all, than one who walks with two.
Precisely so, by the Rood, it stands to reason
That unlettered men will more easily learn one lesson
(The simplest a terrible task!) than be taught two.   40
It is not easy for any man to believe Abraham;
And how much worse – woe's me – to love wicked neighbours!
One more easily believes in three loveable Persons
Than one loves, or lets be, the louts as well as the likeable.
Gang your gate, Hope, for God's sake,' said I.
'Those who learn *your* law will not long observe it!'

    As we thus went our way, reasoning with one another,
We saw a Samaritan sitting on a mule,[4]
And rapidly riding in our direction.
He was coming from a country that men call Jericho,   50
And was jogging off quickly to a jousting in Jerusalem.[5]
Abraham the Herald, and Hope and he, all met together
Where a man was lying wounded, left there by highwaymen.
He could neither stagger nor stand, nor stir hand or foot,
Nor help himself anyhow, for he seemed half dead,
Naked as a needle, and no one to help him.

    Faith had first sight of him, and fled on the other side,
And would not come near him by nine fathoms' length.

    Then Hope came hiking by, he who had boasted
How with Moses' commandments he had saved many men;   60
But as soon as he saw that victim, he dodged aside –
With as much dread, by God, as a duck from a falcon.

    Yet as soon as the Samaritan had seen that man,
He got down off Dapple, and led it by the bridle
To where the man was. He examined his wounds,
And perceived by his pulse that he was in peril of death

And, unless he was rapidly roused, might never rise again.
So he bustled to his bottles, and opened them both,
And washed the man's wounds with oil and wine,
Anointed and bound-up his head, and laid him in his lap,   70
And brought him on the mule to a manor men call Christ's Law,
Some six miles, or seven, from the New Market.
He entered him at an inn, and said to the inn-keeper:
'Take this man in, and tend him till I return from the jousting.
Here is some silver to buy salve for his wounds.'[6]
And he gave him twopence extra towards the man's board,
Saying, 'If he spends more, I will see you repaid later;
I will not delay now.' So, astride on his Dapple,
He rode off in a rush on the direct road to Jerusalem.

   Faith, who wanted to meet him, followed him fast;   80
And Hope made haste, in case *he* had a chance
To overtake him and talk to him before they reached the town.
When I saw this, I did not stay, but started running
In pursuit of that Samaritan who had shown so much pity,
And offered myself as his servant. He said, 'I thank you;
But I offer you, rather, friendship and fellowship in need.'

   I thanked him too, and then began to tell him
How Faith and his friend Hope had fled away
When they found that poor fellow who had fallen among thieves.
'You may excuse them,' said he, 'for their help would not
                                            have been useful;   90
No medicine on Earth may bring that man back to health –
Neither Faith nor Hope – his wounds have festered so,
Except the blood of a boy born of a maiden.
If he is bathed, or baptised as it were, in that blood,
Then plastered with penance, and with the Passion of that child,
He will stand, and step forward; but he will never be stalwart
Till he has eaten all the child, and drunk its blood.
Not one man in the world has passed through that wilderness,
Whether walking or riding, without being robbed and rifled,
Except Faith and his friend Hope and myself as third –   100
And now *yourself*, since you follow suit with us.

   For outlaws lurk in the woods and below the banks,
Where they may see every man, and mark exactly
Who is behind, who before, and who is on horseback

(For a man on a horse has more courage than he who walks).
So when their chief saw me, a Samaritan, pursue Faith and Hope,
On my mount whose name is Flesh (which I got from Mankind),
That whoreson lost heart, and hid himself in Hell.
But I assure you, before three days are over
The felon shall be fettered fast in chains,   110
And never again grieve travellers who go that way.
    Ero mors tua, O mors!
    (Oh death, I will be thy death!)
  Then Faith shall be forester here, and walk this frith,
Escorting common folk who do not know the country
To the way that I went, which leads to Jerusalem.
And Hope shall serve the hosteller, where the traveller lies healing.
All who are feeble and faint, whom Faith cannot teach,
Hope shall lead on with love, as his own law bids;
He shall be their host and their healer through the faith of
                                    Holy Church,
Till I have salves for all sick men; then I shall be seen again:
I shall come again to this country, and comfort all the sick   120
Who crave or covet or cry out for a cure.
For that boy has been born in Bethlehem, whose blood shall save
All who live by Faith and follow his friend Hope's teaching.'
  'Ah, sweet sir, but what *shall* I believe?' said I.
'As Faith and his friend both informed me?
Three separate Persons living perpetually,
All three only one God — thus Abraham taught me.
And, afterwards, Hope instructed me to love
One God with all my might, and all other men afterwards;
To love them like myself, but Our Lord above all.'   130
'Set fast your faith and firm belief
Upon Abraham, that Herald-of-Arms.
And as Hope ordered, so I also say,
Love your fellow-Christians just as you love yourself.
And if Conscience or Common-sense should combat
                                  that teaching,
Or heretics heckle you — show them your hand.
For God is like a hand: hear me, and learn how.
  First is the Father, like a fist with fingers folded —
Until it was His liking to unloose them

And protrude them from the palm whenever He pleased.   140
For the palm is properly the hand, and protrudes the fingers
To make or administer as much as is in its power.
So it truly betokens – and so you may tell them –
The Holy Ghost in Heaven: *He* is the palm.
The fingers are free either to fold or to act,
And so symbolise the Son, who was sent to Earth
And touched and entered (at the Palm's teaching)
St Mary the Maiden, and became a man.
>   *Qui conceptus est de spiritu sancto – etc.*
>   (Who was conceived by the Holy Ghost – etc.)[7]
So the Father is a fist with Fingers that can touch
All that the Palm perceives as proper to handle.   150
>   *Quia omnia traham ad me ipsum.*
>   (I will draw all things unto me.)[8]
Thus all three of them are but one, as the hand is,
And yet are separate selves in a single Being.
Because the palm puts forth fingers and fist as well,
So, in the same way, as we can see is reasonable,
He Who is Holy Ghost puts forth both Father and Son.
   And, as the hand can hold things hard and fast
With four fingers, thumb, palm, and so forth,
So the Father and Son and the Holy Spirit
Hold all the wide world between the three of them:
The windy welkin, the earth and the water,   160
Heaven and Hell, and all that they hold.
Thus it is (and no man need believe any different)
That three Persons are present in our Heavenly Lord
Separate in themselves, yet sundered never –
Any more than my hand can move without my fingers.
My fist is a full hand when folded together;
Thus the Father is fully God, as former and creator:
>   *Tu fabricator omnium . . .*
>   (Thou the Maker of all things . . .)
And all the might He commands is as a Maker.
   The fingers form a full hand, for drawing or painting
Or carving or contriving, for their craft is such: 170
Just so, the Son is the *skill* of the Father,
Yet fully God as the Father is, neither feebler nor stronger.

The palm, that is properly the hand, has power of its own,
Apart from the clenched fist or the fingers' craft;
For the palm has power to project all the joints,
And unfold the clenched fist, for it is the palm's place
To receive or reject what the fingers reach for
When it feels the fist's or the fingers' wishes.

    So the Holy Ghost is God, neither greater nor less
Than Sire or Son, and of the same power.   180
And they are all one God, as my hands and fingers,
My fist, whether folded or unfolded, and my palm,
All form only one hand, however I turn it.
If a man is hurt in the middle of his hand,
It is obvious that he is unable to grasp anything;
For the fingers that should fold, and so form the fist,
Have lost their power, because of pain in the palm,
To clutch or clasp or take a close hold.

    If the middle of my hand were maimed or pierced,
I could retain really nothing of what I reached for.   190
Yet even if my thumb and fingers were all cut-about,
But the middle of my hand without maltreatment,
I might help myself in many kinds of ways –
Though my fingers might ache, I could move and adjust them.

    It seems to me that I see a symbol here:
Whoever sins against the Holy Spirit shall never be saved,
Neither here nor hereafter, as I have heard tell.

> *Qui autem blasphemaverit in Spiritum Sanctum non habebit*
>   *remissionem in aeternum*
>   (He that shall blaspheme against the Holy Ghost hath never
>   forgiveness),[9]

For he who trespasses thus has pierced God's palm.
For God the Father is like a fist, the Son like a finger,
And the Holy Ghost in Heaven is as it were the hand's palm. 200
So to sin against the Holy Spirit, so to speak injures
God in the part He grasps with; and His grace is killed.[10]

    The Trinity is likened also to a torch or a taper,
Which has wax and wick as it were intertwined,
And a flame that comes flaring out from both;
Just as wax and wick and the warmth of fire combine
To form a flame and so light a fire,

So do Father and Son and Holy Spirit
Foster belief and love among folk,
And cleanse all kinds of Christians from their sins.   210
And as you will sometimes see a torch that suddenly
Has the blaze of it blown out, though the wick still burns
Without light or flame to ignite the tinder:
So the Holy Ghost is God and Grace without mercy,
To all who unnaturally wish to destroy
Loyal love or the life that Our Lord created.
　　And as glowing embers are of less relief to workmen
Who must stay awake and work on winter nights
Than a link or a candle that has caught fire, and blazes:
No more do Sire and Son and Holy Spirit   220
Grant any grace or forgiveness of sins
Till the Holy Ghost begins to glow and blaze.
The Holy Ghost will glow as gloomily as an ember
Till true love lies by Him, and blows the flame;
Then He flames like a fire upon Father and Son,
And melts their might into mercy. You may see in winter
How icicles hanging from eaves, when the sun shines out,
Will melt in a minute into mist and water:
So, by grace of the Holy Ghost, the great might of the Trinity
Is melted into mercy – but for the merciful only.   230
And as wax, with nothing else, on a warm ember
Will blaze up and burn because they have met,
And bring solace to those who were sitting in darkness, and see it,
So will the Father forgive folk of humble heart,
Who remorsefully repent and make restitution,
And by making amends inasmuch as they may.
If his assets do not suffice, though he dies in such a mind,
Then Mercy, because of his meekness, will make up the rest.
And as wick and fire will make a warm flame,
And make men cheerful, who were sitting in murk,   240
So Christ of His courtesy (if men cry for His mercy)
Both forgives and forgets, and prays for us too,
To our Father in Heaven, to have forgiveness.
　　But you may hack fire from a flint for four hundred winters,
And unless you have tow or tinder or kindling to catch the sparks,
All your labour and your long toil are lost;

No fire can make flame if it lacks a fellow-substance.
Thus the Holy Ghost is God and Grace without mercy
To all that act against nature — as Christ Himself says:
    Amen dico vobis, nescio vos.
    (Verily I say unto you, I know you not.)[11]
    Be unkind to your fellow-Christian, and you can pray,   250
Deal-out alms, and do penance, day and night for ever,
And purchase all the pardons in Pamplona and Rome,
And no end of indulgences: be ungrateful to your fellows,
And the Holy Ghost will not hear you, nor help you, because of it.
For unkindness quenches Him, so that He cannot shine,
Nor burn or blaze clearly, since unkindness blows Him out.
    Paul the Apostle proves whether I lie:
    Si linguis hominum loquar. . . etc.
    (Though I speak with the tongues of men . . . etc.)[12]
So beware, you wise men of worldly affairs,
You who are rich and can reason, rule your souls well.
I counsel you, be not unkind to your fellow-Christians;   260
For upon my soul, many of you rich men, as men have told me,
May burn, but do not blaze: you are blind beacons.
    Non omnis qui dicit mihi, Domine . . . etc.
    (Not everyone that saith unto me, Lord, Lord, shall enter
        into the Kingdom of Heaven.)[13]
Dives[14] died in damnation for his unkindness
In withholding meat and money from men who needed them.
I recommend all rich men to remember him,
And give their goods back to that God Whose grace provided them.
For those who misuse His people, I hope no better
Than that they dwell where Dives is, all the days of eternity.
Thus unkindness is God's contrary, and kills, as it were,
The Grace of the Holy Ghost, that is God's own nature.   270
What Nature does, unkindness undoes as do those cursed thieves,
Unkind Christians, who for covetousness and envy,
And whether by mouth or by hand, will slay men for their
                                        moveables.
What the Holy Ghost has in keeping, those whoresons destroy;
That is, life and love, and the light in Man's body.
For all good men, in like manner, may be likened to torches
Or tapers, that are offered in reverence to the Trinity;

And whoever murders a good man, so it seems to my conscience,
Puts out the light that Our Lord loves most dearly.
    There are many more ways in which men offend the
                                                  Holy Ghost,   280
But that is the worst way open to anyone,
Of sinning against the Holy Spirit; to destroy, of set purpose,
For covetousness of any kind, what Christ bought dearly.
How can a man ask for mercy, or mercy help him,
Who wickedly and willingly would extinguish mercy?
Innocence stands nearest to God, and it cries day and night,
"Vengeance, vengeance! May it never be forgiven,
The sin that ruined us, spilt our blood, and as it were uncreated us!
    Usquequo, Domine, non vindicas sanguinem nostrum?"
    (How long, O Lord, doest thou not judge and avenge our
      blood?)[15]
Thus, "Vengeance, vengeance!" even Charity may cry;
And since Holy Church and Charity charge this so strongly,   290
I cannot believe that Our Lord will love those lacking charity,
Nor pity them despite their mournful prayers.'
    'But suppose *I* had sinned so and, being about to die,
Were sorry that I had so offended the Holy Spirit;
That I made my confession, and cried to God the Creator for grace
And meekly begged Him for mercy: might I not be saved?'
    'Yes,' said the Samaritan, 'it is possible that you might repent
                              so perfectly
That, through your repentance, the rigour of justice might relax.
But it is seldom seen, after straightforward testimony,
That a criminal once condemned by a King's Justice   300
Is rescued by his repentance, once reasonably found guilty.
For when a plaintiff is the prosecutor, the imputation is so grave
That the King himself cannot pardon unless both parties
                                     come to terms,
And each is equally content, as Holy Writ says:
    Numquam dimittitur peccatum, donec restituatur ablatum.
    (A sin is never remitted until what has been taken is restored.)[16]
Thus those folk fare who, in falsehood all their lives,
Live evilly, and do not leave off until life forsakes them;
Then dread of despair drives away grace,
And mercy may not enter their minds after that;

Hopelessness kills the good hope that should have helped them:
Not because God has no power, or is unable   310
To amend all that is amiss, for His mercy is greater
Than all our ill deeds, as is written in the Scriptures:
   Miserationes ejus super omnia opera ejus.
   (His tender mercies are over all his works.)[17]
But before He turns justice to mercy, men must make
                                        some restitution;
And sorrow will suffice if a man lacks all else.
   There are three things, as the Holy Scripture tells,[18]
That force a man to flee from his own house:
One is a scolding wife who will not be reproved,
And who forces her husband to take flight, for fear of her tongue.
The next is an ill-roofed house that leaks rain upon his bed,
So that he searches elsewhere for a dry place to sleep.   320
The third is when smoke and smoulder smother his eyes –
And that is worse than his wife, or sleeping wet.
For smoke and smoulder will smother his sight
Till he is bleary-eyed and half-blind, and hoarse in the throat,
And coughs and curses, "May Christ send them sorrow,
Who didn't bring in better wood, or blow till it burned well!"
   These three things that I tell of, I interpret thus:
The wife is our wicked flesh, that will not be chastened,
For nature will not leave it, nor cease to war with the soul;
Yet if it falls, we find excuses in its frailty;   330
Fleshly sins are easily forgiven and forgotten
To a man who asks for mercy and means to do better.
   The rain that runs in where we should be resting,
Is the sicknesses and sorrows we so often suffer,
As St Paul the Apostle taught Christian people:
   Virtus in infirmitate perficietur.
   (My strength is made perfect in weakness.)[19]
And though men may make much ado of their infirmities,
And be impatient in such penances, pure reason shows
That they have cause to complain, being sick or sad.
And Our Lord will easily, at the end of their lives,
Have mercy on such men, who bemoaned their suffering.   340
   But the smoke and smoulder that smother men's eyes,

Those are covetousness and unkindness, and they put-out
                                        God's mercy;
For unkindness is the contrary of any kind of reason,
And no one is so sick or sorrowful or so very wretched
That he cannot love if he elects to, and lend from his heart
Good will or good words, and wish for their sake
Mercy and forgiveness for all manner of men,
And love others as he loves himself, and amend his life.
But I must delay no longer.' He laid spurs to his mount,
And went away like the wind. And with this, I awoke.   350

Wool next my skin, and wet-shod, I went on again,
As a reckless rover regardless of misfortune,
Wandering like a wastrel, all my life long,
Till at last I wearied of the world, and was yearning to sleep;
And at one Lent I relaxed, and slept a long time.
So I stayed there, snoring hard, until Palm Sunday,
And dreamed long of Christ's Passion, and His penance that
                              redeemed all people,
And of boys and girls singing *Gloria, Laus*, 'Praise and Glory',
And of how the old folk sang *Hosanna* to the organ.[1]
   Somebody like the Samaritan, yet somewhat like
                              Piers Ploughman,   10
Came riding, bootless and barefoot, on an ass's back,
With neither spur nor spear. But he looked sprightly,
As is the nature of a knight newly coming to be dubbed
And get his golden spurs and gallant shoes.[2]
   Faith stood looking from a casement, and cried out,
                              'O Son of David!'
Like a Herald-at-Arms announcing an adventurer come to joust,
And the aged Jews of Jerusalem sang for joy,
   Benedictus qui venit in nomine Domini!
   (Blessed is he that comes in the name of the Lord!)[3]
   I asked Faith the meaning of all this ado,
And who was coming to joust in Jerusalem. He said, 'Jesus,
To fetch back from the Fiend the fruit of Piers Ploughman.'[4]   20
'Is Piers in this place?' I asked; and his look pierced me:
'Jesus, out of gentilesse, will joust in Piers's blazon,
And in his helmet and hauberk, Human Nature by name,
So that Christ shall not be recognised here as the King of Heaven;
And Jesus shall joust in Piers Ploughman's jerkin,
For no blow He endures can dismay Him in His natural Divinity.'
'And who shall joust against Jesus? The Jews and Scribes?'
   'No; the foul Fiend, False Condemnation, and Death.

Death has threatened to undo and bring down
All things that live or lurk by land or water;   30
Life says that he lies, and has laid Himself as pledge
That for anything Death can do, within three days
He will go and fetch from the Fiend Piers Ploughman's fruit,
And lodge it where he likes, and chain-up Lucifer,
And batter down and destroy Death and Sorrow for ever.'
  Ero mors tua, O mors!
  (O death, I will be thy death.)[5]
Then Pilate came, with a swarm of people, and sat in the
                Judgment Seat
To see how doughtily Death would fight, and to umpire
                 the dispute.
The Jews and the Judge himself sided against Jesus,
And all the Court cried-out shrilly, 'Crucify Him!'
Then a pillager appeared before Pilate, and said,   40
'This Jesus jeered at, and scorned, our Jewish temple;
He said he could destroy it in a day, and after three days
Erect it all anew – and there he stands, who said it! –
And would remake it the same in every measurement,
In length and latitude and loftiness and capacity.'
A constable cried, 'Crucify him! I'll warrant he's a warlock!'
Another cried, 'Off with him! Off with him!' And he took
              some sharp thorns
And twisted their spiny twigs into a chaplet
Which he savagely set on Christ's head, with mocking speech:
'Hail, Rabbi!' said that ribald, and poked reeds at Him,[6]   50
Then nailed Him naked, with three nails. to the Cross.
They pushed poison towards His lips, on the end of a pole,
And bade Him drink His death-draught, for His days were done.
'And if you have magic art, use it to help yourself.'
'If you are Christ, and a King's son, come down from the cross:
Then we shall believe that the Lord of Life loves you, and
              will not let you die!'
  Christ said, '*Consummatum est*,' and commenced to swoon,
As piteously pale as a dying prisoner;
Then the Lord of Life and Light laid His eyelids together.
The daylight withdrew in terror, the sun grew dark,   60
The Temple wall trembled and split, and the whole world shook.

Hearing that din, dead men left their deep graves,
And told why that tempest lasted such a long time.
Said one dead body, 'There is a bitter battle.
Life and Death, in this darkness, are trying to destroy each other,
Nor shall anyone know truly which of them has won,
Until Sunday, around sunrise.' And he sank back into the soil.
Some said Christ was God's son, so finely He died:
    'Vere Filius Dei erat iste.'
    (Truly this was the Son of God.)[7]
But some said He was a warlock, 'And we had better make certain
He is dead indeed, before taking him down.'   70
Two thieves also suffered death on that day,
On crosses beside Christ, as the Common Law then was.
A constable came and cracked the legs of both,
And afterwards the arms of either thief;
But nobody was so bold as to touch God's body:
Because He was a cavalier, and a King's son, Nature forbade
                                for once
That any whoreson should have the courage to lay hands on Him.
   But [Nicodemus says] a knight soon came, with a
                               sharp-ground spear;
Longinus was his name, and long since he had lost his sight.
He came to that place where Pilate and the other people were;   80
And demur as he might, they made him there and then
Take the spear into his hands and tilt against Jesus;
For none who was there, on horseback or foot, had courage
To attack or touch Him, or take Him down from the Cross.
But this blind knight-bachelor drove the blade through His heart
And the blood streamed down the spear and unsealed the
                                knight's eyes.
Then the knight fell to his knees and asked forgiveness:
'Lord, it was not my will to wound you so sharply!'
He sighed then, and said, 'I sorely repent.
For the cruelty I have committed. I cast myself on your mercy.   90
Have pity on me, Just Jesus!' And with this, Longinus wept.
   Then Faith fiercely rebuked the false Jews,
Calling them caitiffs, accursed eternally
For their vile villainy – 'Vengeance light on you all!
To make a blind man strike a bound man was a beastly thought.

You curséd cowards, it was never called chivalry
To abuse a dead body, by night or day.
But despite the great gash, Christ gains the prize;
For your champion of champions, chief knight of you all,
Yields himself recreant, resigned to the rule of Christ.   100
Once this darkness has departed, His death will be avenged;
And you, my lords, have lost, for Life shall be sovereign,
And the freedom of your franchise has fallen into slavery.
You and your children shall be churls, and achieve nothing,
Nor have lordship over lands, nor have land to till,
But be altogether barren, and live by usury –
A life that in all His laws Our Lord has cursed.
Now your good days are done, as Daniel prophesied:
When Christ came, crowning in that kingdom should cease!
  Cum veniat Sanctus Sanctorum, cessabit unctio vestra.'
  (When the Holy of Holies comes, your anointing shall cease.)[8]
 For fear of these phenomena, and the falsity of the Jews,   110
I withdrew through the darkness, and went down to
         the underworld.
And there in good sooth I saw (as we may read in the Psalms)[9]
A wench who came from the west (so went my dream).[10]
She came walking my way, and was looking towards Hell.
This maiden was called Mercy, and was of mild nature,
A gracious girl, and of goodly speech.
 Her sister, as it seemed, came softly walking
Exactly out of the East, and was looking westward:
She was indeed a comely creature, and was called Truth;
By reason of the power surrounding her, she was never afraid.   120
 When these two maidens, Mercy and Truth, had met,
Each asked the other about those great wonders –
The din, and the darkness, and the sudden daybreak –
And what were that gleam and that glory at the gates of Hell.[11]
Truth said, 'I am amazed indeed by all these matters,
And have come thus far to find out the meaning of the affair.'
Said Mercy, 'Do not marvel; it means great joy.
A maiden called Mary, unmeddled-with by man,
Or any kind of creature, has conceived by the Word
And Grace of the Holy Ghost, and grown big with child;   130
Without blame or blemish did she bring him into this world,

And that my tale is true, I take God to witness.
Since the boy was born, thirty winters have gone by;
And he endured death at almost noon today.
That is the cause of the eclipse that occludes the sun;
For its meaning is that Man shall be drawn from his murk,
While this gleam and this glory shall leave Lucifer blind.
Patriarchs and prophets have often preached
That man shall save man through the help of a maiden;
That that which was lost through a tree, a tree should restore,[12]   140
And that a death should raise up those whom Death
                                        brought down.'
    'What you are telling,' said Truth, 'is a tale of mumbo-jumbo.
Adam and Eve, and Abraham and others –
Patriarchs and prophets – that now lie in pain,
Will never be lifted aloft by that light over there,
Nor be heaved out of Hell. Hold your tongue, Mercy!
You are talking trash: I am Truth, and know what is *so*.
He who is once in Hell, comes out no more;
The prophet and patriarch Job disproves your sayings:
        Qui descenderit ad inferos, non ascendet.'
        (He that goeth down to the grave shall come up no more.)[13]
Then Mercy answered mildly, in this manner: 150
'It is experience that makes me hope they shall be saved.
For poison casts out poison, as reason proves:
The vilest of all venoms is that of a scorpion;
No medicine may remedy the part that it stings,
Till the dead creature is laid on the wound, and undoes the harm,
The first venom destroyed by the venom itself.
So shall this death undo, I dare wager my life,
All that Death first undid through the Devil's enticement;
And just as man was beguiled by guile,
So the Grace by which man was begun shall itself beguile well: 160
        Ars ut artem falleret.
        (Art that shall deceive art.)[14]
    Said Truth, 'Let us pause, for I seem to see
(Coming from the nip of the North, and not far away)
Righteousness running towards us: let our argument rest,
For she is our elder, and wiser than we.'
'For certain; and also I see, in the South,

Peace gaily approaching, robed in patience.
Love has longed for her so lastingly, I believe no less
Than that He sent her a message about what this light means,
That hovers over Hell: perhaps she will tell us.'
  When Peace, robed in patience, had approached the others,   170
Righteousness did her reverence for her rich dress,
And prayed Peace to tell her where she planned to go
In those gay garments, and whom she had hoped to greet.
  'I will away,' she said, 'to welcome all those
Who have long been hidden from me by the hell-dark of sin:
Adam and Eve, and many more in Hell,
Moses among them, shall have mercy shown them.
And I shall dance at the sight – sister, dance too!
For since Jesus jousted well, joy's dawn begins.
    Ad vesperum demorabitur fletus: et ad matutinum laetitia.
    (Weeping may endure for a night, but joy cometh in the
      morning.)[15]
Love, who is my belovéd, sent a letter to me,   180
Saying Mercy my sister and I should save Mankind;
That God has given and granted to Peace and Mercy
To be Mankind's mainpernors, now and for ever more.
See here the letters-patent!' said Peace. '*In pace in idipsum*;
And, that this Deed shall endure, *dormiam et requiescam.*'
    (I will both lay me down in peace, and sleep.)
  Said Righteousness: 'Are you raving? Or roaring drunk?
Do you believe that that light can unlock Hell,
And save men's souls? Sister, never believe it!
God, in the beginning, gave this judgment Himself,
That Adam and Eve and all that came after them   190
Should die downright, and dwell in anguish afterwards,
If they touched a certain tree, and tasted its fruit.
After this, Adam, against that forbiddal,
Did feast on that fruit, and forsook, as it were,
The love of Our Lord, and His Law also,
And did as the Devil taught, and Eve desired,
Against all reason. I, Righteousness, record for certain
That their pains will be perpetual, and no prayer help them:
Let them chew as they chose; and let us not chide, sisters,
For what they bit off was a bane no balm will cure.'   200

'I shall prove,' said Peace, 'that their pains must have an end,
And woe turn to weal when the time is ripe;
For had they never known grief, they could not know happiness –
No man knows what weal is, who has not met woe,
Nor what it is to hunger, who has never lacked food.
If there were no night, nobody, I believe,
Would understand entirely what is meant by day;
Nor any really rich man, living in rest and comfort,
Understand any distress, were natural death done away with.
So God, by Whom all began, of His great goodness   210
Became a man, born of a maiden, to save all men and women,
And allowed Himself to be sold, to learn the sorrow of death
That unravels all regret, and is the arrival of rest.
For until we meet meagreness, I may tell you,
None of us knows what "enough" may mean.

    Therefore God in His goodness gave the first man, Adam,
A condition of comfort and of complete bliss;
But soon He allowed him to sin, and experience sorrow,
So as to know within him the nature of happiness.
And then He set Himself at risk, and assumed Adam's nature,   220
So as to know his suffering, in three separate places –
In Heaven and on Earth and soon, he intends, in Hell,
To learn what utter woe is, Who knows utter joy.
So shall these folk fare; their folly and sin
Shall teach them torment first, then eternal bliss.
No person, where peace reigns, can appreciate war,
Nor utter contentment until *welladay* teaches him.'

    And now there appeared a person with two wide-open eyes;
Book was this bishop's name, a man of bold speech.
'By God's body,' said this Book, 'I will bear witness   230
That when this Boy was born, a star blazed forth,[16]
And all the wise men in the world were of one opinion –
That a boy had been born in Bethlehem city
Who should save men's souls and overcome sin.
And all the elements,' said Book, 'bear witness to it.
The airy sky first announced Him as God Who made all:
Those that were in Heaven took a starry comet
And lit it like a torch in tribute to His birth;
And the light followed the Lord to lowly Earth.

The water bore witness He was God, for He walked on it;   240
And the Apostle Peter perceived His approach
As He walked on the water, and knew Him well, and said,
  "Jube me ad te venire super aquas."
     (Lord, bid me come unto thee on the water.)[17]
And lo! the sun has locked-up its light in itself,
At seeing Him suffer, Who made sun and sea.
The Earth, unhappy at seeing Him suffer,
Quakes like a living creature, and crushes the rocks.
Lo! Hell could not hold fast, but opened at His Passion,
And let out Simeon's sons,[18] at seeing Him hang on the Cross;
And Lucifer now must believe this, loth though he may be.
For Jesus the Giant has projected an engine   250
To break and beat-down all that may be against Him.
And let me, Book, be burned unless Jesus rises living,
With all the mights of Man, to make His Mother glad
And comfort all His kindred and carry them out of sorrow,
And leave all the joy of the Jews disjointed and shattered;
And unless they revere His Rood and His Resurrection,
And believe in a new Law, they are lost, body and soul.'
   'Stay a while,' said Truth, 'for I can both hear and see
A spirit that speaks to Hell, and bids them unbar the gates.'
From within the light, a loud voice cried to Lucifer: 260
     *Attollite portas principes vestras, et elevamini, portae: aeternales;
     et introibit rex gloriae.'*
     (Lift up your heads, O ye gates, even lift them up, ye ever-
        lasting doors; and the King of Glory shall come in.)[19]
'Princes of this place, unpin and unbar your portals!
Here comes, crowned, the King of Glory!'
Then Satan sighed, and said to them all,
'Such a light, without our leave, stole Lazarus away;
Discomfort and care are coming towards us.
If this King comes in, he will carry off mankind,
And lead them where he likes, and have little trouble in
                                                        binding me.
Patriarchs and prophets have proclaimed this for years,
That such a light and a lord should lead them all hence.'
   'Listen,' said Lucifer.[20] 'This lord is known to me –   270
The lord and the light as well – from long ago.

Neither Death nor devils' tricks can do him harm,
And he walks as he wishes. But he'd better beware of dangers:
If he robs me of my rights, he robs me by force.
By right and reason, all the rabble in Hell
Belong to me, body and soul, both the good and the wicked.
He himself said, the Sovereign of Heaven,
That if Adam ate the apple, all men should die
And dwell with us devils; thus did he threaten.
He who is Truth, he spoke those words.   280
And since I have had seisin these seven hundred winters,
I believe the Law will not allow him a jot.'
    'That is so,' said Satan. 'But I'm seriously worried
Because you gained them by guile – and broke into his garden
In the semblance of a serpent, and sat in the apple-tree,
And egged-on Eve, when alone, to eat,
And told her a tale full of treacherous words.
That is how you had them out, and brought here at last;
And to what is gained by guile, there is no good title.'
'God will not be beguiled,' said a goblin, 'nor befooled.[21]   290
We have no true title to them; it was treachery that damned them.'
    'That is so,' said Satan, 'and I fear Truth will steal them.
These thirty winters, I think, he has walked the world, preaching;
I have tested him with temptations, and one time asked him
If he were God or God's son – and I got a curt answer.[22]
And so he has traipsed around these thirty-two winters.
And when I saw things were so, in her sleep I went
And warned Pilate's wife what kind of man Jesus was.[23]
For though the Jews hated him, and have put him to death,
I would have had him live longer. I believed if he died   300
His soul would suffer no sin to be in its sight;
For his body, when flesh and bone, was busy all the time
To save men from sin, if they themselves were willing.
And now I see a soul come sailing towards us
Amid glory and great light: it is God, I well know.
My advice to us all,' said he, 'is to get out fast;
We'd be better off dead than be seen by *him*.
Your lying, Lucifer, has lost us all our prey.
It was your fault that we first fell from High Heaven –
Because we believed your lies, we all leapt out with you.   310

And now, because of your latest lie, we have lost Adam,
And all our lordship, I believe, over land and water:
    Nunc princeps hujus mundi ejicietur foras.'
    (Now shall the prince of this world be cast out.)[24]
  Again the Light bade them unlock; and Lucifer answered.
'What lord art thou?' asked Lucifer. '*Quis est iste?* (Who is this?)'
'*Rex gloriae,*'the Light said at once. 'The King of Glory,
The Lord of might and mastery and all manner of virtues.
Dukes of this dark place, undo these gates,
That Christ may come in, the Son of the King of Heaven.'[25]
At His breath, Hell broke open, for all Belial's bars,
And the gates went wide despite their warders.   320
  Patriarchs and prophets, 'the people who sat in darkness',
Sang the song of St John, 'Behold the Lamb of God'.[26]
Lucifer could not look at them, for the light had blinded him.
Then Our Lord lifted up into His light all those that loved Him,
And said to Satan: 'Lo! Here is my soul as ransom
For all souls of sinners, to save those who deserve it.
They are mine, and part of me; my claim to them is better.
Though Reason may rule, and I myself recognise,
That from eating of the apple all must die,
I did not order them held here in Hell for ever.   330
For the deed that they did was incited by deceit;
With guile you gained them, against all justice;
In my palace of Paradise, in the appearance of an adder,
You treacherously took from me the two that I loved.
  There like a lizard with a lady's face[27]
You wrongfully robbed me. The Old Law reads
That beguilers shall be beguiled, and that is good sense:
    Oculum pro oculo, dentem pro dente.
    (Eye for eye, tooth for tooth.)[28]
Therefore, soul shall buy soul, and sin shall cure sin;
All that Mankind has misdone, I as man will amend.
Member for member was the Old Law's "amends",   340
And life for life also: by that Law I claim
Adam and all his issue, to be at my will for ever.
What Death has undone in them, *my* death shall restore,
And shall quicken and requite all that is quenched.
Good law demands that grace shall undo guile:

Never believe, then, Lucifer, that I unlawfully seize them;
By reason and by right I ransom my vassals:

    Non veni solvere legem, sed adimplere.

    (I am not come to destroy the law, but to fulfil.)[29]

Falsely and feloniously, in my own fields,
Against all equity, you stole my own. Now in law
I recover them by ransom, and by no recourse else,   350
So that what you gained by guile is regained by grace.
You, Lucifer, in the likeness of a loathsome adder,
Got by guile that which God loved;
And I, Who am Heaven's Lord, in human likeness,
Have repaid your guile with grace — let guile combat guile!
And as a tree caused the death of Adam and all his seed,
So a tree shall make Adam and all his seed alive again;
Thus guile is beguiled, and its own guile traps it:

    Incidit in foveam quam fecit.

    (And is fallen into the ditch which he made.)[30]

Now your guile begins to turn against you,
And my grace to grow greater and wider.   360
The bitter draught you brewed, now you must brook:
You who are Doctor of Death — drink your own potion!

    For I who am Lord of Life, *my* drink is love;
And for that drink, today, I died on Earth.
I fought so for Man's souls, I am still athirst;
No drink may refresh me, nor slake my thirst,
Till it is vintage time in the Valley of Jehoshaphat,
And I drink the ripe grape of the resurrection of the dead.[31]
Then I shall come as a King, with a crown of angels,
And hoist all human souls out of Hell.   370
Fiends and fiendlets shall stand before me
And be at my bidding and go about my business.
My human nature demands I be merciful to Mankind,
For we are blood-brothers, though not all of one baptism.
But none who are my brothers both in blood and in baptism
Shall be damned to the death that has no ending.

    Tibi soli peccavi.

    (Against thee only, have I sinned.)[32]

On Earth it is not the custom to hang a criminal
Twice, if the first time fails; not even a traitor;

And if the King of a country should come in time
To the place of execution or of other punishment,   380
The law says the man shall live if the King but looks at him.[33]
    I, who am King of Kings, shall come at such a time,
When all the wicked are doomed to death and damnation;
And if the law lets me look at them, it will lie with my mercy
Whether they die or do not, for their evildoing.
And if they have paid in part for their presumptuous sins,
I may rightfully use mercy, yet all my words remain true.
And though Holy Writ requires my revenge on evildoers –
        Nullum malum impunitum
    (No evil unpunished)[34] –
They shall be cleansed completely, and washed clean of iniquity
In my prison called Purgatory, till pardon behoves,   390
And my mercy shall be shown to many of my brethren;
For kinsmen may let kinsmen go cold or hungry,
But cannot without compassion see kinsmen bleed.'
        Et audivi arcana verba, quae non licet homini loqui:
    And I heard unspeakable words, which it is not lawful for a
        man to utter.[35]
'But my righteousness and my right shall rule all Hell,
And my mercy rule all mankind before me in Heaven,
How unkind a King I should be, not to help my own kin,
And especially in such straits as most sorely need help –
        Non intres in judicium cum servo tuo, Domine:
    Enter not into judgment with thy servant, O Lord.[36]
Thus it will be by law that I shall lead hence
Those that loved me and believed in my coming.
And, Lucifer, for the lies that led Eve astray,   400
You will bear a bitter sentence!' And He bound him in chains.
Ashtaroth[37] and the rest of his rout ran off to hide in corners,
For the boldest of the lot dared not look at Our Lord,
But left Him to do as he liked, and lead off whom he pleased.
    Then many hundreds of angels harped and sang the hymn
        Culpat caro, purgat caro;
        Regnat deus dei caro.
    (The flesh offends, the flesh atones;
        The flesh of God now reigns as God.)[38]
And Peace played on her pipe to this piece of poetry:

'*Clarior est solito post maxima nebula Phoebus,*
Post inimicitias clarior est et amor . . .'[39] said Peace,
'After sharp showers, does the sun show fairest;
No weather is warmer than after watery clouds;   410
No love is liever nor friendship loyaller
Than after warfare and woe, when Love and Peace are the captains.
Never was war in this world, nor wickedness so bitter,
That Love, if He liked, could not change it into laughter,
And Peace, by means of patience, prevent its perils.'
Then Truth called a truce: 'Your words are true, by Jesus!
Let us clasp each other in covenant, sealed with a kiss!'
'And let no person,' said Peace, 'perceive that we ever disputed;
For nothing is ever impossible to the Almighty.'
  'You are in the right,' said Righteousness, and reverently
                                          kissed her;   420
And Peace kissed *her*, saying, 'Now let peace be perpetual!
  Misericordia et veritas obviaverunt sibi, justitia et pax
    osculatae sunt.'[40]
  (Mercy and truth are met together; righteousness and peace
    have kissed each other.)
Then Truth blew a trumpet and sang *Te Deum laudamus*;
And Love played on the lute, loudly singing the Psalm
  Ecce quam bonum, et quam jucundum, habitare fratres in unum.
  (Behold, how good and how pleasant it is for brethren to
    dwell together in unity.)[41]
Then until day dawned, these damsels danced.
  But then the bells rang out for Easter, and rapidly woke me.
So I called to Kitty my wife and Colette my daughter,
'Arise, and do reverence to God's resurrection!
Creep to the Cross on your knees, and kiss it as a jewel!
For it bore God's bless̀ed body for our redemption;
And it frightens the Fiend, for such is its might   430
That no grisly ghost dares glide into its shadow!'

So I awoke, and wrote down what I had dreamed,
Put on my most expensive clothes, and proceeded to church,
To hear the whole Mass, and later have the Eucharist.
In the middle of Mass, when men went to make their offerings,
I suddenly fell asleep again, and soon after dreamed
That Piers the Ploughman appeared, as if painted with blood,
And carrying a cross, before the common people,
And like in all his lineaments to Our Lord Jesus.
I called upon Conscience to make the meaning clear.
'Is this Jesus the Jouster?' I asked, 'Whom the Jews killed?   10
Or is it Piers Ploughman? And who painted him red?'[1]
Quoth Conscience, and knelt, 'Those are Piers's coat-of-arms,
His colours and bearings; but he who is here bloodstained so,
Is Christ with His Cross, the Conqueror of the Christians.'
'Why do you call Him Christ, when the Jews called Him Jesus?
Patriarchs and prophets have prophesied in the past
That every kind of creature should incline and kneel
Whenever men named the holy name of Jesus.
Therefore no name can match the name of Jesus,
Nor is any so necessary to name by night or day.   20
For all dark devils dread to hear it,
And sinners are solaced and saved by that name.
Yet you call Him Christ: for what cause, I beg?
Is Christ a name of more power or more worth
Than Jesu or Jesus, from whom all our joy comes?'
    'Now, you know very well, and are not without reason,
That cavalier, king, and conqueror may be one person.
To be called a cavalier is fine, because men will kneel to him;
To be called a king is fine, for he can *make* knights;
But to be called a conqueror comes only by special charisma,   30
And from uncommon courage, and the courtesy of knighthood;
He makes lords of low folk in the lands that he conquers,
And foul thralls of freemen that refuse his laws.

The Jews had been like gentlefolk; but, Jesus once despised,
And His love and His law, are now like lowly villeins:
Through all the wide world, not one of them lives
Except under tribute and tax, like tillers and peasants.
But those that became Christian, as counselled by the Baptist,
Are like freemen and franklins, from the virtues of baptism,
And are gentlefolk with Jesus (for Jesus was baptised,   40
And on His Cross upon Calvary was crowned King of the Jews).

It is fitting for a King to defend and maintain,
In lands he has conquered, his laws and his liberties.
Jesus did so for the Jews; He justified and taught them
The laws of that life that lasts for ever;
He defended them from foul evils such as fevers and fluxes,
And from fiends that possessed them, and from false beliefs.
Then the Jews called Him Jesus, a gentle prophet,
And King of their Kingdom – though His crown was of thorns.

Then on the Cross He became a great conqueror,   50
Whom Death could not bring down or undo for ever;
For He arose and reigned, and ravaged Hell.
He was called the Conqueror then, of the quick and the dead,
For He gave bliss to Adam and Eve and many others
Who had long been lying in Hell as Lucifer's slaves.
And since, to His loyal liegemen, He has given great largesse –
Such as places in Paradise when they depart this world,
He may well be called Conqueror, because that is the
                                          meaning of "Christ".[2]
And the cause that He comes thus to us, with the Cross of
                                                    His Passion,
Is to teach us, when we are tempted, to use the Cross   60
And let it fight for us and defend us from falling into sin,
And to see by His suffering that whosoever wants happiness
Must first apply himself to penance, and to poverty also,
And be willing to endure in this world a wealth of woe.
But now to speak more of the name, and why Jesus was named so,
To be fair, it is a fact that He was first called Jesus,
When He was born in Bethelehem, as the Bible tells,
And came to redeem Mankind. Then Kings and angels
Reverenced Him royally with all Earth's riches.
Angels came down from the skies, and knelt and carolled   70

Gloria in excelsis Deo
(Glory to God in the highest).
   Afterwards Kings came and kneeled, carrying gifts
Of myrrh and much gold, and demanding no thanks,
Nor any kind of recompense, but acknowledging His kingship
Over sun and earth and sea. And so they went back
To their kingly kinsmen, conducted by angels.
And there the words of which you spoke were fulfilled:
   In nomine Jesu omne genu flectatur coelestium, terrestrium, et
      infernorum.
   (At the name of Jesus every knee should bow, of things in
      heaven, and things in earth, and things under the earth.)³
For all the angels of Heaven kneeled at His birth,
And the wisdom of the world was in those three kings;
Reason and Righteousness and Ruth were their offerings,⁴
Which is why the wise men of those days –   80
The Masters, and men of letters – called them Magi.
   The first King came with Reason, represented by incense.
The second king offered, in sooth, when he came,
Righteousness, Reason's colleague, in the form of red gold;
For gold is likened to Loyalty that lasts for ever,
And Reason to the rich gold of truth and righteousness.
The third King came, and likewise kneeling,
Presented Him with Pity in the appearance of myrrh;
For myrrh means mercy, and a tongue of mild speech.
Thus were three things of like worth offered at once   90
By rulers of three races, kneeling from respect for Jesus.
   But, for all these precious presents, Our Lord Prince Jesus
Was neither King nor conqueror till the coming of the time
That He moved towards manhood, and to much wisdom.
Now, it becomes a Conqueror to know cunning skills,
And have many wiles and much wisdom, if he wants to lead men;
Jesus did have these, in His days, had I time to describe them:
Sometimes He suffered, and sometimes He hid Himself;
Sometimes He fought fiercely, and fled at other times;
Sometimes He gave gifts, and granted health too,   100
And restored life or limb however He liked.
Jesus came among men in the manner of a conqueror,
Till all were His, for whom His blood was shed.

When He was a young man, Jesus went to a Jewish feast
And there turned water into wine, as we are told in the Scriptures; [5]
It was then that God of His grace began to Do-Well.
For wine is an emblem of the Law, and a life of holiness,
And the Law then was lacking, for men did not love their enemies.
But Christ both counsels and commands us,
Lettered and unlettered alike, to love our enemies.   110
Therefore it was at this feast first, as I said before,
That God began of His grace and goodness to Do-Well.
As yet He was not called or accounted Christ, but Jesus,
As a fine young fellow, and full of wisdom, and Son of Mary.

    He worked this miracle in his mother Mary's presence
So that she, first and foremost, should firmly believe
That He was begotten by God's grace, and by none other;
And He worked it, not by some sleight, but only by His word,
Accordant to the Nature He came of. So He commenced
                               to Do-Well.
    When He had grown to more manhood, away from
                                His mother, 120
He made lame men leap, and gave light to the blind,
And fed with two fishes and five loaves
More than five thousand folk who were truly famished.
Thus He comforted the careworn, and acquired a greater name,
Wherever He went; and that was *Do-Better*.
For His deeds made the deaf to hear, and the dumb to speak;
And all whom He healed and helped asked for His grace.
So the common people of His country called Him,
Because of the deeds he did, "Jesus, Son of David".
For David, in his own day, did the doughtiest deeds,   130
So that maidens sang, "Saul has slain his thousands, and
                        David his ten thousands."[6]
Therefore He came in that country to be called "Son of David",
And they named Him after Nazareth, and thought none worthier
To be King and Kaiser of the Kingdom of Judah
And the Jews' Chief Justice, than Jesus was.

    Caiaphas and his Jewish company became envious of this;
And to do Him to death, they conspired day and night.[7]
They killed Him on a cross at Calvary, one Friday,
Then buried His body, and bade certain men

To keep it from night-comers, with a company of armed men,   140
So that no friends should fetch it away. For prophets had

                                 told them

That the Blessed Body should arise from burial
And go to Galilee and gladden the Apostles
And His mother Mary: so men had believed.
    The soldiers set to guard it themselves confessed
That angels and archangels, before the arising of the day,
Had come and knelt to the corpse, singing *Christus resurgens*
    (Christ being raised from the dead dieth no more).[8]
And that He rose alive before them all, and went forth with them.
The Jews begged the guards to be discreet, and besought them
To tell the common folk there had come a company of Apostles   150
That bewitched them while they watched, and stole away

                                 the corpse.

    But Mary Magdalen met Him by the roadside,
Going towards Galilee as both God and man,
Alive and alert; and loudly she cried
To all company she came into, *Christus resurgens!*[9]
Thus it came out that Christ had conquered, recovered, and lived:
    Sic oportebat Christum pati, et resurgere a mortuis tertia die.
    (Thus it behoved Christ to suffer, and to rise from the dead
      the third day.)[10]
For what a woman knows cannot well be concealed!
    Peter perceived all this, and pursued Mary Magdalen,
With James and John, to seek Jesus out;
Thaddaeus was with them, and Thomas of India,[11] and ten others.   160
Then, as all these wise ones were together,
Shut in a building, behind bolted doors,
Christ came in to them, through the closed gates and doors,
And said, "Peace be unto you!" to Peter and the Apostles.
He took Thomas by the hand, and told him to search
And feel with his fingers the flesh of His heart.
    And Thomas touched it, and his tongue exclaimed,
    "*Dominus meus, et Deus meus.*
    (My Lord and my God.)
You are my Lord, and I believe, O Lord God Jesus!
You suffered and died, and will be deemster of us all;
For now you are alive and alert, and will live for ever!"   170

Then Jesus gently rejoined to him,
"Thomas, because you attest this now, and truly believe it,
You shall be blessèd both now and for ever.
And blessèd shall all be, in body and soul,
Whose sight is never set on me, as *you* see me now,
Yet loyally believe all this: I love them and bless them.
     Beati, qui non viderunt, et crediderunt."
     (Blessed are they that have not seen, and yet have believed.)
   And when He had done this, He taught the disciples Do-Best,
And gave Piers the power to grant pardon
And mercy and forgiveness to all manner of men,
And authority to remit all sins of whatever kind,   180
So long as men acknowledged to his entire satisfaction
His pardoning-power and its proviso – *Pay back what you owe.*[12]
   So Piers has power, his pardon thus paid for,
To bind and unbind both here and elsewhere,
And set men free of all sins save only that of debt.
   And soon after this, on high into Heaven
Christ went, and will dwell there, but at last will come
To reward all men who *pay back what they owe* –
That is, pay completely, as pure honesty dictates.
Any person who does not so pay, Christ means to punish: 190
On Doomsday He will be Deemster of both quick and dead,
And send the good up to God and to great joy,
And the wicked to dwell in woe without end.'
   Thus Conscience discoursed to me of Christ and of the Cross,
And bade me do it obeisance. But then in my dream
The Paraclete came to Piers and his companions;[13]
In the likeness of lightning He alit on them all,
And made them understand and interpret many tongues.
I wondered what it might be, and touched Conscience
                                        with my arm,
Being afraid of that light – for now in the likeness of fire   200
The Spirit of the Paraclete had quite overspread them.
   Quoth Conscience, and knelt, 'That is Christ's Messenger;
He comes from the great God, and His name is Grace.
Kneel, and if you can sing, let *Veni Creator Spiritus,*[14]
"Come, Holy Ghost", be your hymn to welcome and
                                        worship Him.'

So I sang that song, and so did hundreds of others,
And cried, together with Conscience, 'God of Grace, help us!'
Then Grace began to go along with Piers the Ploughman,
And counselled both Piers and Conscience to summon
                                                    the common people;
'For I shall distribute today a division of Grace   210
To all sorts and species of creatures that have five senses:
Treasure to live by until the end of their life,
Weapons to fight with that will never fail.
For Antichrist and his apostles shall harm all the world
And overmaster you, Conscience, unless Christ comes
                                                    to your aid.[15]
   And many false prophets, and flatterers and fakers,
Shall come with Cure of Souls over Kings and earls,
And Pride shall be made Pope, the Prince of Holy Church,
With Covetousness and Unkindness as his Cardinal Counsellors.
Therefore I, Grace, will give you treasure before I go,   220
And weapons to fight with when Antichrist attacks you.'
And He gave every man a grace by which to guide himself
Lest Idleness or Envy or Pride overcame him.
        Divisiones vero gratiarum sunt, idem autem Spiritus.
        (There are diversities of gifts, but the same Spirit.)[16]
   To some He gave wisdom, and a way with words,
And eloquence by which to live in such worldly callings
As priests and preachers and apprentices to the Law.
All these should live uprightly by the labours of their tongues,
And use intelligence to teach others as Grace taught *them*.
To some He taught subtlety and keenness of sight,
To earn their daily bread by buying and selling;   230
To some He taught labouring, an honest and excellent life;
Others He taught to delve, to ditch, or to thatch –
And earn their living by the lore they learned from Him.
Some He gave knowledge of numbers, in all kinds of computing;
He taught some to compose clever pictures, and mix colours;
Some to foresee and foretell what should befall –
Whether for weal or woe, to give warning beforehand,
As astrologers do by their art, and subtle philosophers.
   Some He taught how to ride, and recover the spoils of robbery,
Getting them back by the use of bodily ability,   240

Forcing them from those felons by lynch-law.
With some he left the wish to be in another world,
Here to live in poverty and penance, praying for all Christians.
He told all to live in unity, trades loving each other,
Forbidding all disputes or debates between them.
'Some crafts are cleaner than others, as you can well see;
But I could have put the cleanest worker to the filthiest
                                        occupation.
I gave you, by my grace, such gifts as you have:
Be like brothers, then, to each other, none calling another base;
    Let whoever masters most skills be mildest of manners;   250
Crown Conscience as your king; make Capability your steward;
And as Capability counsels you, clothe and feed yourselves.
I appoint Piers the Ploughman my agent and bailiff,
And my registrar for the receipt of *Return what you owe*.
My purveyor and ploughman, too, shall Piers be on Earth,
And he shall have an ox-team to till Truth's field.'
So Grace gave Piers a team of four great oxen.
The first was Luke, a large beast, but of gentle looks;
Then Mark, and Matthew for a third, both mighty beasts;
And to them he added John, the gentlest of all,   260
The prize beast of Piers's plough-team, surpassing the others.
    And Grace in his goodness gave Piers four stots[17]
To harrow all the land that his oxen had ploughed.
One was called Augustine, and Ambrose another,
And Gregory (a great scholar), and good Jerome;
These four followed Piers's team, for teaching the faith,
And harrowed in half no-time all Holy Scripture,
With two harrows that they had, an old and a new,
    Id est, vetus Testamentum et novum.
    (That is, the Old Testament and the New.)
    And Grace gave Piers grains of corn, called the
                                        Cardinal Virtues,[18]
To sow in men's souls; and he explained their names.   270
The Spirit of Prudence, the first seed was called;
And whosoever ate it would use his imagination,
And consider the outcome before committing himself to action;
Thus, learned men buy a ladle with a long handle
To collect floating fat, and keep their crocks in good order.

The second seed was called the Spirit of Temperance.
Whoever ate of that seed acquired such a nature
That his stomach would never swell from excess food or drink,
And no scorning or scolding spoil his even balance,
No winning of wealth or of worldly riches   280
Make him waste idle words or use wicked speech:
No uncommon clothing would ever come on his back,
Nor the meat in his mouth have been spiced by master-cook John.
    The third seed that Piers sowed was the Spirit of Fortitude.
Whosoever ate of that seed would be always strong-hearted
To suffer all that God sent of sickness and misfortune;
No lying or libel, nor loss of worldly goods,
Could move him to mourning, nor make his soul un-merry;
He was dauntless and enduring under all indignities,
To pass them off in patience with *parce mihi, Domine,*   290
And cover himself with the counsel of Cato the Wise:
    Esto forti animo, cum sis damnatus inique.
    (Be strong in courage when unjustly condemned.)[19]
    The fourth seed that Piers sowed was the Spirit of Justice,
And he that ate of that seed would always be honest
Towards God, and fear only guile, giving way to no fear else;
For guile goes about so secretly, that sometimes good faith
And the Spirit of Justice itself cannot be seen.
The Spirit of Justice is unsparing to punish
Those that are guilty, or even to correct
The King himself if he falls into malfeasance or sin.   300
For he counts the King's wrath as nothing, when he sits in Court
As a Justice, to judge cases; just so, he never fears
A Duke, or Death itself, but does as Law demands;
He cares nothing for presents or prayers, or princes' letters;
He gives equity to all, to the full extent of his power.
    Piers sowed these four seeds, and set about harrowing them
With the Old Law and the New Law, so that Love might
                            sprout up
Among the four virtues, and the vices be destroyed.
For it is common in the country that kexes and weeds
Grow among the fruits of the field, and foul *their* growth;   310
And that is what vices do to worthy virtues.

Said Piers, 'Harrow all who have mother-wit, with these
                                        Doctors' teachings,
And cultivate, by their counsel, the Cardinal Virtues.'
   Said Grace, 'Before your grain begins to grow ripe,
Piers, you should build yourself a barn to bestow your corn safely.'
   'By God, Grace,' said Piers, 'then you must give me the timber,
And act as architect yourself, ere you depart.'
   So Grace gave him the Cross and the Crown of Thorns
From which Christ had suffered on Calvary for the sake
                                        of mankind;
And from the water of His baptism, and the blood He bled
                                        on the Cross,   320
Grace made a kind of mortar; and Mercy was its name.
With these Grace began to make a good foundation.
Then he walled it and wattled it with Christ's pains and Passion,
And afterwards made a roof out of all Holy Scripture;
And he called that house Unity – or in English, Holy Church.
   And when these deeds were done, Grace devised
A cart, called Christendom, to carry Piers's sheaves;
And he gave him caples for his cart, named Contrition
                                        and Confession,
And made Priesthood his hay-warden while he himself went
Over the width of the world, with Piers, to cultivate Truth.   330
   Piers having gone to plough, Pride saw his chance,
And gathered a great host in order to march against
Conscience, all Christians, and the Cardinal Virtues –
Which he meant to beat-down and bruise, and bite their
                                        roots apart.
So he sent forth Surquedry,[20] his Sergeant-at-Arms,
And his spy Love-Spoiler Speak-evil-behind-men's-backs.
These two came to Conscience and the Christian people,
And Surquedry told them their tidings. 'You are to lose
The seeds that Piers sowed, that is to say, the Four Virtues;
Piers's barn shall be broken down, and all who may be in Unity   340
Shall be scattered. And, Conscience, your two caples
Confession and Contrition and your cart of the Faith
Shall be coloured so cunningly, so concealed under sophistry,
That you cannot contrive to tell by Contrition,
Nor by Confession, who is Christian or unChristian,

Nor any merchant-man who handles money,
Whether what he earns is won fairly, or unfairly by way of usury.
　　In such camouflage and cunning does Pride come armed,
Together with Lord Lechery who lives for bodily lust,
To lay waste the whole world, in a little while,   350
By using their wits, with luxury and wicked ways.'
　　Quoth Conscience then to all Christians, 'My counsel is to go
As quickly as we can into Unity, and keep inside,
And pray for peace in the barn of Piers the Ploughman.
For I am certain that we two have not strength between us
To go forth against Pride, unless Grace is with us.'
　　Then Commonsense came to advise Conscience,
And cried out his command to all Christian people –
That they should dig a deep dyke around Unity,
So that Holy Church might stand in Unity like a stela.   360
　　So Conscience commanded all Christians to delve
An immense moat, such as might make a fortress
To help Holy Church and her guardians.
Then every kind of Christian except common whores
Repented, and repudiated sin: all but those, and rogues,
False men such as flatterers, and filchers and usurers,
False-witnesses, and jurymen who were often forsworn
And wittingly and wilfully sided with injustice,
Forswearing for silver what they knew to be so.
　　No Christian creature that knew Commonsense,   370
Except such ill-doers as those I have spoken of,
But lent a helping hand to enlarge the Moat of Holiness:
Some by telling beads, and some by pilgrimages,
Others by private penance or by gifts of their few pence.
Then the water came welling up, as wicked deeds
Started it streaming saltily from men's eyes.
The pure lives of laymen and of clergy alike
Soon had Holy Church standing amidst the Moat of Holiness.
　　Said Conscience, 'I care not though Pride *should* come now,
And the lord of lust shall be hindered all this Lent, I hope.   380
Come, then, all you Christians; now we can dine,
All who have laboured loyally throughout this Lent.
Here is blest bread, that conceals God's body:
Grace, by God's word, gave Piers the right

And might to make it, and men then to eat it
To aid their souls towards health, once in a month,
Or as often as they need, if they have paid
For Piers Ploughman's pardon, with *Repay what you owe*.'
    Then the common folk cried, 'What? You require us to
                                                      pay back
All that we owe anyone, before we go to Mass?'   390
'I counsel and require,' said Conscience, 'and so do the
                                                Cardinal Virtues,
That all men forgive each other; and the Pater-noster asks it:
    *Et dimitte nobis debita nostra, sicut et nos dimittimus debitoribus
        nostris.*
    (And forgive us our debts as we also forgive our debtors.)
Only after this may you be absolved, and make true Communion.'
    'Ah, bah!' said a brewer, 'I won't be ruled,
By Jesus, for all your jabber, by any "Spirit of Justice",
Nor by Conscience himself, by Christ, while I can sell
Both dregs and draff, and draw from the same hole
Both thick ale and thin; for that's my nature,
And I don't haggle around after holiness: hold your tongue,
                                                Conscience,
You talk a lot to no purpose about "Spirit of Justice".'   400
    'You paltry poltroon!' said Conscience. 'You profane wretch!
You are unblest, brewer, unless God be your rescuer;
Unless you live by love of the Spirit of Justice
(The chief seed that Piers sowed), you will never be saved.
Unless Conscience and the Cardinal Virtues feed the common folk,
(Indeed believe it!) they are lost, both life and soul.'
    'Then many a man,' said an unlearnèd vicar,[21] 'must be lost!
I have Cure of Souls in Holy Kirk, and there never in my
                                                time came to me
Anyone able to tell me about cardinal virtues,
Or who cared a cock's feather – or a hen's either – for
                                                Conscience. 410
The only cardinals *I've* come across came from the Pope;
And we clergy, *when* they come, have to pay for their keep –
And all their fine furs and their palfreys' fodder, and the
                                                pillagers that follow them!
Every day I can hear the common folk cry out against them,

That the country is accursed into which cardinals come,
And that where they linger longest, lechery reigns.
Therefore I would wish, as God is my witness,
That no cardinals came among the common people,
But that they held fast in holiness to their habitation
At Avignon, among the Jews[22] –   420
    Cum sancto sanctus eris!
    (With the holy thou shalt be holy!)[23] –
Or in Rome, where their own Rule says they should guard
                                      the Relics.
And you, Conscience, should stay at King's Court for ever;
So should that Grace you grind on about, as guide to the clergy;
And Piers with his new plough and his old one also
Should be Emperor of all Middle Earth, to make all men Christian.
   That's an imperfect Pope who should help all people
Yet sends men to slay those whom he should be saving.[24]
I wish well to Piers Ploughman, who imitates God in his works,
    Qui pluit super justos et injustos:
Who sendeth rain on the just and the unjust alike,[25]
And sends the sun to sweeten a sinner's tilth   430
With as bright a blaze as for the best man or woman.
Just so, Piers the Ploughman takes pains, and tills
No worse for the wastrels or the brothel-wenches
Than for himself and his servants – though those *are* served first.
And he toils and tills just as hard for a traitor,
And at all times, as for a true and trusty man.
And worshipped be He Who made all, both heinous and good,
And lets sinners go on living, so that at last they may repent.
And may God improve the Pope, who pillages Holy Church,
And claims, above the King, to be keeper of all Christians: 440
Yet accounts it nothing when Christians are killed and robbed,
And even furnishes forces to fight and spill Christian blood,
Against both Old Law and New, as St Luke bears witness:
    Non occides . . . Mihi vindicta:
    That shalt not kill . . . Vengeance belongeth to me, I will
      recompense, saith the Lord.[26]
It seems that so long as he himself has his will,
He doesn't care a curse for the rest of Creation.
And may Christ in His courtesy save the Cardinals too,

And turn their quick wits towards wisdom, and the welfare
of souls!
As for the common folk, they feel very little
The counsels of Conscience or of the Cardinal Virtues,
Unless they catch sight of something that will serve their ends.   450
Dishonesty or deceit do not trouble them at all;
For the Spirit of Prudence among the people is *guile*,
And all those lovely Virtues appear as vices.
Everyone schemes some deceit by which to hide sin,
And passes it off as pure art, and honest practice.'
    A lord who heard this, laughed, and said, 'By this light,
I think it right and reasonable to take from my Reeve
All that my auditor, or it may be my steward,
Records in his accounts, and my clerks write out.
With the Spirit of Wisdom they search the Reeve's rolls,   460
And with the Spirit of Fortitude I scrape in the cash!'
    Then a king came there, and said, 'By my crown,
I was crowned king to rule the common people,
And defend Holy Kirk and her clergy against criminals.
And whatever livelihood I lack, the Law lets me take it
Where I can most quickly come by it; for I am the head of
the Law;
You are only the limbs, and I am above you all.
Now, since I am head of you all, I am also your healer —
The chief helper of Holy Church, and headman of the Commons.
What I take from those two, I take at the teaching   470
Of the Spirit of Justice; for I am Judge over you all.
So I may have Communion freely, for I borrow from no man.
Nor cadge from the Commons except as required by my rank.'
    'Upon condition,' said Conscience, 'that you can duly defend
And rule your realm well, by reason and by truth,
Then your Law allows you to claim what you need —
within reason.
    Omnia tua sunt ad defendendum, sed non ad depredandum.'
    (All things are yours for defending, but not for despoiling.)
The vicar, being far from home, took friendly leave.
Thereupon I awoke, and wrote down what I had dreamed.

Passus 20

Well, having thus awakened, on my way I went,
My expression mournful, and misery in my heart;
Nor did I know where to eat, nor where to find food.
When it was nearly noon, I met with Need,
Who accosted me with abuse, and called me an impostor.
'Could you not have excused yourself, as the King and others did,
That only out of necessity did you take food and clothing,
As taught and told by the Spirit of Temperance,
And never took any more than directed by Need –
Need who knows no law, nor acknowledges any debt?   10
For he makes free of three things for his life's preservation.
The first is food, if man refuses him it and he has no money
And no one will go bail for him, and he has nothing
                                                    worth pawning.
  If he is caught in such a case, and acquires food by theft,
He certainly commits no sin by getting it so.
And he may acquire clothing so, if he cannot bargain better:
Need will soon stand his surety in such a case.
And if his lips long for water, the Law of Nature
Will make him drink from any ditch rather than die of thirst.
So Need, in real necessity, may annex things to himself   20
Without consulting Conscience or the Cardinal Virtues,
So long as he submits to the Spirit of Temperance.
  For no virtue is so sovereign as the Spirit of Temperance,
Neither the Spirit of Justice nor the Spirit of Fortitude;
For the Spirit of Fortitude fails very often
By being immoderate, as may be often seen:
It may have men beaten too badly, or not beaten enough,
Or give men greater grief than good measure suggests.
And the Spirit of Justice must judge, willy nilly,
According to the King's Council, or the Commons' wish.   30
And the Spirit of Prudence will in many points fail
When it wants to foresee the future, for that rests with wisdom;

Opinions are not always wise, nor informed guesses, either:
Man proposes, God disposes – and governs all good virtues.
And Need is near God in this: that he humbles men in a moment,
And makes them as meek as lambs when they miss necessities.
Wise men have forsaken wealth, wishing rather to be needy;
They went to live in wildernesses, and would not grow rich;
God left His great joy and spiritual good,
Assuming human nature, and becoming needy –   40
So needy, as the Scriptures say in sundry places,
That He Himself said in His sorrow on the Cross,
"Both foxes and fowls of the air may creep or fly to shelter,
And the fishes have fins that take them fleetly to rest;
But Need has so seized me here, that I must needs stay
And suffer most bitter sorrows, that will soon turn to joy." [1]
So do not be bashful about begging and being needy, [2]
When He Who made all the world was needy from choice –
Never a man more needy, nor who died poorer.'
When Need had so reproved me, I soon fell asleep,   50
And had a most marvellous dream: that in Man's shape
Antichrist came, and tore up by the roots
The tender crop of Truth, turned it upside down
And made falsehood spring up and spread and serve men's needs.
In every quarter he came to, he cut away Truth,
And made Guile grow in its place, as if it were good.
The friars followed this fiend, for he gave them vestments,
And the religious orders reverenced him, and rang all their bells,
And whole convents came out to welcome that tyrant
And all his hangers-on, too – except the fools, [3]   60
Which fools preferred to die first, rather than live
Any longer, since Loyalty was so insulted,
And the false fiend Antichrist ruled over all folk.
For these fools were mild and holy men, fearing no misuse,
Defying all falseness, and the folk who practised it;
And should any king comfort or consort awhile with such men,
Antichrist's crowd would curse him, and their counsel,
                              whether cleric or layman.
  So Antichrist soon saw hundreds follow his banner.
Pride bore it boldly all about,
Beside the Lord who lived for bodily lust,   70

And who came to fight Conscience, that safe-keeper and guide
Of the Christian Company and the Cardinal Virtues.

    Said Conscience, 'I counsel all you fools to come with me
Into Unity, Holy Church's stronghold, and hide there,
And cry unto Nature to come and keep us fools safe
From the limbs of this fiend, for love of Piers Ploughman.
Let us call to the common people that they come into Unity,
To abide there and battle against Belial's children.'

    Nature heard the cry of Conscience, and came out of
                             the planets [4]

And sent forth his fore-runners, fevers and fluxes,   80
Coughs and carditises, cramps and toothaches,
Rheums and retinitises, and running sores,
Boils and blains and burning agues,
Frenzies, and other foul evils. These fore-runners of Nature
Pierced and preyed-upon great presses of people
Till a legion, more or less, had soon lost their lives.
Then were heard cries of *Woe's me!* and *Help! Here comes Nature*
With dreadful kinds of death, to undo us all!
And the Lord that lived for lust cried aloud
To Comfort, his knight, to come and carry his banner.   90
    'To arms, to arms!' cried that Lord, 'Every man for himself!'
The two sides met each other before the trumpets could sound
Or Heralds-at-Arms call out the titles and names of the lords.
Hoary Old Age came, and he was in the spearhead,
Bearing the banner before Death, as by right he could.
Nature followed near him, with a flock of fierce diseases,
Such as poxes and pestilences, that undid many people.
Thus Nature's contagions killed whole companies –
Death came driving after him, and dashed into dust
Kings and cavaliers and kaisers and popes;   100
Learnèd or unlettered, he let no man stand
That once he had hit, for he never stirred again.
Many a lovely lady, and many knights' lemans,
Dropped senseless, and died, from the bitterness of Death's blows.

    Now Conscience, in pure kindness, requested Nature
To pause and be patient, and see if such people
Would secretly leave Pride's party, and become perfect Christians.
So Nature held his hand, in hope that folk would reform.

But then Fortune began to flatter those few left alive,
Promising them long lives. And she sent out Lust   110
Among all sorts of men, married or single,
And he gathered a great host to fight against Conscience.[5]

    This Lust laid about him with cheerful looks,
And with secret speeches and subtle words,
And armed himself with idleness and with arrogance.
He bore a bow in his hand, and many bloodstained arrows
That were feathered with fine promises and not a few
                              false betrothals.
With his unchaste chatter he often troubled
Conscience and his companies the teachers of Holy Kirk.

    Then Covetousness came, and cast about for means   120
Of overcoming Conscience, and the Cardinal Virtues.
He armed himself in avarice, and lived as if ravenous.
His weapons were wiles for winning and hoarding:
With feigning and falsehood he fooled all the people.
Simony had sent him to assail Conscience,
And these two preached to the people, and chose prelates for
                              themselves
Who would take Antichrist's side, to save their temporalities.
He came to the King's Court as a cruel baron,
And in that Court kneeled to Conscience before the
                            whole company –
And made Good Faith flee the place, but Falsehood remain;   130
He boldly overbore with many bright gold-pieces
Much of the worth and wisdom of Westminster Hall.
He would jog up to a Justice and joust at his ear,
Unseating Honesty with, 'Take this to amend your judgment';
Then would afterwards be off in haste to the Archbishop's Court,
There turning Civil Law towards Simony, with a bribe
                            for the officer.
For a mantle of miniver he would make a true marriage
Disband before Death came, and frame a divorce.

    Quoth Conscience, 'Alas! I wish Christ, of His grace,
Had made Covetousness a Christian, he fights so keenly   140
And is so bold and stubborn while there's money by him.'

    But Life only laughed, and had scallops cut in his clothes,
And armed himself hastily in whorish words,

Thinking sanctity absurd, and courtesy wasteful;
He thought Loyalty a labourer, and Liar a freeman;
Conscience and Good Counsel he counted as fools.
Thus, with a little luck, Life was revived,
And pranced away with Pride, praising no virtue,
Nor caring how Nature can slay, and will come at last
To kill all earthly creatures except only Conscience.   150
No; Life leapt away and found himself a light-of-love.
Said he, 'Health and I, and high-heartedness,
Will save you from dread of Death or of Old Age;
You shall forsake all sorrow, and think nothing of sin.'
    Life and his leman, Fortune, liked this very well;
Till at last they begat in their glory a lazy lout
Called Sloth, who was to cause much calamity.
He matured amazingly fast, and was soon a man;
Then he wedded a brothel-wench who name was Despair.
Her sire had been an Assize-juror who was always foresworn,   160
A certain Tom Two-Tongues, attainted at every inquest.
Sloth was a wary warrior, and made himself a sling
That cast the dread of Despair a dozen miles round.
    Conscience, in consternation, called upon Old Age,
And bade him make efforts to fight, and frighten Despair away.
Old Age hefted the sword of Good Hope, and made ready
                                              in haste;
He drove Despair into outlawry, and did battle with Life.
Life fled away in fear, and sought help from Physic,
And begged for salvation from some of his elixir,
And gave him hard-earned gold that gladdened his heart;   170
And for this gold, Physic gave him a cap of glass.[6]
Life had faith that Physic's art could foil Old Age,
And drive away Death with doses and drugs;
But Old Age attacked Life again, and at last chanced to hit
A physician in a furred hood, who fell into a palsy;
And that doctor died not three days later.
    Said Life, 'Now I see that neither Physic nor Surgery
Is even a ha'porth of help against Old Age.'
But in hope of healing he took good heart,
And rode to the house of Revel, a rich and merry mansion: 180
'The Company of Comfort', men sometimes call it.

Soon after, Old Age attacked *me*, and walked over my head,
And battered me bald in front and bare on the crown;
He rode so rough-shod on my head, I shall bear the marks for ever.
'Sir Ill-bred Old Age,' I said, 'may bad manners attend you!
How long have you had right-of-way over men's heads?
Could you not have had the courtesy,' quoth I, 'to ask leave?'
He answered, 'Ah, so? Be quiet, you oaf!' And attacked me
                                                    with ageing.
He hit me under the ear, and now I'm hard of hearing;
He beat me about the mouth, and battered my teeth out;   190
He fettered me so firmly with gout, I can't stir from home.
And for all the woe I was in, my wife too was sorry,
And wished with all her heart that I were in Heaven;
For the limb she loved me for, and delighted to feel –
At night in especial, when we were naked –
By no means could I manage to make it to her liking:
Old Age, and she, had entirely undone it.
    Then, as I sat there in sorrow, I saw Nature pass by,
And Death drew near me. I shook with dread,
And cried out to Nature to cure my cares: 200
'See how Hoary Old Age has handled me!
Avenge me, if it be your will, for I long to get away!'
    'If you want revenge, you must go into Unity,
And stay there, without stirring out, until I send for you;
And be careful to learn some craft, before you do come out.'
'Counsel me, Nature,' quoth I. '*What* craft shall I learn?'
    'Learn to love, and leave all else aside.'[7]
'But how shall I gain goods, and get food and clothing?'
'If you love loyally, you shall never lack
A meal or a worldly garment while your life lasts.'   210
    So on Nature's advice I set out to wander
Through the lands of Contrition and Confession, till I came
                                                    to Unity.
Conscience was its Constable, the saviour of Christians,
But I saw it was besieged by seven great giants,
Who in Antichrist's company harassed it hard.
Sloth with his sling made a fierce assault;
And proud priests, more than a thousand, accompanied him
In bum-freezers and pointed boots, and with bloody great knives:[8]

These came against Conscience, in company with Covetousness.

   'By Mary!' said a banned priest from the Irish border,   220
'So long as I get silver, I set Conscience at no more
Than I do to drink a draught of good ale!'
And so said sixty more from the same country,
And sent showers of shot at him, and many sheaves of oaths,
Broad-barbed arrows like 'By God's heart and nails!',
And they almost had Holiness and Unity helpless.

   Conscience cried, 'Help, Clerisy, or I shall fall
Before these perverted priests and prelates of Holy Church!'
The Friars heard his cry, and came to his help;
But they knew their business badly, and Conscience
                               abandoned them.   230

   Then Need came near, with news of a warning for Conscience,
That they had come out of covetousness, in hope of a curacy:
'Because they are poor, perhaps, and have no patrimony,
They flatter rich folk for the sake of good living.
But since they *chose* the chill of wretched poverty,
Let them chew the mouthful they chose – and charge them
                                 with no parish!
He is likelier to lie, who must beg for his living,
Than he who labours for his living and lets beggars share it.
Since friars forsook the felicities of this world,
Let them live as beggars – or eat angels'-food only!'   240

   When he heard this counsel, Conscience commenced laughing,
And courteously comforted the friars, having called them in,
Saying, 'Sirs, you are certainly all welcome
To Unity and to Holy Church. But one thing I beg of you:
That you remain in Unity, and keep yourselves from envy
Of lettered folk or lay, and live according to your Rule.
Then I will be your bailsman; you shall have bread and clothing
Enough, and your other necessities; you shall not lack
If only you leave your logic and learn how to love.
For love they gave up lordship and lands and learning,   250
Friars Francis and Dominic – for the love of holy living.

   If you long for livings, take a lesson from Nature:
God made in their proper measure all manner of things,
And set them at certain decisive numbers,
And gave new things names, and numbered the stars:

Qui numerat multitudinem stellarum: et omnibus eis nomina vocat.
   (He telleth the number of the stars; he calleth them all by
     their names.)[9]
   Kings and cavaliers, likewise, keepers and defenders,
Have officers under them, all in fixed numbers;
And for costing a campaign, one must record men's numbers,
Or no purse-bearer will pay them, however hard people fight –
Others who might be on the battlefield would be thought
                                    bandits,   260
Pillagers and armour-plunderers, in all places accursed.
   What is more, monks and members of all Religious Orders
Are required by their Rule to restrict their numbers:
Of learned and unlearned alike the Law demands
A certain quota for each class – except only friars.
I may tell you, then, by Christ, Mother Wit informs me
That it would be wicked to give you wages, for you are
                         growing innumerable!
The Heavenly Host is numbered, but not that of Hell;[10]
And so I especially wish you were all well registered,
And numbered under a notary's seal, neither more nor less!'   270
Envy heard this, and had friars haste off to school
To learn logic and law – and contemplation, too –
And preach to men about Plato, and prove it by Seneca,
That everything on Earth ought to be common property.[11]
   Yet he lies, I believe, who preaches this to unlettered men,
For God made a law for Man, and Moses taught it:
   Non concupisces domum proximi tui . . . nec omnia quae illius sunt.
     (Thou shalt not covet thy neighbour's house . . . nor
       anything that is thy neighbour's.)
But how ill is this observed in the parishes of England!
For parsons and parish priests, who should be the people's
                              confessors,
Are called 'curates' because they must know and heal
All their parishioners, and impose penances on them,   280
And make them ashamed in their shrifts; but that shame
                            makes men go
Fleeing off to the friars, as defaulters do to Westminster
(Bearing borrowed money there, then begging the lenders
Frantically for forgiveness, or a few more years' grace;

But while they are at Westminster, they will go to work hard
To make themselves merry on other men's goods).[12]
   So it fares with many folk who confess to the friars –
Like assizers and executors, who will award the friars
A few pence to pray for a dead man, then proceed to make merry
With the remains of the riches that the other had drudged for.   290
Thus leaving the dead man in debt until the Day of Doom.
On this score, Envy abhorred Conscience,
And founded a school for teaching the friars philosophy.
   Meanwhile, Covetousness and Unkindness were attacking
                                           Conscience;
But he held firm in Unity and Holy Church.
He appointed Peace his Portress, to bar the gates
Against all idle tale-tellers and hesitants.
Hypocrisy and she had a hard struggle,
For Hypocrisy made a heavy assault on her gates,
And wickedly wounded many wise teachers   300
Who accorded with Conscience and the Cardinal Virtues.
Conscience called for a Doctor skilled in hearing confessions:
'Go, give your salve to those who are sick, and wounded by sin.'
Doctor Shrift prepared painful salves, and made the sick
                                       do penance,
Every man of them for the misdeeds they had committed,
Till Piers's pardon had been paid for by *Repay what you owe*.
   Some found this treatment distasteful, and sent letters to discover
If any surgeon there besieged used less stringent cures.
Sir Like-to-Live-in-Lechery lay there and groaned,
For fasting on a Friday made him feel like death: 310
'There *is* a surgeon in this seat who deals more softly,
And knows far more of physic, and plasters a fellow more gently.
He is called Friar Flatterer, Physician and Surgeon.'
Contrition said to Conscience, 'Have this man come to Unity,
For here we may have many men whom Hypocrisy has hurt.'
Quoth Conscience, 'There is no need. I know of no better healers
Than the parson, the parish priest, the bishop, or the
                                Grand Penitentiary – [13]
Except Piers Ploughman, who has power over them all,
And may deal men indulgences unless they are in debt to him.
Still, since you so wish, I am willing to sanction   320

That Friar Flatterer be fetched, and physic your patients.'
    The friar had heard of this, and went in haste
To My Lord Bishop, for a licence giving him leave to *cure*
Just like a *curate*. So he came with his certificates,
As boldly as you like, to the Bishop; and he soon had his brief
To hear confessions in whatever quarter he came to.[14]
So he came to where Conscience was, and knocked to come in.
    Peace, the Portress of Unity, opened the gate,
And hurriedly asked him what he might want.
The friar said, 'In faith, both for profit and for health,   330
I would like to converse with Contrition. That is why
                                                    I have come.'
Said Peace, 'He is sick, and so are many others.
Hypocrisy hurt them so badly, they will hardly recover.'
'I am a surgeon, and understand salves;
Conscience knows me well, and can vouch for my skill, too.'
Peace then said, 'I pray you, before you proceed,
What is your name? Please tell it, and not conceal it.'
    'Certainly!' said his friend, 'It is Sir Slip-into-Houses.'[15]
'Ah, so! Then gang your gate, by God, for all your physic;
Unless you have learned something better, I shall not let you in!   340
I knew such a one as you, not eight winters ago,
Who came, in such a cope, to a Court where I dwelt.
He was doctor to My Lord and to My Lady too;
And at last this licenced beggar, when My Lord was away,
Gave our women-folk such *salves*[16] that some grew with child!'
    But Courtesy commanded Peace to cast the gates open:
'Let in the friar and his friend; give them full hospitality;
He may know this or that, and there is no telling
But that Life may learn from him to leave Covetousness,
To be in dread of Death, and withdraw from Pride,   350
And come to accord with Conscience, and all kiss each other.'
And so, because of Courtesy, the friar came in
To where Conscience was, who greeted him warmly.
Quoth Conscience, 'You are welcome! Can you heal the sick?
My cousin Contrition is confined here wounded:
Comfort him if you can, and take care of his sores.
The parson's plasters and powders are too mordant;
And he leaves them on too long, being loth to change them –

From one Lent to the next Lent he will let them burn.'
The licentiate said, 'That is too long. I shall amend it.'   360
   So he goes and fingers Contrition, and gives him a plaster
Called Private-Payment, and says, 'I shall pray for you,
And for all those whom you love, all my life long.'
And to Peace, 'You, my lady, shall have Matins and Masses.
And the fellowship of our fraternity – for a little silver.'[17]
So he creeps around collecting cash, and cajoling whom
                                                 he confesses,
Till Contrition has quite forgotten to cry out, or weep,
Or be wakeful for his wicked acts, as he had once done.
In the comfort of a mild confessor, he was contrite no more,
Though that is the most sovereign salve for all sins.   370
   Sloth saw this, and so did Pride,
And they came back with cruel intent to the attack on Conscience.
Conscience cried out again for Clerisy to help him,
And called on Contrition to keep the gates.
But Peace said, 'He's asleep and dreaming, and so are many others.
That friar has bewitched these folk with his physic,
And salved them so mildly that they fear no sin.'
   Said Conscience then, 'By Christ, I will become a pilgrim,
And walk as wide as the whole world stretches,
To find Piers the Ploughman, who may overthrow Pride   380
And find fitter work for the friars who flatter for their keep
And run counter to me, Conscience. I call Nature to avenge me
And send me happy fortune and health, till I have found
                                                 Piers Ploughman!'[18]
And while he was crying out for grace, I awoke.

Explicit hic dialogus Petri Plowman.
(Here ends the discourse concerning
Piers Ploughman.)

APPENDIX

The 'Autobiographical Episode'

C, 5, 1–104

Thus I woke up, God knows, when I lived in Cornhill,
Kit and I in a cottage, clothed as a loller,[1]
And not highly thought of, trust me, it's true,
By lollers of London and ignorant hermits,
Because I wrote about them as Reason taught me.
For as I came by Conscience I met with Reason
In a hot harvest when I had my health
And limbs to labour with and loved to live well
And to do nothing but drink and sleep.
I was sound in mind and body and someone questioned me;   10
Roaming in remembrance, thus Reason rebuked me.
'Can you serve,' he said, 'or sing in a church,
Put the hay into haycocks or pitch it into carts,
Mow or stack or make bindings for the sheaves,
Reap or oversee the reaping and rise early,
Or have a horn and guard the hay and sleep out at night
And keep my corn in my croft from cadgers and thieves?
Or make shoes or cloth, or tend the sheep and cattle,
Hedge or harrow or drive the hogs and geese,
Or any other craft the community needs,   20
To improve the life of those who provide for you?'
'Surely,' I said, 'so God help me,
I am too weak to work with the sickle or the scythe,
And too tall,[2] trust me, to bend over low.
If I worked as a workman I wouldn't last long.'
'Then have you lands to live on,' said Reason, 'or a rich family
To find you your food? For you seem an idler,

A spendthrift who has to spend or a timewaster.
Or do you beg for your living at people's doors
Or con them at churches on Fridays and feast-days?   30
That is the life of lollers and it's praised little
Where Righteousness rewards men right as they deserve.

> *Reddet unicuique iuxta opera sua*

>   (He will repay every man in accordance with what he has
>   done.)

Or perhaps you are maimed in body or member,
Or injured in some accident which might be an excuse?'
'When I was young,' I said, 'many years since,
My father and my family sent me to school
Until I knew certainly what Scripture meant
And what is best for the body, as the Bible says,
And safest for the soul, so long as I continue.[4]
And I never found, in faith, since my family died   40
Any life that pleased me but in these long clothes.[5]
And if I ought to live and earn my living by labour,
I should live by the labour that I learned best.[6]

> *In eadem vocacione in qua vocati estis*

>   ([Remain] in the same state to which you are called.)

And so I live in London and in the land round it;
The tools that I toil with and take my wages with
Are *Pater-Noster* and my primer[7] and *Placebo* and *Dirige*
And my psalter sometimes and my seven psalms.
These I say for the souls of such people as help me,
And those who provide my food promise, I believe,
That I'll be welcome when I come, once a month or so,   50
Now to him, now to her; in this way I beg,
Without bag or bottle but only my belly.[8]
And also, moreover, it seems wrong to me, Sir Reason,
To constrain clerks to do the work of common men,
For by the law of Leviticus[9] that our Lord ordained,
Tonsured clerks, by common understanding,
Should neither sweat at manual work nor swear oaths at inquests
Nor fight in the front line nor injure the foe.[10]

> *Non reddas malum pro malo*

>   (Do not return evil for evil.)

For those who are tonsured are the heirs of heaven,

And in choir and in church the ministers of Christ.[11]   60
   Dominus pars hereditatis meae. Et alibi: Clemencia non constringit
   (The Lord is the portion of my inheritance. Mercy is not
      constrained.)
It is fitting for clerks to serve Christ
And for untonsured lads to labour on the land.
For no clerk should be crowned with the tonsure unless he has come
From franklins and free men and folk who are married.
Bondsmen and bastards and beggars' children,
These belong to labour and lords' kin to service
Of God and good men, which goes with their rank,
Some to sing masses or sit and write,
Read and receive what Reason ought to spend.
But since bondsmen's children have been made bishops   70
And their children's bastards have become archdeacons
And cobblers and their sons knights on payment of silver,
And lords' sons their labourers, pawning their lands
To ride against our enemies for the right of this realm
For the comfort of the commons and the king's worship.
Since monks and nuns, who should feed the mendicants,
Have made their kin knights and purchased knight-fees,[12]
And popes and patrons have spurned poor nobles
And taken the sons of Simon[13] to keep the sanctuary,
Life-holiness and Love have been long distant,   80
And will be till it's over or changed some other way.
   So please don't rebuke me, Reason, I pray,
For in my conscience I know what work Christ wants of me.
The prayers of a perfect man and his wise penance
Are the dearest labour that pleases our Lord.
Truly "Man does not live",' I said, ' "by bread alone"[14].
The prayer "*Pater-Noster*" provides proof of that:
"Thy will be done" will look after us in all things.'
'By Christ,' said Conscience, 'I can't see that this lies.[15]
But begging in cities doesn't seem perfect   90
Unless one's in an order, obedient to prior or abbot.'[16]
'That is true,' I said, 'and so I acknowledge
That I have wasted time and I have misspent time.
And yet, I hope, like a man who has ventured his money
And always lost and lost, and at last struck lucky

And made such a bargain he was better off for ever,
And at last wrote off his losses as light,
His winnings were so great through the words of grace.[17]

    Simile est regnum celorum thesauro abscondito in agro.

      Mulier qui invenit dragmam . . . etc.

  (The kingdom of heaven is like a treasure hidden in a field.

    The woman that found a silver coin . . .)

So I hope to have of him who is almighty
A gobbet of his grace and begin a time   100
That all times of my time to profit shall turn.'

  'I counsel you,' said Reason, 'to get on with beginning
The life that is laudable and lawful for your soul.'
'Yes, and continue in it,' said Conscience, and I went to church.

NOTES

Prologue

The poet sees, in a dream, the whole maze of activity that constitutes 'Middle Earth' – a plain lying between Heaven and Hell (lines 13–16). Corruption is everywhere, nowhere more flagrantly than in the Church: all men's standards – including, we detect, his own – are materialistic rather than spiritual. Already, however, we meet honest ploughmen, since one of them is not only the 'hero' of the poem but is also to be an instrument of human salvation.

1 The citation is inexact, but there are similar passages in several epistles, notably Ephesians 5:4.

2 The shrine of St James the Greater, at Compostela.

3 The site of a popular shrine dedicated to the Virgin.

4 A pardoner was originally a man (usually lay or in minor orders) licensed to give papal indulgences that remitted temporal penalties for sins. Gradually, pardoners began selling what they claimed were plenary remissions of the consequences of sins (past, present or to come), besides arrogating to themselves other privileges and powers. Cf. Chaucer's Pardoner in *The Canterbury Tales*.

5 The Black Death, at its worst during 1348–50, killed off so many people that many parishes could not support a priest.

6 Consistory Courts were episcopal courts of great power in cases involving the clergy. Langland often uses them as emblems of Judgment Day.

7 Matthew 16:19.

8 'Cardinal' does in fact derive from the Latin *cardo*, 'a hinge'. The four Cardinal Virtues are Fortitude, Temperance, Prudence and Justice (see Passus 19, lines 269ff.). Langland glances satirically at the other meaning of *Cardinal*.

9 There follows an allegorical account of England's political structure and situation in the 1370s. The king was still a child, so that the country was in theory ruled by a Council of Peers. In fact, however, much of the power lay with John of Gaunt, Duke of Lancaster, and his overbearing followers. In the fable of lines 146–207 (after a sketch of the duties of king, nobles, clergy and commons), the Cat represents John of Gaunt, with Richard II as the Kitten. The Rats are probably the upper-class members of Parliament, the Mice rich

City merchants. The whole fable represents a plea for maintaining the present situation for fear of creating a worse.

10 Usually a lapsed cleric turned wandering poet.

11 Ecclesiastes 10:36.

12 'God preserve you, Dame Emma.' Some lost song – possibly about the sorceress of Passus 13, line 340?

Passus 1

Passus 1 constitutes a moralising commentary on what Langland has described in the Prologue. We are given, as it were, the spiritual aspects of, and background to, what has so far been observed temporally and materialistically. By association, rather than by argument, Lady Holy Church draws us towards the basic theme of the poem: the identity of Truth and Love, and their personification in Christ as the incarnation of God. Langland is quick to ask the question upon which the whole epic hangs – 'How shall I save my soul?' He receives, but does not yet recognise, the same answer as crowns his entire long quest.

1 For the edifying story of Lot, see Genesis 39. The quotation is from verse 32.

2 For the conspiracy of World, Flesh and Devil against mankind, see also Passus 16, lines 24–52.

3 Matthew 22:17–22.

4 Langland's phrase (here as in the Prologue) is *kynde witte*, which might also be rendered as 'natural – or innate – intelligence', implying an inborn sense of right and wrong.

5 The elder-tree is apocryphal, but the belief was widespread, perhaps because of the tradition that the Cross was made of elder-wood (though a Celtic tradition has it made from the wood of a descendant of Adam's tree). For the hanging itself, see Matthew 27:3–5. See also Bennett.

6 The *locus classicus* is 1 John 4:16.

7 St Luke (apparently Langland's favourite evangelist) does not say so. Langland may still be thinking of the context cited above.

8 This anachronism, common medieval currency, may be variously interpreted; but it probably refers to 2 Samuel 23:8 ff.

9 The seven lower orders of faithful angels are Thrones, Dominions, Virtues, Powers, Principalities, Archangels, Angels. The rebellious angels, that became fiends, fairies and other supernatural beings, form a tenth order.

10 A misquotation, occurring elsewhere in the poem, from Isaiah
    14:13–14.
11 Cf. Deuteronomy 10:2.
12 Cf. Isaiah 53:2.
13 John 1:14.
14 Matthew 7:2. The Latin, below, is the Vulgate of this passage.
15 James 2:26.

Passus 2

Having been instructed in the recognition of Truth, the Dreamer
must now learn how to recognise Falsehood (personified in the
Devil). Holy Church shows him (on the ill-omened left side, which in
this case is the North – the Devil's quarter) several examples of
personified evil. Gradually, these begin to act out their allotted parts.

1 Langland uses *Fauvel* to mean – primarily – Flattery. The name
   may ultimately derive from the Latin *fabella*, 'fable, invention, lie',
   but Langland will probably have borrowed it from the earlier
   fourteenth-century *Roman de Fauvel*, by Gervais du Bus. In this
   poem, the name is made cognate with *fauve* and *faux*, 'tawny' (a
   colour of deceit), and 'false'. The name is also an acronym – which
   must be slightly adjusted, in English – of Flattery, Avarice,
   Uncleanness of heart, Variety (fickleness), Envy and Lachete
   (baseness of soul).
2 Properly speaking, 'weed' means simply 'reward' – including fair
   payment for honest work. Langland uses personified Meed to
   represent *corrupt* payments of all kinds. Her clothing may be
   intended to suggest the Scarlet Woman, the Whore of Babylon
   (though she is introduced as a maiden – since she cannot properly
   be said ever to have belonged to any man). She is in any case the
   enemy and antithesis of Holy Church.
3 The first phrase is proverbial, the second from Matthew 7:17.
4 Psalm 15:1ff. – one of Langland's favourite texts.
5 The suggestion of incest is quite possibly intentional. Cf. line 25.
6 Assize-jurors were originally witnesses, upon oath, but had begun
   to move towards the present-day function of jurors; they were in
   either case susceptible to bribery. Summoners were officers of the
   Church whose duty was to bring sinners before ecclesiastical courts.
   Their corruption and venality were notorious: cf. Chaucer's
   Summoner in *The Canterbury Tales*. Pre-emptors were 'purveyors',
   royal officials who oppressed market-folk by buying-up their goods

(at arbitrary low prices), during a royal progress. Provisioners, 'vitaillers', were those who did this with foodstuffs. 'Brokers' here means marriage-brokers – professional go-betweens. The Court of the Arches was the London law-court of the Archbishop of Canterbury. Its (clerical) lawyers charged high fees.

7 What follows is a gorgeous parody of the 'deeds of gift' that often accompanied marriage-settlements.

8 'Pauline' may be a reference to the Crutched Friars ('crutched' = 'crossed' – *cruciati*, from the crosses on their clothes and staffs), a theoretically mendicant order that busied itself in lawsuits. But it is difficult to see a pardoner in such an Order or function; and the reference may be to the preaching that was common at Paul's Cross (pardoners, of course, having no right to preach: see Prologue, line 68; cf. also Passus 10, note 9). All such, together with beadles and reeves and millers, were proverbial for greed and dishonesty.

9 In the passage that follows, Langland (through the mouth of Theology) makes play with the double meaning of 'weed' noted above. Theology's at first surprising defence is of honest payment for services rendered; not of bribery and corruption. Hence his contradictory account of her ancestry.

10 Luke 10:7.

11 What I have called 'pope's-priests' were 'prouisoures' – clerics arbitrarily given benefices, over the heads of other eligible priests, by the pope or by his delegates. Such appointments were open to accusations of simony. Note that in the whole of this splendidly satirical passage, *all* the officials (clerical or not) who ride or are ridden to the King's Court at Westminster, are implicitly accused of corrupt venality. It may also be a fresh satirical touch that it is *Fauvel* who orders the mounts: in Gervais du Bus he is himself a tawny stallion.

12 The Commissary was an episcopal officer to whom bishops delegated special legal powers outside the Consistory Court itself.

Passus 3

Meed is brought for trial before the King at Westminster. She is treated at first as an innocent victim of unscrupulous people; but very soon the venal frequenters of the Court are 'making up' to her. In this Passus, the attack upon Meed by Conscience is a counterbalance to her defence in Passus 2 by Theology. It constitutes the Dreamer's first ideally spiritual – as distinct from piously practical – advance.

1 It was a fairly common practice, for people who could afford it, thus to decorate and restore a Friary or its church – and have one's name and portrait recorded there in stained glass. To be one of the Friars' Lay Sisters was to become, with no further effort unless a little more money, a participant in their spiritual privileges. Langland several times mentions the practice, with disapproval.

2 Cf. Matthew 6:1–4. The Vulgate quotation and Authorised Version paraphrase after line 72 are from the same source.

3 Pillories were at this time used to punish various kinds of dishonest trading, especially those involving food. The 'penal stools' were ducking-stools, an equivalent punishment for female offenders.

4 Not Solomon, but Job 15:34. I have not given the Authorised Version, since Langland himself at once paraphrases the passage.

5 There is no known historical connection between bribery and the dethronement and murder of Edward II – the king presumably referred to.

6 Again, no literal connection can be made with the poisoning of a pope; but see Passus 15, lines 521–2, and the notes on that couplet.

7 A reference to the secret and illicit use of the Privy Seal for the obtaining of benefices.

8 Love-days were sessions of the Manorial Courts, for the settling of minor local disputes.

9 Meed is referring to the disastrous French Campaign by Edward III, 1359–60, which resulted in his signing away most of his French possessions – for money – and in which the troops were indeed demoralised by great storms. It is hard to see how *Conscience* can be blamed for any of the misfortunes and misdeeds alleged by her; and while meed *as soldiers' pay* is certainly a great heartener of troops, it was meed *as pusillanimous greed* that caused Edward to sign the Treaty of Brétigny. Perhaps Langland intends Meed's arguments to be confused and false? Later in her defence, however, she copies Theology in assuming the righteous interpretation of her name; and for a while, this convinces the king.

10 Psalm 15 again, as are the texts after lines 234 and 240.

11 A reference to Luke 6:38, and to the bottomless greed of the corrupt.

12 Psalm 26:10.

13 Matthew 6:5.

14 The story is in 1 Samuel 15, *et seq.*

15 Ibid.

16 Isaiah 2:4.

17 Ibid.

18 This is a parody, but a half-serious one, of fake astrological predictions. There is no point in attempting a Nostradamian interpretation for every detail; the purport is plain enough – eventual salvation for all the peoples of the world.

19 Proverbs 22:1.

20 Langland paraphrases the Vulgate of Proverbs 22:9. The Authorised Version differs. The joke, expounded by Conscience, is that Meed's mock-bashful claim to be unlearned is howlingly confirmed: the last phrase of (Vulgate) 22:9 is by no means to Meed's purpose, and is quoted by Conscience after line 345. It is not found in the Authorised Version.

21 Thessalonians 5:21.

22 See note 20.

Passus 4

Meed's trial, or rather examination, is suspended while Conscience rides away to bring Reason back to Court. Meanwhile, there has begun a case that is to end in the overthrow of Meed and most of her adherents. The king pledges himself to reform the State, and to use Conscience, Reason and Obedience to that end – and also for the reformation of society *per se*. Note that all moral advances are still those of *practical* good behaviour, and imply no real spiritual change.

1 'Cato' refers to neither of the great Romans, but to a collection of moral proverbs called *Catonis Disticha* – 'Cato's Couplets'. They are the work of one Dionysius Cato, *fl*. fourth century AD. They formed part of every grammar-school curriculum, and were a favourite source of quotations for Langland. The point is that basic education (Cato) is the servant of Reason (see Bennett). 'Tom True-tongue (etc.)' represents decent and sensible conversation. The horse represents watchful patience, and its girths are *good advice*. Its bridle must be heavy so as to encourage humility.

2 These two represent *worldly* wisdom and native cunning (Bennett).

3 Romans 3:16–17.

4 Ibid., verse 18.

5 'Wrong' is no longer the Devil, as in Passus 1, but a purveyor (see Passus 2, note 6). 'Peace' is here an oppressed farmer.

6 This was another abuse – under-payment by a tally that could in theory, but not always in practice, be off-set against taxes.

7 Because when criminals were convicted in Royal Courts, all their property escheated (was forfeited) to the Crown – unless, as Wisdom hints, the criminal could buy himself off. Later, Wisdom suggests to the king another such transaction: that Wrong be released by Mainprise (or suretyship); that is to say, upon bail which he would promptly skip. Meed shall be his mainpernor, or surety, after which no more need be said about his crimes.

8 Emblem of a proudly-dressed woman. Cf. Passus 5, lines 26 and 63.

9 Religious who forsake their cloisters either for pure pleasure, or to go on needless pilgrimages, such as (lines 126–7) to the shrine of St James at Compostela.

10 Perhaps meant literally; but most likely a reference to fees taken by officials or the Papal Court in exchange for judgments or benefices.

11 See Passus 2, note 11.

12 The riddle derives from a precept of Pope Innocent III's: that that man is a just judge *qui nullum malum praeterit impunitum, nullum bonum irremuneratum* – who lets no evil go unpunished, no good unrewarded.

Passus 5

This Passus marks the beginning of the true quest, Reason's sermon moving everyone to repentance; the poet puns on his name, Will, to show that human resolve is beginning to reform. The goal is now spiritual as well as practical. The Seven Deadly Sins, personified, confess and repent and are shriven. Christ's aid must be enlisted before Truth can be found and redemption achieved; and meanwhile, who can guide the world along the right path? Not the false palmer (lines 523ff. – the corrupt Church), but the true pilgrim – Piers. At this stage, he personifies natural and instinctive goodness (as described by Holy Church in Passus 1). Further, as a ploughman, he represents honest and productive toil, which Langland repeatedly maintains to be the root and bedrock of sincere practical Christianity. Piers Ploughman's description of the Way to Truth is an allegory of spiritual progress, and leads to an allegorical description of the human soul itself.

1 The Plague was by now very seldom quite absent; but there were serious outbreaks on at least four occasions between 1369 and 1375. There was a great storm on Saturday, 15 January 1361 (1362 by modern reckoning).

2 See Passus 4, note 8.

3 To beat his wife so as to save her from the ducking stool that was the fate of scolds.

4 Half-a-mark was 6s.8d., or nearly 34p in modern currency. A mark was a good month's wages for an artisan.

5 Proverbs 13:24.

6 Matthew 25:12.

7 The Holy Ghost.

8 Here, the personified Sin of Pride.

9 Since Envy was a sin commonly attributed to friars (Bennett).

10 Sugar was considered medicinal. I have used 'twisted canes of candy' to translate Langland's *diapenidion*, a medical form of barley-sugar (Bennett).

11 It is noteworthy that Wrath is not presented as himself an angry man (as, in fact, Envy *is*), but as a cause of anger and contention in others.

12 Limiters were friars licensed to beg only in specific areas. 'Lectors' *may* here mean 'lecturers'; but a Lector is one of the lowest Minor Orders of the Church.

13 This must be meant allegorically, for of course he had no right within the convent walls (for, in fact, despite line 136, as a gardener he would have been a layman; and even friars needed a special dispensation).

14 It was Gregory IX (Pope 1227–41), not St Gregory I or St Gregory VII, who forbade abbesses to hear confessions.

15 Probably a reference to 1 Peter 4:7.

16 The purpose of this portrait is to demonstrate that every trade and profession uses dishonest tricks to increase profits; hence the diverse occupations pursued by Covetousness and his wife. For no clearly known reason, Langland in line 189 calls him 'Sir Harvey'.

17 So that it would stretch.

18 Pudding-ale was thick and inferior, but she sold it mixed with smaller quantities of good ale (Bennett).

19 In other words, at nearly three times the normal price for good ale.

20 Strictly 'regrater' – one who buys cheaply and gains a local monopoly, then sells dearly.

21 The priory of St Andrew, near Bromholm in Norfolk, had a cross reputed to have been made from the True Cross. It was not far from the shrine at Walsingham, a favourite resort for pilgrims (Goodridge & Bennett).

22 Punning on *French* in its meaning of 'cant' or 'jargon'. Norfolk was supposed to be a particularly dishonest county.

23 Even more than the Jews, whom at this period they outnumbered in England, the Lombards were hated as extortionate money-lenders.

24 The 'cross' was the 'heads' side of a coin (the reverse being *pile)*. The pun is of course on Christ's Cross.

25 I do not know the origin of this couplet.

26 From St Augustine's *Epistles* (Bennett).

27 Psalm 51:6. The 'gloss' will be the *Glossa Ordinaria* (see Bennett).

28 Psalm 18:25–6; but the Authorised Version does not translate *sanctus*, 'holy'.

29 Psalm 145:9.

30 Nowhere literally in the Scriptures. 'Scintilla' really means *spark*.

31 These bits-and-pieces are too trivial to interfere with his fast – or so she would persuade him.

32 This curious game was a kind of barter in which appointed judges estimated the difference in value to be paid by one or other owner of two articles offered for exchange. Here, the difference in value between Hicks's hood and Clement's cloak is only a mug of ale – which was no doubt the primary purpose of the game.

33 Robin Hood was a real person, alive and in trouble with the law in the early thirteenth century. His exploits, of course, are fictitious. It is doubtful which Randolph of Chester Langland had in mind; but it is interesting to learn that ballads about both people were already current. Cf. Bennett & Goodridge.

34 Duty should have called him to *early* Mass, and at his parish church. Even at the Friary Mass he arrives only when it is virtually over.

35 The opening phrases of Psalms 1 and 128.

36 Langland calls this person *Vigilate*, 'Be watchful', in reference either to Mark 13:35–7, or to Matthew 26:41. *Leveilleur* = 'the waker'.

37 Romans 13:7. The theme of *restitution* is central to the two closing Passus, but is in a sense basic to Langland's view of Christianity.

38 This is the name given, in the apocryphal Gospel of Nicodemus, to the penitent thief, though his name also appears as Dimas and even Titus. (The impenitent one was Gestas or Gesmas.) For the canonical account of the incident, see Luke 23:39–43, as also for 'remember me' in line 474.

39 *Latro* is Latin (and masculine) for 'robber'. It is the word used in the Vulgate for Christ's fellow-sufferers on Cavalry.

40 Genesis 1:26.

41 1 John 4:16. The Latin before line 499 is from Ephesians 4:8.

42 Isaiah 9:2.

43 Mark 16:9, etc.

44 Luke 5:32.

45 John 1:4.

46 Psalm 71:20 – though the Authorised Version differs.

47 Psalm 32:1.

48 Psalm 36:6–7.

49 A representation of the kerchief reputedly lent by Veronica to Christ, to wipe His face – which left its likeness on the cloth.

50 That of St Thomas à Becket, in Canterbury. As perhaps the most popular in England, it was notable for its rich endowments.

51 Exodus 20:12. Others of the Ten Commandments are paraphrased in the lines that follow. Cf. also Deuteronomy 5:7–21.

52 The human soul.

53 A theme often found in medieval literature. Cf. the ninth-century hymn *Ave maris stella* – 'Hail, Star of the Sea' – stanza 1, line 4: in this the Virgin is called *felix coeli porta*, 'blissful gate of Heaven'.

54 Cf. Hosea 13:3.

55 That is, your soul may linger in Purgatory.

56 Seven Virtues (though not the conventional list) to balance the Seven Deadly Sins.

57 Bishops' bulls were letters authorising the sale of indulgences.

Passus 6

As we have seen, Langland believed honest labour to be an essential part of practical Christianity. Those people who agree to follow Piers, in search of Truth, must work in his field until the harvest is complete. Piers's 'half acre' of course represents all Middle Earth; and, while both work and harvest are *literally* meant, they are also emblematic of spiritual cultivation. Human nature being what it is, the whole project quickly comes to a standstill.

1 Luke 14:10.

2 But not for the profitless, dishonest and immoral callings that he lists: they are *ipso facto* damned, short of repentance and amendment. Cf. the Prologue, lines 35–45.

3 Psalm 69:28.

4 Ibid.

5 Cf. Deuteronomy 24:10–13. Again the theme of restitution.

6 An eighth-century image of Christ, crucified but regally dressed, in Lucca Cathedral.

7 Perhaps an uncloistered monk, or a goliard.

8 Bretons, like Gascons at a later period, had a reputation for boasting.

9 Bayard was a common, and hence generic, name for a horse. The food is presumably bran-mash, since *baken*, like modern German *backen*, did not have the limited meaning of modern English 'bake', though I have used that word for convenience,

10 Galatians 6:2.

11 Hebrews 10:30 and Romans 10:19.

12 Luke 16:9.

13 Genesis 3:19.

14 Proverbs 20:4.

15 The image of a man, or of a man's face, was the emblem of this evangelist.

16 See Matthew 25:14ff.

17 Ibid., verse 29.

18 Psalm 128:2.

19 I do not know what particular kind of fur *Calabrian* fur was, except that it was grey (Bennett); but physicians were a byword for (ill-gotten) wealth.

20 From *Cato's Couplets*. See Passus 4, note 1, and Bennett.

21 The ineffective Statutes of Labourers attempted to halt the increased demands of workmen (prompted by the scarcity of labour, and the widespread emancipation of villeins, after the Black Death). But Hunger's Law, says Langland, is always observed.

22 As with the 'prophecy' in Passus 3 (see note 18 on that Passus), there is little point in labouring for detailed explanations of this passage. But a few points may be noted. 'Waken with the waters' does suggest the floods of line 326; Saturn is (astrologically) malignant, and associated with winter, famine and certain diseases. The sun standing awry suggests an eclipse (there was one in 1377); and the monks' heads remind us of the lack of charity in the Church. The maiden having mastery refers to Meed and her continuing reign with even greater power. Further suggestions are made by Bennett and Goodridge.

Passus 7

Piers's project having broken down, all thoughts of a literal pilgrimage, even within the terms of allegory, have been abandoned (except, in later Passus, for Langland individually; and even that is emblematic). The precept now is to be: *Cultivate your own fields; save your soul at home, by honest labour, humble devoutness and practical charity.* This will prove more effective than all the indulgences and false pardons that you may purchase: there is a *true* pardon, summed-up in the words 'Do well'.

This Passus ends the first part of the epic, but with hints of what is to come – namely, Langland's quest (within himself) for the *meaning* of 'Do-Well', personified, and his companions Do-Better and Do-Best. The later significance of Piers is also foreshadowed: already he is offering himself as a mediator for the salvation of others.

1 Such a plenary (and hereditary) pardon is beyond the power of any Church official, even the highest: only God can remit the guilt itself, as well as the punishment for it.

2 Goodridge says that this means the two divisions of the Ten Commandments – those relating to God, and those relating to our neighbours. Bennett says it means Canon Law and Civil Law. Most probably it refers to the Old and the New Testaments, as elsewhere in the poem.

3 A misquotation from Psalm 15:5.

4 Not in the Bible.

5 Psalm 15:5. Substituted for Langland's 15:1.

6 'Very small'.

7 Matthew 7:12.

8 Cato here is the Cato who wrote the *Disticha* or Couplets. See notes above. The 'Clerk of the Stories' was the twelfth-century Peter Comestor, who wrote an *Historia Scholastica* which was a (legendarily) expanded version of the Bible (Skeat).

9 Not Gregory, but Jerome in his commentary on Ecclesiastes (Bennett).

10 Luke 19:23.

11 From St Jerome's Epistles (Bennett).

12 Psalm 37:25.

13 Cf. the Athanasian Creed, and its basis in Matthew 25:46. Piers is infuriated (line 116) because this is *not* a full pardon for all his helpers, but merely a restatement of what he and they have already been taught: it is valid as a pardon *only conditionally* – upon good

behaviour. Piers thereupon resolves to live like a hermit, offering his own piety on behalf of mankind.

14 Psalm 23:4. This verse has sometimes been interpreted as a resolve to live faithfully and piously, without fear, even when surrounded by malicious unbelievers (Goodridge). If that is its import here, it may mean that Piers rejects the Priest's casual dismissal of the pardon – which, though not what Piers expected (see previous note), is nevertheless a guarantee of salvation *upon terms*.

15 Psalm 42:3.

16 A paraphrase of Matthew 6:31.

17 Psalm 14:1.

18 I have corrected Langland's misquotation of the Vulgate (Proverbs 22:10).

19 Langland is here muddling Daniel 2 with Daniel 5. The dream cited by him in fact concerned Belshazzar.

20 Genesis 37:9–10, 41:39–41, and succeeding chapters.

21 Biennial and triennial masses were those endowed, for such periods, on behalf of a dead person. For Bishops' Bulls, see Passus 5, note 57.

22 Matthew 16:19.

23 By the Four Orders, Langland means the Augustinians, Carmelites, Dominicans and Franciscans. Friars could give lay people (sometimes whole families) 'letters of fraternity', thus creating them 'confraters' or associate-members of the Order. Cf. Passus 3, note 1. This gave them the privilege of being prayed for during life and after death; but it cost money. The Provincial was the monastic head of a given district, and had the power to distribute letters of indulgences. Such indulgences (see note 1) were in fact limited; but pardoners, and others, let it be thought that one could thus buy one's way into Heaven.

Passus 8

This Passus describes the Dreamer's hesitant beginning in his quest for Do-Well, Do-Better and Do-Best. Passus 7 was the start of a transition from *temporal* to *spiritual* concerns (hints of which had been given in earlier Passus). But, misled by his encounters with the two Friars, and with Thought, the poet still continues for several Passus (*a*) to believe that Do-Well, Do-Better and Do-Best are *separate* modes of life (only towards the end does he see that, like the Trinity itself, they are triune); (*b*) to look for them in the worldly and practical kind of Life that he has explored in the Prologue and the first seven Passus, rather than looking for them in spiritual development. He must learn that they are not constituted by *actions*, merely, but by an attitude of mind that must necessarily *bring about* good actions.

Langland sees quite easily through the Friars' facile and superficial complacency. But Thought is harder to reject, since he represents the limit of the Dreamer's present ability. Only Reason, says Thought, can teach Langland how to *apply* his moral principles.

1 Franciscan Masters of Divinity.
2 Latin: 'On the contrary!' This was the formal signal of a rebuttal in the debates or 'quodlibets' of the Theological Schools.
3 Proverbs 24:16.
4 An echo of Luke 16:9. Cf. Passus 6, line 230.
5 2 Corinthians 11:19. Langland misunderstands, or perhaps for dramatic reasons allows Thought to misunderstand, St Paul's *statement* – and takes it to be an injunction. See also Passus 20, note 3, and Goodridge.
6 The word in Langland is *Witte*, which throughout the poem has many shades of meaning. In this context, the name could also be rendered as Intelligence or Native Good Sense.

Passus 9

Reason's answer to Will's question begins as an allegory of the human body – for it is in the healthy interaction of the natural human faculties (bodily and mental) that Reason claims Do-Well is to be found. Most of the evil in the world, he says, arises from the misuse of one or more of these faculties: Do-Well is rational obedience to God's laws; and whatever is contrary to Nature and Good Sense, is criminal. Do-Well is therefore basically spiritual in origin, though physical in its effects.

1 In Langland, *Kynde* – another word with several shades of meaning. It can mean 'Nature', 'human nature', 'all that is naturally ordained', 'all that is innate'. Therefore, 'unkynde' can mean *unnatural* as well as *cruel* (Langland would have found the difference very slight, in any case). In this context, of course, Kynde (or Nature) means *God*.
2 The doctrine of Empedocles, that all things were composed of various admixtures of four 'elements'. My translation modifies Langland's text: he omits Fire, since for him *eyre* meant the fire of the upmost atmosphere, whereas the air that we breathe he called *wynde*.

3 The human soul.

4 Satan. See John 12:3.

5 That is, Do-Well guards the frontiers of body and soul from the invasion of evil.

6 For metrical convenience (and anyway not without justification!) I have thus translated Langland's *Inwitte*, which might also be rendered as Good Sense, and elsewhere also carries the modern meaning of conscience.

7 Psalm 148:5.

8 All three Persons of the Trinity acted simultaneously in creating Man. 'Let *us* make . . . ' (Genesis 1:26) implies this. Langland's text is very confused, but not in fact contradictory, since the Word may be used either as an intermediary or as part of a simultaneous act. See Goodridge.

9 The word used here by Langland is the same *Inwit* (so spelt in this context) as in line 18; but it does not refer to the *person*.

10 Philippians 3:19.

11 1 John 4:16.

12 Matthew 25.12 and Psalm 81.12, respectively.

13 St Jerome, St Gregory, St Augustine and St Ambrose. Cf. Passus 19, lines 262–8.

14 'There is nothing directly relevant in Luke. Goodridge suggests Acts 6:1–4 or James 1:27.

15 Both quotations are from Peter Cantor's *Compendium* (Goodridge).

16 Proverbs 9:10.

17 James 2:10.

18 Psalm 34:10.

19 At the marriage at Cana. John 2:1–10.

20 It was believed that Cain was conceived during a time when his parents should by duty have abstained from intercourse (in penance for their sin). Though, in any case, Jewish law too proscribed certain times. Cf. Leviticus 12:2–5 and 15:16–28, etc. This meant that he was born cursed with wickedness, and all his descendants would be cursed and wicked too.

21 Psalm 7:4.

22 This tradition is not in canonical scripture; but it was believed that Genesis 6:1–4 referred to the intermarriage of Cainites with Sethites.

23 Genesis 6:6–7.

24 Genesis 6:14–20.

25 Ezekiel 18:20.

26 Matthew 7:16.

27 John 14:6 – I am the way and the truth.'
28 An ancient Essex ceremony, still observed, was that if a couple
   could swear that they had never quarrelled, nor regretted their
   marriage (and could maintain their word under severe cross-
   examination), they would be awarded with a flitch – a whole side,
   salted and cured – of bacon.
29 Goodridge says that the Latin is by John of Bridlington.
30 On days of fasting or other penitence.
31 1 Corinthians 7:2.

Passus 10

Reason's speech displeases his wife, Dame Study. She believes
Langland to be a sensual hypocrite merely toying with amateur
theology, rather than genuinely seeking Do-Well. She attacks all
quibbling arguments and fine distinctions unless they are undertaken
by serious, expert and devout scholars. When Langland protests his
own earnestness, she relents and sends him off to her kinsfolk Clerisy
(or Learning) and his wife Scripture (which means not merely the Old
and New Testaments, but all sacred or devout writings). Together,
this couple imply *all* knowledge proper for a Christian to possess. It
should be noted that Langland has gained virtually nothing from
Reason and Study, but still clings to his intellectual preconceptions.
Even from Clerisy and Scripture he gains little more save to be driven
into the opposite camp and to regard faith alone (without intellect or
learning) as Do-Well.

1 Matthew 7:6.
2 'Gem' derives from the Latin *gemma*, a bud – and reflects the belief
  that such stones grew organically.
3 The 'love-days' previously noted (Passus 3, note 8).
4 Cf. Job 21:7 ff. and Jeremiah 12:1.
5 Psalm 73:12.
6 Psalm 11:3 in the Vulgate; but both the Prayer Book and the
  Authorised Version differ from the Latin.
7 Cf. Passus 2, line 111.
8 Psalm 132:6. Langland has completely misunderstood the text. As
  the biblical 'gloss' points out, and the New English Bible makes
  plain, David is talking about a new home for the Ark of the
  Covenant. Langland believes the text to imply that God Himself is
  found among the fields and woods, and their inhabitants, rather
  than among rich townsfolk.

9 Not in the Cathedral, but outside, at St Paul's Cross.

10 Isaiah 58:7.

11 The Apocrypha rather than the Bible properly so called. Tobit 4:8.

12 Ezekiel 18:20.

13 Galatians 6:5.

14 The English is Authorised Version, Romans 12:3. The words of the Vulgate mean 'not to have more wisdom than it is proper to have'.

15 Langland's word is *clergye* – 'clerkship', not necessarily implying ordination, but only the state of being literate and well read.

16 Medieval education comprised two main groups of studies. The Trivium consisted of grammar, logic and rhetoric; the Quadrivium, of arithmetic, geometry, astronomy and music.

17 This is again Cato of the *Disticha*. But cf. Passus 18, note 14.

18 Galatians 6:10.

19 Romans 12:19. See also, as previously noted, Hebrews 10:30.

20 Do-Well, in short, is adherence to Christian faith. Although Will comes to embrace this as the literal and exclusive nature of Do-Well, he is not much advanced by it – nor by Clerisy's denunciation of corruption in the Church (which he himself has already denounced).

21 John 14:9–10.

22 A dictum of St Gregory's (Goodridge).

23 I cannot trace the quotation verbatim; but the motto is familiar enough.

24 Again untraceable by me.

25 Matthew 7:3.

26 Ibid., verse 4.

27 Not Mark, but Luke 6:39.

28 The story is in 1 Samuel 4.

29 Psalm 50:21.

30 Isaiah 56:10.

31 Cf. the Prologue to *The Canterbury Tales*, lines 177–82. The origin of the saying appears *not* to be Gregory, but Gratian's *Decretum*. Still, the 'fish out of water' simile is widespread.

32 Matthew 21:12; Mark 11:15; Luke 19:45.

33 Psalm 1:1.

34 Psalm 20:7–8.

35 An allusion to the pretended Donation of Constantine (d.337), by which the Emperor allegedly endowed Pope Sylvester and his successors in perpetuity with wealth and temporal power. Cf. Passus 15, lines 519–23. It was Gregory who sent Augustine to

Britain, where he founded monasticism; hence 'Gregory's godchildren'. See also Passus 15, note 50.

36 An old and rich abbey, taken as typical.

37 Isaiah 14:4–5.

38 Here an emblem of Antichrist, who shall eventually be defeated by the King of Heaven and His loyal followers – not, as Will here supposes, by secular power.

39 1 Timothy 6:9–11.

40 Ecclesiasticus 10:9.

41 From Cato's *Disticha*.

42 James 2:5–6. Also Luke 16:19ff. – the parable of Dives and Lazarus.

43 Cf. note on Passus 8, line 20.

44 There is nothing explicitly to this purpose in either Peter or Paul. Perhaps Langland was thinking of Mark 16:16.

45 Colossians 3:1.

46 Exodus 20:13 – the sixth Commandment. See also Deuteronomy 5:17.

47 Romans 12:19, with the Authorised Version and (lines 370–1) with Langland's gloss. See also Hebrews 10:30.

48 Cf. Revelation 20:12–15.

49 John 3:13 – i.e., a man's fate is known only to God.

50 Even in Minor Orders, Langland must have known that the Church *could* not pronounce finally on such a matter.

51 Matthew 23:2.

52 Psalm 36:6.

53 See Luke 23: 39ff. The Harrowing of Hell – the release from damnation of certain patriarchs, prophets and others – is not specifically recounted in the canonical Gospels, but in that of Nicodemus (which was, in the Middle Ages, accorded virtually canonical respect).

54 Ecclesiastes 9:1.

55 Latin and early Middle French. Origin unknown to me.

56 The Latin, 'nobody good', is too terse for a certain attribution. Psalm 14:1? Matthew 19:17? The latter is likelier.

57 Langland's paraphrase of Mark 13:9–11.

58 Langland's paraphrase of Psalm 119:46.

59 Cf. Passus 9, line 72, and note 13 on that Passus.

60 Matthew 20:4.

Passus 11

Langland has in effect rejected secular power, learning and reason, and even good works, as fallible if not fallacious means to Do-Well. For this, he is rebuked by Scripture. Now thoroughly discouraged, he abandons his quest for many years – which he spends in idle and lascivious pleasure. He is pulled up sharply, however: first by fear, then by Loyalty (which in this context means general uprightness and honest living, and adherence to the basic tenets of the Church). Now he is made to see that all that he has rejected *may* be valid, but only if inspired and infused by love – by *caritas*, or Christian charity and loving-kindness. Also, he must stop *questioning* everything for a reason. This he cannot yet do, until brought by Imagination into a broader view both of the world and of the inner self (the process only begins in this Passus, and belongs chiefly to the next).

1 From St Bernard.
2 See 1 John 2:16. The phrase 'pride of perfect living' does not occur there in the Authorised Version, nor in the Vulgate. The New English Bible renders the phrase as 'all the glamour of [the world's] life'.
3 Not Plato, but a familiar adage perhaps derived from Proverbs 16:9.
4 Perhaps based upon Matthew 6:34.
5 Complex puns are involved here. 'Reason' – *witte* – is both the Dreamer's, and generically human, good sense, and the character called by me *Intelligence* (and by Langland Witte) in Passus 8 and 9. 'Will', as on certain other occasions – as in Passus 5, line 62 – puns upon the Dreamer's name and on childishly human obstinacy and self-seeking.
6 See Passus 3, lines 35ff., and elsewhere, for the notoriously easy penances given by well-fed friars. Cf. Passus 7, lines 191–3, for Provincials' letters, pardons and acceptance into Fraternities. See *passim* for friars' venality!
7 Untraced by me in this form, but related to the basic theme of *restitution*. But cf. Passus 5, note 26.
8 But of course Langland knows that their motive was the high burial-fee that they would charge.
9 Untraced by me; but, again, related to the theme of penitence and restitution. See note 7.
10 John 3:5.
11 There is nothing quite like this in either of Peter's Epistles or any

of Paul's. The general principle may, however, be found in several texts; and as the words stand, they are a misquotation of Leviticus 19:17. Langland is punning (I believe he is pretending to do so naïvely) upon the Latin *frater*, which translates both as *brother* and as *friar*.

12   Matthew 7:1.

13   I follow Goodridge here in replacing Langland's repetitive *Non oderis fratrem* – 'Thou shalt not hate thy brother' – with 1 Timothy 5:20, which is more to the poet's point.

14   Psalm 50:21.

15   They must observe the seal of the Confessional.

16   Untraced by me.

17   The reference is to Matthew 22:1–14.

18   Isaiah 55:1.

19   Mark 16:16. The second, unquoted, part of the verse is also meant to be in readers' minds: 'but he that believeth not shall be damned'.

20   Psalm 145:9.

21   The account given by Langland, and by Trajan himself, closely follows a widespread medieval legend. The point is that St Gregory's prayers for Trajan's salvation would not *in themselves* have sufficed to redeem an unbaptised misbeliever; but Trajan's own instinctive excellence of character, *plus* the prayers, *did* suffice. Some versions have it, however, that he first had to be restored to life, and baptised.

22   See Passus 10, note 16.

23   1 John 3:14.

24   Luke 14:12–13.

25   Cf. 1 Peter 2:2.

26   John 8:34.

27   Galatians 6:2.

28   The story is in Luke 7:37–50.

29   Matthew 7:2.

30   See Luke 24:13–31.

31   Luke 10:38–42.

32   Obviously, therefore, not Matthew. This quotation is from the same source as the last.

33   Proverbs 30:8.

34   Again, not Luke; it is Matthew 19:21.

35   Psalm 37:25.

36   Based upon Matthew 17:20.

37   Psalm 34:10.

38 Psalm 43:1.

39 Langland misquotes the Vulgate, giving *Deo*, 'God', instead of *Domino*, 'Lord'. It is Psalm 37:3.

40 James 2:10

41 Psalm 47:6–7

42 Here, as sometimes elsewhere, to be taken as God the Creator.

43 A superstition traceable, like so many, to Aristotle.

44 It was believed that the lecherous peacock sought out the eggs of his hen so as to break them – thus inducing her to fresh copulation; see Skeat.

45 Adjured by St Paul (1 Corinthians 4:5), Reason must suspend judgment and so must Langland.

46 1 Peter 2:13.

47 Ecclesiasticus 11:9.

48 Genesis 1:31.

49 Genesis 1:22–6.

50 Boethius, Book One, Prosa 7. Cf. Chaucer's version: 'This feynede philosophre took pacience a litel while; and when he hadde resceyved wordes of outrage, he, as in stryvynge ayen and rejoysynge of hymself, seide at the laste ryght thus: "undirstondistow nat that I am a philosophre?" The tother man answerede ayen ful bytyngly and seyde: "I hadde wel undirstonden it yif thou haddest holde thi tonge stille." '

Passus 12

Imagination is to set Will's muddled and extremist thoughts in order; he sorts out, for the poet, the tangled strands of various theories, relates them to each other, and leads the dreamer towards *acceptances* – towards something like Keats's 'Negative Capability', the ability to remain in uncertainty.

1 Luke 12:38.

2 A misquotation of Revelation 3:19. Cf. also Proverbs 3:12.

3 Psalm 23:4. Langland misunderstands the *protective* purpose of the shepherd's crook and staff, which he takes to be instruments of (loving) punishment.

4 1 Corinthians 13:13. I have not quoted the Authorised Version, since Langland himself immediately paraphrases the text.

5 Rochemadour was a shrine of the Virgin, near Cahors.

6 These are all examples of straying from one's proper concern and duty.

7   Aristotle, as a heathen, could in any case be *presumed* to be damned. Hippocrates murdered his nephew, the even greater physician Galen. Virgil (not the poet, but the medieval necromancer) was carried off by Satan. Alexander died young, murdered by poison.

8   Felicia was the hero Guy of Warwick's wife, who plagued her husband until he deserted her. Rosamund, for centuries a fabulous beauty, was Henry II's mistress until poisoned by his wife.

9   I have not traced this.

10 Luke 6:38.

11 A misquotation of Luke 12:47. I have translated Langland's Latin, and ignored the Authorised Version.

12 1 Corinthians 8:1.

13 John 3:8.

14 John 3:11.

15 John 3:8 again.

16 Leviticus 20:10 is the passage Langland has in mind, but it does not specify death by stoning. Cf. Deuteronomy 22:20–24.

17 John 8:3–11. That Christ wrote *something* on the ground, is canonical; that He wrote about the Jews' sins, is not.

18 Matthew 7:1.

19 One must not partake of Holy Communion if in a state of sin. Cf. 1 Corinthians 11:27–9.

20 Cf. Numbers 1:50–3.

21 1 Samuel 13:9–14.

22 2 Samuel 6:6–7 gives one example.

23 Psalm 105:15.

24 1 Corinthians 3:19.

25 Luke 2:15.

26 Matthew 2:1.

27 This belief is based on the word 'house' in Matthew 2:11 (Goodridge).

28 Luke 2:7, with a comment perhaps of Langland's own.

29 'Glory to God in the Highest!'

30 Psalm 32:1.

31 Matthew 15:14.

32 All who could read must be tried by ecclesiastical courts (if at all), not by secular; thus they escaped hanging. Tyburn, of course, was long one of the most famous gibbet-sites. The quotation from Psalm 16 suggests that this was used as a test of literacy; but the more famous 'neck-verse' (the implication is obvious!) was Psalm 51.

33 Ecclesiasticus 5:5.

34 Psalm 62:12.

35 Psalm 135:6.

36 It is not known to which poet Langland refers – he tends, in any case, to use the word 'poet' loosely – as, for instance, of Plato.

37 Not in his *Logic*, but in his *Natural History*.

38 1 Peter 4:18.

39 I have not been able to identify this and the next Latin quotation.

40 Psalm 23:4.

Passus 13

In this Passus, the Dreamer's quest moves even farther from *literal* towards *spiritual* concepts of 'doing'. The pilgrim called Patience reaffirms that *to love* is to 'Do Best'; and in token of this, the name of Piers Ploughman is heard again: he is now the embodiment of the *caritas* that may save mankind, and of the unpretentious life of the devout poor. In addition to this, the Dreamer himself learns patience and humility. To emphasise the importance of this achievement (and, indeed, of the Passus itself), Langland reintroduces the Seven Deadly Sins by way of Haukyn, the man of Active Life. Haukyn symbolises all worldly, superficial, venal thought and activity – and therefore all the sins that arise from these. He does this very neatly by way of his own inveighing against both laymen and clergy. Gradually, Conscience and Patience begin the cleansing of his coat – the reformation of his sins; his penitence, and his redemption.

1 Luke 10:7.

2 That is to say, after death such sinful friars as this Master (cf. Passus 8, lines 8ff.) will suffer in Purgatory or even in Hell unless they repent and do penance.

3 I do not know the origin of this quotation.

4–9 All these emblematic dishes are phrases from penitential psalms. See Passus 12, note 32 for 4, which is Psalm 51:1, the 'neck-verse'. The remainder are all from Psalm 32.

10 Psalm 51:17.

11 Isaiah 5:22.

12 See 2 Corinthians 11:24–8.

13 Ibid. As earlier, Langland plays on the double meaning of *frater* – either 'brother' or 'friar'.

14 I cannot identify the quotation; but see previous note.

15 *The Apocalypse of Gluttons* was written by Walter Mapes (*c.*1140–1209), who eventually became Archdeacon of Oxford. He

contributed to some versions of the Arthurian Legend, as well as composing this and other satirical works (this one contains specific descriptions of clerical gluttony). By contrast, St Aurea was an eleventh-century Spanish anchoress of (literally) legendary abstemiousness (Goodridge).

16 Matthew 5:19.

17 The first quotation is universal; the second is from Psalm 15:1.

18 This is a riddling way of saying that he carries with him, as a talisman, an image of the *Agnus Dei*, 'the Lamb of God which taketh away the sin of the world' (John 1:29). The days mentioned are those of Easter Week – the Saturday being Passover Day. It was on this day that the pope ritually blessed the *Agnus Dei* images; and it 'starts the calendar' because it was the first day after the redemption of mankind on Good Friday. The 'middle of the moon' will be Easter Day. On Easter Wednesday, church services concentrated upon the neophytes who had been baptised on the preceding Saturday: that in itself was a kind of 'passing over'. Cf. Goodridge.

19 1 John 4:18.

20 See Mark 14:3–9. Though unnamed in that context, the woman is traditionally assumed to have been Mary Magdalen.

21 Luke 19:2–8.

22 Luke 21:1–4.

23 A glancing reference to James 1:3–4.

24 This is Haukyn. In line 221 he looks like a minstrel because of his disreputable clothing (see below). He *calls* himself one because he envies their pay and their abilities (which he affects to despise); but his dissolute life also makes him resemble those minstrels decried in the Prologue, lines 35–9. In fact (line 226) he is a 'waferer': besides being an ordinary baker, he also bakes both sweet wafer-bread and what will become Holy Wafers. I am not sure what allegorical subtlety lies behind these facts, except the (as it were) two-faced nature of his business; but bread' in line 243 means – astonishingly for this period! – *money*. Haukyn is named Active Life *not*, as he claims, because he is a busy and honest trader (and a helper of Piers Ploughman: cf. lines 236–40), but because he interferes in all men's business – for his own aggrandisement (lines 283–313).

25 These are of course *household* minstrels, not itinerants.

26 The heads of St Peter and St Paul on the seal of a papal indulgence.

27 Mark 16:17–8.

28 Acts 3:6. It is perhaps needless to remark that all this argument

(including, I think, the recantation in lines 256–8) is Langland's irony rather than Haukyn's naïvety.

29 Stratford-at-Bow (the odd French of which was spoken by Chaucer's Prioress). It was a busy bread-making centre just outside London (Skeat).

30 Which is very good history. The reference is to John de Chichestre.

31 The first quotation is a slight misrendering of part of Galatians 1:10. The second is Matthew 6:24.

32 The first quotation is slightly misremembered from Psalm 10:7; the second is from Psalm 57:4.

33 Unidentified people, and perhaps imaginary.

34 Matthew 6:21.

35 Luke 6.25.

36 According to Skeat, not a quotation but a general maxim.

37 Psalm 101:7; but both Prayer Book and Authorised Version differ considerably from the Vulgate (and each other). I have given a slightly paraphrased version of the Vulgate.

38 Not John, but Luke 10:16.

Passus 14

The active and sinful life of the world, as allegorised in Haukyn, begins to give way. In its place come the spiritual values – and *techniques* – taught by Patience. These are: patience itself, humility, contrition, happy poverty and, above all, *faith and love (caritas)*.

1 Luke 14:20.

2 The three phrases between lines 17 and 23 constitute the three aspects or acts of Contrition. Sacramental Penance is indeed often referred to as Satisfaction – see line 94.

3 The first part is from Matthew 6:25–6; the second is Langland's (and Patience's) recurrent motto.

4 A slightly garbled version of John 14:13.

5 Matthew 4:4.

6 I do not know the origin of this Leonine hexameter.

7 Psalm 148:5.

8 Psalm 145:16.

9 Exodus 17:6. For the forty years in the wilderness (line 63), see Deuteronomy 1:1–3.

10 Kings 17 and 18.

11 These were the legendary Seven Sleepers of Ephesus. The legend

varies from one source to another, but all agree that seven young Christians fell asleep and were walled up in a cave. The length of their sleep and their eventual fate also vary from one account to another, but the period usually given is two hundred years.

12 A very confused memory of Ezekiel 16:49–50.

13 Sodom and Gomorrah, the Cities of the Plain. See Genesis 18:20 to 19:25.

14 Psalm 32:1.

15 Luke 16:19ff. Neither Vulgate nor Authorised Version has the *name* Dives; it is a Latin adjective, meaning 'rich', misinterpreted as a personal name. *La dolce vita* – 'the pleasant life' – is perhaps more familiar to modern ears than Langland's medieval French equivalent, *douce vye*.

16 Psalm 76:5 – but Vulgate, Prayer Book and Authorised Version all differ widely in their wording. I have made my own translation.

17 Psalm 73:20. Again, the three sources mentioned differ widely. I have used the Prayer Book version.

18 Source dubious, though the spirit is that of Matthew 19:23–4.

19 I have corrected the Latin, which Langland badly misquotes from Isaiah 30:15.

20 Langland is (reverently) parodying the formal introduction to a legal certificate, patent or declaration – that mankind is redeemed by the death of Christ.

21 See above, Passus 3, note 1 – and elsewhere.

22 Langland's Latin reads *Ita impossibile diviti, etc.* – 'Thus it is impossible for a rich man, etc.' – which occurs nowhere in the Bible but is obviously a sketch of Matthew 19:23–4. So I have substituted that, as above.

23 Revelation 14:13.

24 Langland's Latin corresponds exactly neither to Luke 6:20 nor to Matthew 5:3, but is much nearer the latter, which I have substituted.

25 Strictly speaking, it was St Paul who said it, in Philippians 2:7.

26 According to Skeat, this derives from Vincent de Beauvais's *Speculum Historiale* (a paraphrase, says Goodridge). Vincent was a thirteenth-century Dominican, whose major work was this outline of world history – with many legends included.

27 A notorious haunt of robbers, between Surrey and Hampshire (Skeat).

28 Not Seneca, but another quotation from the main Latin passage above; and the Latin after line 305 is from Juvenal's Tenth Satire (Goodridge).

Passus 15

Almost stealthily, as it were, the true concept of Do-Well has been arrived at; and this long Passus is a kind of prologue to Do-Better. Though the Dreamer is rebuked for insatiably wanting to *know*, he is taught that knowledge and learning are perfectly good in themselves *provided* that they operate together with charity (which again, as nearly always in this poem, means *caritas* – though 'charity' in the more usual sense is of course one practical expression of loving-kindness, and is often implied by Langland). And charity can truly operate only through Piers Ploughman – who is now explicitly identified as Christ (line 206).

The perspective of the poem, and of the Dreamer, broadens to take in – for the Church and for all mankind – a vision of this loving-kindness working hand-in-hand with learning, wisdom, contented poverty and the virtues already learnt. The personal and purely temporal are being more and more transcended: we are now concerned with the possibility of universal salvation, by means of Charity; and the Dreamer is almost ready for the vision (in the next Passus) of Piers tending the Tree of Charity.

1 Peter is 'porter', of course, by virtue of his holding the keys of Heaven (Matthew 16:19). St Paul's falchion is an emblem of his martyrdom.

2 An example of Langland's shaky Latin. His source (Isidore only, not Augustine as he claims: see Goodridge) has *recolit*, 'remembers', which makes sense of *Memoria*. Langland confuses the verb *recolo* with some other that means 'to complain' – perhaps *recuso*, 'to object, to take exception'. Strictly speaking, moreover, even *recolo* (used figuratively as here) means less 'recollect' than 'turn over in one's mind'.

3 This is of course the passage in Isidore *(Etymologiarum Liber)* cited earlier by Langland.

4 *Presul* (Classical Latin *praesul*) originally meant a public dancer; did it acquire its clerical meaning from the story of David's dance before the Ark of the Covenant (2 Samuel 6:14)? *Pontifex*, originally 'bridge-builder', came to mean 'high-priest', hence 'pontiff', 'archbishop' and even 'pope'. A metropolitan bishop *(metropolitanus)* is also an archbishop, the bishop of a metropolis. *Episcopus* is the general term for a plain diocesan bishop. *Pastor*, 'shepherd', can mean any cleric with Cure of Souls, but specifically an ecclesiastical Visitor, or inspector, who would usually be of episcopal rank.

5 Isaiah 14:14.

6 Proverbs 25:27.

7 In St Bernard's *Epistles* (Goodridge).

8 Unidentified by me, but of course referring to Genesis 3:1–19.

9 The Latin is Romans 12:3. But see Passus 10, note 14.

10 Psalm 97:7.

11 Psalm 4:2; but I have substituted 'lying' for the Authorised Version's archaic 'leasing'.

12 In other words, 'Go to St Augustine's commentary, and check whether I am a heretic.'

13 The Latin is a misquotation from either James 2:1 or Deuteronomy 16:19. I have opted for the latter. Cf. also Leviticus 19:15.

14 I do not know where; but the likeness to a 'whited sepulchre' (not as in Langland) is in Matthew 23:27; and there is a 'whited wall' in Acts 23:3.

15 Not in fact from his works, but from an anonymous set of homilies (Goodridge).

16 A baselard was a kind of dagger, or sometimes a short sword. Priests were in fact forbidden to wear either weapons or frivolous adornments (see also below, lines 120–1, and elsewhere in the poem).

17 'Sir' was formerly a title of priests as well as of knights.

18 Matthew 18:3.

19 1 Corinthians 13:4–5 (slightly compressed).

20 The quotation is from 1 Corinthians 13:12. 'Mirrored in me' implies *both* Christ's assumption of human form, *and* that Will can understand Christ as perfect Man, but not as Charity incarnate.

21 A tunic from Tartary would probably be of silk, and a costly rarity. At this time, 'scarlet' was not necessarily red, but a particular kind of fine cloth, of any colour.

22 Obscure. Perhaps it means simply that he is devoted to prayer, of which he 'makes a fine art'.

23 The laundry is of course a symbol for contrition and penance (it is often forgotten that 'contrite' derives ultimately from the Latin *tero*, 'to rub, as in cleaning', and *contero*, 'to wear away by rubbing or battering' – still methods of laundry in Ireland and Egypt). The quaint locution 'a mile's length', as a measure of *time*, may refer to the time it takes an average man to walk a mile; but this does not seem a very long period of contrition.

24 The original line ends in Latin – *laboravi in gemitu meo*, 'I am weary with my groaning', from Psalm 6:6.

25 Psalm 51:17.

26 Matthew 9:4. This quotation, as applied to Piers, prepares us for the *identity* stated in line 206.

27 Langland gives the last four words in Latin: *petrus, id est, Christus.* This is done deliberately, to recall 1 Corinthians 10:4 – *'petra autem erat Christus'* – 'and that rock was Christ' (which itself echoes the well-known pun in Matthew 16:18: *'tu es Petrus, et super hanc petram aedificabo ecclesiam meam'* – 'thou art Peter, and upon this rock I will build my church'.

28 The Lollards ('idlers', or possibly 'canters') were followers of Wycliffe. While they decried the same Church abuses as those attacked by Langland, unlike him they also disbelieved in transubstantiation and clerical celibacy. They were peripatetic preachers. For 'landloping hermits', see Prologue, lines 53–7 and elsewhere.

29 Matthew 6:16.

30 Edmund, King of the East Angles, was allegedly martyred by the Danes in 869. Edward may be either Edward the Confessor (1004–66), who is more likely, or Edward the Martyr (962–78) – unjustly so called.

31 Cyprus was a thin silken fabric, usually black, resembling crape, often confused with the tree *cypress*. For Tartary cloth, see note 21 on this Passus. The point, from lines 219–24, is that charity may be found with high-ranking priests or monks, but never with mendicant friars,

32 Ecclesiasticus 31:8.

33 Psalm 4:8.

34 This is the earliest St Antony, the lavishly-tempted hermit, who died at about the middle of the fourth century. He spent much of his life in the Egyptian desert. St Aegidius, or Giles, was French; he is known almost only from a tenth-century (and self-evidently spurious) 'Life' – which embodies the tale cited by Langland.

35 St Paul of Thebes, traditionally the Christian proto-hermit (although he died only a few years before Antony, he was a centenarian even senior to that saint). St Jerome wrote a chimerical 'Life' of him: one would have expected few pleachable leaves, and less moss, in the Theban desert.

36 No; he made tents (Acts 18:3).

37 Cf. Matthew 4:18. But Andrew was in fact Peter's *brother*.

38 A widespread and quite uncanonical legend.

39 Job 6:5, followed by a gloss.

40 Psalm 112:9.

41 Partly from Peter Cantor, partly from Jerome (Goodridge).

42 See above for the Medieval Seven Arts (Passus 10, note 16). The
    Masters and Doctors had theoretically qualified in the higher
    studies of philosophy and medicine.

43 This refers to the hymn by St Thomas Aquinas, *Pange, lingua,
    gloriosi corporis mysterium* ('Declare, oh tongue, the Mystery of the
    glorious Body'). Stanza Four reads, in part:

> *Fitque sanguis Christi merum;*
> *et, si sensus deficit,*
> *ad firmandum cor sincerum*
> *sola fides sufficit.*

It is tempting to render this as English verse; but it means: 'And the
pure wine becomes the Blood of Christ; and, if the understanding
fails [to grasp this], faith alone suffices to support the untainted heart.'

44 What follows, about Mohammed, is common medieval legendary
    material.

45 For Antony, see above, note 34. St Dominic (1170–1221) was the
    founder of the Order of Friars Preachers, and a model of frugal
    living. *Francis* here means St Francis of Assisi (1181–1226), founder
    of the Friars Minor (Minorites), who were originally itinerant and
    penniless. The Benedict intended here (480–547) founded the
    monastery of Monte Cassino. Bernard of Clairvaux (1090–1153)
    founded the Cistercian Order.

46 Matthew 7:7.

47 Matthew 5:13.

48 Ibid.

49 Of course, the Apostles except Judas; but Langland must have
    been aware that a good deal of this work was delegated.

50 St Gregory the Great (540–604) despatched Augustine and forty
    other monks to convert Britain (596). St Augustine of Canterbury
    (d. 605) soon converted Ethelbert, and became Canterbury's first
    archbishop.

51 See Matthew 22:2–14. For Langland, the wild game signified the
    heathen; the tame fowls, oxen; and 'fatlings' (calves, piglets, etc.,
    specially fattened for the table) are young neophytes that need
    particular attention.

52 As in Leviticus 11, and elsewhere.

53 Psalm 132; but see Passus 10, note 8.

54 Mark 16:15.

55 Honorary, not to say imaginary, bishoprics in the Holy Land –
    necessarily treated as sinecures, despite Langland's missionary zeal.

56 John 10:11.

57 Matthew 20:4.

58 Matthew 7:7.

59 Galatians 6:14

60 The military Order of Knights of the Temple was founded in 1118. Though they had begun as an order practising poverty, their wealth and influence increased rapidly: they were soon objects of jealousy and therefore of calumny. It is certain that some corruption had crept into the Order, but equally certain that none of the panoramic atrocities alleged against them was true. Nevertheless, after and amid many and great barbarities, the Church suppressed the Order in 1312.

61 Her 'rightful possessions', beginning with the 'Donation of Constantine'. See lines 519–23, and Passus 10, note 35.

62 Luke 1:52.

63 Deuteronomy 12:6. A 'heave-offering' was usually a lamb's (or sheep's, or other animal's) shoulder, held up as a sacrifice.

64 A widespread, now forgotten, legend. Cf. Passus 3, note 6.

65 See above, note 55, and below, lines 557–8.

66 See above, note 4.

67 This is fabled to have happened at Mailapur (or Mylapore) in India, after Thomas had baptised the ruler and many of his subjects.

68 Deuteronomy 23:25.

69 Isaiah 3:7. In this and the last quotation, I have corrected Langland's Latin.

70 Not Hosea, but Malachi 3:10.

71 Cf. Leviticus 19:18, as well as the better-known Matthew 19:19

72 Matthew 14:15–21.

73 John 11:43.

74 Distantly based upon Daniel 9:24–7.

Passus 16

We now re-encounter Piers, in his new role – that of Christ Himself (though somewhat ambiguously) – as Keeper of the Tree of Charity. This Tree represents many things, all of them under constant threat from the Devil. It is the growth of goodness and holiness in this world from the Jewish patriarchs onwards; it is the growth of the Church with all the saints (and other holy folk) borne by it as fruit; it is the growth of goodness – Do-Well, Do-Better and Do-Best – in the soul of Man (which is imperfect, however, until crowned with the 'theological' virtues of Faith, Hope and Charity). Personifications of these we shall soon encounter, after this vision of how Charity grows

in the world. All three of the main emblematic *themes* of the Tree
combine in the life of Christ, of which Langland now has a vision. Just
before Passiontide, he meets Faith (in the person of Abraham), and is
confirmed in his belief in the Trinity.

1 Psalm 37:24, slightly altered by Langland. I have correspondingly
  altered the Authorised Version.

2 The first part of the Latin comes from Matthew 12:32. The second
  part is apparently Langland's gloss: that voluntary sin is tantamount
  to sin against the Holy Ghost, Whose help could always have been
  sought against temptation (Goodridge).

3 Skeat mentions a legend that the tree from which the Cross was
  made grew in three stems (as emblem, presumably, of the Trinity).
  There is also, however, a Celtic legend (see the Cornish *Ordinalia*,
  and Passus 1, note 5) that Adam's tree gave rise to three others: one
  from which Noah's keel was built, one which formed the roof-tree
  of Solomon's temple and one from which the Cross was made. The
  three staves, of course, are themselves symbols of the Trinity.

4 The three *physical* states correspond, in ascending order of
  excellence, to three *social* states (matrimony, chaste widowhood,
  virginity), and to the three *spiritual* states of Do-Well, Do-Better
  and Do-Best. Later (lines 200ff.), the Trinity itself is symbolically
  tied into the analogy. See also Goodridge.

5 That is to say, not in *deep* Hell, but in Limbo.

6 Cf. Galatians 4:4. Cf. also the *Pange, lingua* hymn by Venantius
  Fortunatus (*c.*530–610), line 10 of which reads: *Quando venit ergo
  sacri plenitudo temporis* . . . ('When, therefore, the fullness came of
  [that holy] time . . .).

7 See Luke 1:28–38.

8 Piers, in this passage, is not strictly speaking Christ Himself, but
  His Divine destiny.

9 Matthew 9:12.

10 John 11:33–8.

11 John 10:20.

12 John 2:13–16.

13 John 2:19–21, though the end of the speech belongs to the next
   note.

14 Matthew 21:13.

15 'Maundy', which gives its name to Maundy Thursday (the day
   before Good Friday), was the ceremony of washing the Disciples'
   feet (John 13:5–15), and is now a ritual washing of the feet of the

poor. The word comes from *mandatum*, 'a command', because of the injunction at the end of the above passage and in verse 34 of the same chapter.

16 Langland's version of John 13:21 and of Matthew 26:21–5 (whence also line 145).

17 Langland's expansion of Matthew 26:48–50.

18 Does not belong in this context at all: it is Matthew 18:7.

19 John 18:8–9.

20 See 1 Corinthians 15, *passim*, and Hebrews 2, *passim*.

21 The Parable of the Hand, elaborated by Charity in Passus 17, lines 136 and 202, to explain the Trinity, is a kind of expansion of this obscure passage. Though the Trinity is triune, Son and Holy Spirit are *in some sense* dependent upon the Father. In this context, 'what both suffer' implies such interdependence – though Langland's human analogy is inexact. The passage that follows (cf. note 4, above) symbolically, in various ways, relates human life to the Trinity. Further, it continues the symbolism of the Tree of Charity: all human life, says Faith, depends upon *trinities* of things.

22 Matthew 27:46 – though Christ was in fact quoting Psalm 22:1.

23 Not biblical, but it echoes God's command to Noah and his family in Genesis 9:1.

24 Jesus, as a man on earth, must have a mother; as the Son of God in Heaven, He needs a Father only.

25 See Genesis 18:1–8. The incident is written as the entertainment of three angels; Langland – I do not know with what authority – treats it as *really* having been a visit of the Trinity, in person and speaking to Abraham *directly* rather than through the mouths of messengers (which is what I take 'And the Lord appeared . . . and the Lord said . . . ' to mean).

26 Genesis 22:1–12. Langland's chronology goes awry here: see next note.

27 These events are recounted earlier, in Genesis 18:23–4.

28 Genesis 12:2–3, referred to in Romans 4:13.

29 Luke 1:55.

30 Genesis 14:18–20. This is held to foreshadow the Last Supper and the Mass – hence, also, Christian priesthood. Thus Abraham, 'Faith', is linked both to the New Law of Christ and to Piers.

31 Abraham's function as herald and protector of the righteous is justified by the previous note. See also Luke 16:22–3, Romans 4:9–14 and, of course, lines 254–69 of this Passus.

32 John 1:29.

Passus 17

Faith has been established; we await Hope and Charity. Hope appears
in the person of Moses: though the recorder of the Old Law, he
nevertheless foreshadows the New Law of *caritas*. In Langland's
opening line of this Passus, Hope calls himself 'a spye' – a scout or
explorer – in search of Christ the Combatant. The Dreamer's last
intellectual (and moral and emotional) difficulties begin to crumble
with the appearance and doctrine of Charity – here personified in the
Good Samaritan, himself treated as an emblem of Piers/Christ.
Charity, of course, preaches the doctrine of that Love which proceeds
from God and should imbue all mankind. And he practises it, while
Faith and Hope remain inactive (lines 52–78).

1 The Old Law shall be consummated, and the New Law (springing
   from it) be validated, by Christ upon the Cross.

2 The 'piece of hard rock' refers back to the Two Tables brought
   down by Moses from Mount Sinai (Exodus 31:18). But it is also
   symbolic of the *permanence* of the Law inscribed on it (which is
   adumbrated by Leviticus 19:18 and Matthew 19:19; but see next
   note).

3 Matthew 22:37–40.

4 For the parable of the Good Samaritan, see Luke 10:30–7.

5 This 'jousting' is Christ's Passion, represented as a tournament in
   which He overcomes the Devil, Hell and Death.

6 This whole episode (lines 52–123) is emblematic of Christ's
   Ministry, of that of the *righteous* Church, of the Passion and
   Resurrection and of the Second Coming. Lines 93–7 refer to
   Baptism and the Eucharist (as well as to confession and penance).
   Lines 98ff. mean that hitherto the path to Heaven has been so beset
   by the Powers of Hell that only the faithful (or those that in
   righteousness *seek* the true faith) could pass it. But the Incarnation
   of Christ, and His imminent Passion, have made it safe for all who
   follow in His footsteps. The Latin after line 111 (more than once
   quoted by Langland) is from Hosea 13:14. 'Jerusalem' in line 114
   implies the New Jerusalem – Heaven.

7 From the Catechism.

8 The Vulgate *omnia* means 'all things', which I have retained. The
   Authorised Version reads 'all men' (John 12:32).

9 Mark 3:29.

10 Cf. 1 Thessalonians 5:19 – which is also relevant to the succeeding
   passage likening the Trinity to a taper, ignited (for the individual)
   only by *caritas*.

11 Matthew 25:12.

12 1 Corinthians 13:1.

13 Matthew 7:21.

14 See Passus 14, note 15.

15 Revelation 6:10, misquoted and greatly shortened by Langland. I too have given a compressed version.

16 A rhyming adage, rather than strictly 'Holy Writ'. But cf. Passus 5, note 26.

17 Psalm 145:9.

18 The passage that follows is a conflation of, and gloss upon, four texts in Proverbs: 10:26; 19:13; 21:19 and 27:15 (Goodridge).

19 2 Corinthians 12:9.

Passus 18

This Passus gives us Will's vision of the Passion and the Harrowing of Hell. The Samaritan, Piers Ploughman and Jesus fuse into one personage, who will 'joust in Piers's blazon' (line 22 – i.e. in human flesh and nature) and overthrow the powers of Hell: cf. preceding Passus, note 5. The doctrine of atonement and redemption is expounded; Christ justifies His release of the Righteous from Hell; and the reconciliation of Mercy, Truth, Peace and Righteousness (= Justice) reflects the reconciliation of conflicts within Will himself. The redemption of all mankind is hinted at, and Christ's absolute victory on the Day of Judgment is foretold. The Dreamer wakes, finds it is (for himself, personally, an important piece of symbolism!) Easter Day; and he calls his family to worship. Though he has more *practical* lessons to learn, he has come *spiritually* almost as far as he ever will.

1 These are references to the service for Palm Sunday (the Sunday before Easter, and so-called from the strewing of palm-leaves before Christ at His entry into Jerusalem – John 12:13).

2 'Gallant shoes' in Langland is *galoches ycouped* – shoes with ornamentally slashed uppers. The golden spurs were emblems of new knighthood.

3 Matthew 21:9 – and also from the antiphon hinted at in line 8.

4 Cf. Passus 16, lines 40–52.

5 Hosea 13:14, and also from an antiphon for Holy Saturday.

6 Langland's account of the trial and crucifixion is a mixture of all four gospels (which are in some respects contradictory), with some additions of his own. No gospel, however, mentions *poison* (line 52); the vinegar and/or wine, variously admixed or not, is claimed

by Robert Graves to have been a merciful anaesthetic. See *The Nazarene Gospel Restored*, p. 988. The soldier with the spear, in John 19:34, was expanded in the apocryphal Gospel of Nicodemus into the whole legend of Longinus (lines 78–91).

7 Matthew 27:54.

8 As elsewhere in the poem, a garbling of Daniel 9:24ff.

9 The whole encounter of Mercy, Truth, Peace and Righteousness is based upon Psalm 85:10–13.

10 The four maidens arrive from different quarters of the globe not merely because of their different natures, but in order to emphasise the universality of their coming reconciliation.

11 We must remember that Will is now *underground*, on the borders of Hell; the 'daybreak' and the glory are Christ's invasion of that kingdom.

12 Another quotation from Venantius Fortunatus's *Pange, lingua* hymn to the Holy Cross, lines 5–6. This hymn lies in the background of both the 17th and 18th Passus.

13 Badly misquoted from Job 7:9. The Vulgate *inferos* means, as Langland intends, 'the underworld'; but the Authorised Version reading, 'the grave', is also relevant, of course.

14 Again from Venantius Fortunatus's hymn, line 8 – slightly misquoted by Langland, and paraphrased by me.

15 Psalm 33:5. Lines 184–5 quote Psalm 4:8.

16 Matthew 2:2.

17 Matthew 14:28.

18 The Simeon of the *Nunc dimittis* (Luke 2:25–35) is said, in the Gospel of Nicodemus (which, as has already been shown, was treated in the Middle Ages as virtually canonical), to have had two dead sons who resurrected at the Crucifixion.

19 Psalm 24:9. It should be noted that most of Langland's quotations throughout this Passus are relevant to one or more church services between Palm Sunday and Easter Monday – or later.

20 In common with many medieval writers, Langland treats Lucifer and Satan as different personages; nor does he make it clear which (if either!) he thinks of as *the* Devil. Even up to the seventeenth century, and after, demonology remained confused, not to say illiterate, to the point of extravagance.

21 Apropos of the preceding note, Langland has *Gobelyn* as a proper name.

22 Matthew 4:3–7.

23 Matthew 27:19. Medieval literature (cf. the Cornish Passion

sequence) attributed this dream to diabolical intervention with exactly the motive to which Satan here admits.

24 John 12:31.

25 This dialogue is based upon Psalm 24:7–10.

26 Line 321 from Isaiah 9:2, quoted in Matthew 4:16. Line 322 from John 1:36.

27 We must not expect modern precision in distinguishing the reptilian orders from writers to whom a dragon could be a 'worm'. Not only the Serpent in Eden, but other snakes, were often represented with forefeet, and sometimes with hindfeet as well. The 'lady's face' is also traditional, but much harder to explain. Originally it may not have been that of a woman at all, but the last relic of a fallen (but not yet utterly damned) angel – though the Serpent is described in line 352 as a loathsome adder. The Vulgate word, *serpens*, means any creeping thing, and is common to both the masculine and feminine genders, though there treated as masculine.

28 Exodus 21:24, repeated in Deuteronomy 19:21 and quoted in Matthew 5:38.

29 Matthew 5:17.

30 Psalm 7:15. Note, in the preceding line, another reference to the *Pange, lingua* hymn.

31 A double reference, Joel 3:2 and 11–16, for the Valley of Jehoshaphat as the site of the Last Judgment. For the beautiful (in the original!) line 368 – 'That I drynke righte ripe must *resureccio mortuorum*' – see Matthew 26:29.

32 Psalm 51:4. (And therefore, the argument runs, pardon rests with me alone.)

33 None of this (lines 377–81) was ever actually Law; but examples have been known of popular insistence on royal prerogative being so used.

34 See Passus 4, note 12.

35 2 Corinthians 12:4. I follow Langland's slight misquotation.

36 Psalm 143:2. Again slightly misquoted by author and translator.

37 Cf. note 20. Ashtaroth = Astarte (among other versions) was in fact a moon-goddess – and one aspect or avatar of the White Goddess particularly celebrated by Robert Graves. Yet (like *Mahound* = Mohammed) the name often turns up as that of a male demon.

38 From an Ascension Day hymn.

39 Paraphrased by Langland in the lines that follow. Origin uncertain; but the idea of *Amantium irae redintegratio amoris'* – or 'The falling out of faithful friends is the renewing of love' (Richard Edwards, 1523–66) – is of course immemorial.

40 See note 9.
41 Psalm 133:1.

Passus 19

Christ having risen, the foundation of Holy Church can begin; and this is the subject of Will's next vision. Piers Ploughman now changes from Christ Himself (at the opening of the Passus), to Christ's Vicar on Earth – St Peter and his papal successors – under the image of a faithful ploughman and sower of seeds in God's field. But already the corruption of the Church, and the coming of Antichrist, are casting their shadows before. In some ways we are moving back to earlier Passus, even to the maze of the Prologue itself (though the return of the Seven Deadly Sins, and the full war against them and Antichrist, belongs to Passus 20). It is already apparent, however, that Do-Best will see active engagement in that war. Piers vanishes; and the Church – and Will – are left in conscious imperfection, to defend themselves as best they may.

1 Cf. Isaiah 63:1–3. Apropos of that passage, it may be noted that *Edom* (like *Adam*) comes from a root meaning *red*. Cf. also the Cornish Ascension episode in the *Ordinale de Resurrexione Domini Nostri Ihesu Christi*. Christ, reaching Heaven, is greeted by a succession of angels with various forms of the question, 'Wherefore are thy garments red?' His answers are precisely those that apply in these lines of the Passus to Christ in Piers's armour (i.e. in human flesh). He has been scourged; He has worn a crown of thorns; He has been crucified; and so forth.

2 It is not, of course; 'Christ' means 'anointed'. Nevertheless, as established in the previous Passus, Christ Crucified, Christ the Harrower of Hell, must be regarded as both King and Conqueror.

3 Philippians 2:10.

4 This symbolic interpretation of gold, frankincense and myrrh is traditional, and relates to three essential qualities of kingship.

5 John 2:1–10. Wine is called an emblem of the Law (in line 107) because this, Christ's first miracle, was an emblem of the New Law of *caritas* – as, indeed, John implies in verse 11.

6 1 Samuel 18:7.

7 Cf. Matthew 26:3–5 or John 18:13–14.

8 Romans 6:9.

9 Mark 16:9–10 or John 20:14–18.

10 Luke 24:46. The reference there is to Daniel 9:24–7.

11 There is no canonical evidence that 'doubting' Thomas evangelised India; but see Passus 15, note 67. For the incidents and quotations given in lines 158–77, see John 20, especially verses 19–29 (which Langland has garbled).

12 This (derived from Matthew 18:28–35) is in a sense the theme of the entire epic, and especially of the two closing Passus: the dangers into which the Church, and the soul, fall, are due not merely to sin *in itself*, but to their neglect to *make restitution*, literally as well as spiritually, to Man and to God. Cf. Passus 5, line 232, and many other contexts.

13 Acts 2:3–4 and 17–18. Piers has now become St Peter.

14 The Pentecostal hymn ascribed to Hrabanus Maurus (d.856).

15 Cf. 1 John 2:18–22.

16 1 Corinthians 12:4.

17 'Stots' are *young* oxen, fit only for lighter work. Those given to Piers are the four greatest Fathers of the Church, often cited by Langland, either separately or together.

18 Cf. Prologue, lines 100–10.

19 From one of the *Distichs* of Cato. Latin, line 290, 'Spare me, O Lord!'

20 'Surquedry' is often translated as 'arrogance', but is in fact closer to 'overweening' or 'presumption'.

21 This vicar is 'unlearned' *(lewed)* only in the sense that he is uncontaminated by 'the dirty devices of this world'. Unlike the still-complacent Conscience, he sees clearly what is *really* wrong with the Church – and the world.

22 Many cardinals preferred to station themselves at Avignon rather than at Rome, and their presence there contributed to the Great Schism of 1378–1417. Urban VI was elected Pope in Rome, Clement VII in Fondi. Clement and his Court later moved to Avignon, where they were largely supplied – and partly financed – by Jewish merchants, who received special privileges.

23 Psalm 18:25 – though the Authorised Version differs from the sense of the Vulgate. I have given the Prayer Book version.

24 Urban VI declared a crusade against his rival, and the Roman supporters almost at once did battle with the French. In any case, Langland would have preferred the crusades in the Holy Land, to say nothing of those against such heretics as the Albigenses, to have been crusades not of destruction but of conversion: see Passus 15, lines 561 to end; and cf. lines 483–94 of the same Passus.

25 Matthew 5:45.

26 St Luke has nothing to do with either quotation. The first is
   Exodus 20:13 and Deuteronomy 5:17; the second Hebrews 10:30
   (and elsewhere).

Passus 20

At last all the agents of Antichrist march forth against the Church.
Conscience calls upon Nature (here, God) for help, and great
afflictions are sent to turn men back to righteousness. Though many
sins are resisted, many return; and the Church and its flock are at last
undone by folly, hypocrisy, greed and the complacency that
Conscience has shown earlier. The end of the epic is inconclusive:
Conscience, and Will himself, have still to search the world anew for
Piers Ploughman and redemption.

1 Langland's expansion (and attribution out of context) of Matthew
   8:20.
2 As Goodridge remarks, Will's chief remaining fault is the *opposite* of
   those that he has previously shown: he has replaced arrogance and
   despair with excessive meekness and trust. (Not *all* action is evil!)
3 A reference to 1 Corinthians 1:19–27 and 2 Corinthians 11:19.
   With what authority, I do not know, but Robert Graves suggests
   (in *King Jesus*) that there may have been punning, among the early
   converts, upon *Christian* and *Chrestian* – the latter deriving from
   chrestos, which can mean 'foolishly simple' as well as 'worthy,
   wholesome, useful'.
4 'Out of the planets' because in traditional astrology their positions
   affect (under God's preordinances) all human good and bad fortune.
5 It is true that the plagues, particularly the catastrophic 'Black
   Death', caused a relaxation of morality in some people (and a
   greater strictness in others). But copious venery was by many
   believed to be a prophylactic. See Nohl's book on the Black Death
   (or, indeed, others).
6 That is to say, a useless medicine or formula – or talisman – against
   disease and old age.
7 Will's last lesson, learned in old age, is virtually the same as his first,
   insufficiently understood by him from Holy Church's teaching in
   Passus 1.
8 Their short (secular) coats, their weapons and their ornamental
   footwear were forbidden to priests. Cf. Passus 15, lines 118–21.
   'Bloody great knives' appears to me a fair modern version of
   Langland's *pisseres longe knyves*.

9 Psalm 147:4.

10 There is good Scriptural evidence (including the above reference) that Heaven, and the affairs of Heaven, are orderly, proportionable, symmetrical and precise; whereas (pace Dante!) Hell is equivalent to uncharted and unmeasured chaos. The point is that the friars are – hellishly – multiplying beyond control.

11 The citations of Plato and Seneca are – at any rate in this context and intention – either meaningless or satirical. They are in any case put down by the quotation that follows line 276 (Exodus 20:17 and Deuteronomy 5:21 – the Tenth Commandment). Christian community of goods is another matter; it is of the non-observance of this among the learned, and the danger and difficulty of trying to make the unlearned understand it, that Langland is complaining.

12 That is to say, friars are bribable for easy penances (passim throughout the poem), as Westminster judges are bribable for favourable decisions. In each case, the money belongs rightfully to someone else – the parish priest or the defrauded creditor.

13 A specially appointed (and usually very senior) cleric who heard the confessions of magnates or of very grievous sinners.

14 Such licences and abuses have been condemned passim throughout the poem. The signalled (by me) pun in lines 323–4 is in Langland: the friar is wrongfully being granted a parish priest's (or higher cleric's) cure of souls.

15 As previously noted (cf. Passus 8, lines 8 ff., and Passus 13, lines 40 ff.), though my translation somewhat obscures the latter, friars tended to travel in pairs. This particular friar's name derives from 2 Timothy 3:6.

16 A salve is a soothing balm – the word used here with both sexual implications and those of mild penances – see above. It is also the Latin greeting Salve! – 'Hail!' – as in the antiphon Salve Regina, addressed to the Virgin Mary. This is one of Langland's most complicated and bitterly ironical puns.

17 A further reference to the selling, by friars, of honorary fellowship in their Order; and the lines that follow repeat the accusations made frequently above (e.g. note 12, or Passus 3, note 1)

18 Lines 380–3. Pride is recognised as the basis for all sins – of course including the primal sin, that of Lucifer's rebellion. 'Nature', in this context, still means God – whose help must be sought until Piers Ploughman (once more a merging of Christ, the righteous Church and its priests, and the actively devout Common Man) may return to Earth.

The 'Autobiographical Episode'

1 The word 'loller' means wastrel or vagabond. During the fourteenth century a similar word 'lollard' was borrowed from the Dutch *lollaert,* a devout layman, and applied to the followers of Wycliff. These words were sometimes confused. Langland was not a Lollard but the piety, satire and indignation of the poem might have suggested a false connection to his contemporaries as they did to Robert Crowley, his sixteenth-century Protestant editor.

2 Will describes himself as 'to long', too tall. His nickname is Long Will.

3 Matthew 16:27.

4 'Continue' in the sense of persevere. Conscience repeats the word at line 104.

5 The clothes of a cleric.

6 1 Corinthians 7:20.

7 A book of basic religious instruction and prayer. *Placebo* and *Dirige*: antiphons in the Office for the Dead. Will's main service to others is prayer for the dead.

8 Will justifies his begging as due always to immediate necessity. He fills 'only [his] belly' and does not save anything in bag or bottle.

9 Leviticus 21.

10 1 Thessalonians 5:15.

11 Psalm 15:3, a text used in the ceremony of tonsuring.

12 'The amount of land for which the services of an armed knight were due to the sovereign' (*Oxford English Dictionary*).

13 The 'sons of Simon' are followers of Simon Magus (Acts 8:18) and practise simony, traffic in sacred things.

14 Matthew 4:4.

15 'Lyeth' could be one of two verbs. I take it to mean 'lies' but it is usually translated as 'applies'. If the former is right, the next word 'Ac' (90) has the adversative sense 'but'; if the latter, the connective sense 'and'.

16 As often, the unstructured and individualistic nature of Will's profession and piety is questioned. Conscience suggests that a life of contemplation and mendicancy is more obviously legitimate for those in religious orders.

17 Matthew 13:44, Luke 15:10.